To Martin

Christmas 1995

from

Colin

The T.Q.M. Toolkit

The T.Q.M. Toolkit

A GUIDE TO PRACTICAL TECHNIQUES FOR TOTAL QUALITY MANAGEMENT

....

Jenny Waller,
Derek Allen
& Andrew Burns

KOGAN
PAGE

First published in 1995

Apart from any fair dealing for the purposes of research or private study, or criticism or review, as permitted under the Copyright, Designs and Patents Act, 1988, this publication may only be reproduced, stored or transmitted, in any form or by any means, with the prior permission in writing of the publishers, or in the case of reprographic reproduction in accordance with the terms and licences issued by the CLA. Enquiries concerning reproduction outside those terms should be sent to the publishers at the undermentioned address:

Kogan Page
120 Pentonville Road
London N1 9JN

© Jenny Waller, Derek Allen and Andrew Burns, 1995

British Library Cataloguing in Publication Data
A CIP record for this book is available from the British Library.

ISBN 0 7494 1280 1

Designed and typeset by Information Design Unit, Newport Pagnell

Printed in England by Clay's Ltd, St Ives plc

Contents

Introduction

The role of tools in management

Tools are an important part of every profession. Having the right tools, and knowing how to use them, marks out the professional from the amateur, enabling the professionals to be better, faster and more competent. Management is no exception. Indeed management consultants rely heavily on tools, often ones they have developed themselves and which constitute valuable intellectual property. If managers want to be professional at what they do, and not just gifted amateurs, they need to have tools.

How tools work

Tools increase individuals' power, sometimes marginally, sometimes enormously. Just as physical tools can help to bang in nails or build bridges, management tools can help to solve small local problems or re-engineer the whole business. Whatever their level of operation, tools enable people to understand, shape and control situations which are too complex to manage through individual effort or insight. For all the complexity of human minds, and their supremacy in many areas of perception and cognition, people have great difficulty in remembering and processing large amounts of information. Without tools, the complexity of modern systems and organisations may make them intractable and not susceptible to control.

What tools achieve

Management tools focus or direct information for a particular purpose. The Impact Chart we use in this book is based on what the tools do:

• Some tools bring information together.
• Others begin to analyse and shape it.
• A few of the more sophisticated are for analysing and shaping the organisation itself.

By selecting and presenting information in particular ways, the tools provide routeways through complexity.

Selecting the right tools

There are, of course, a lot of tools to choose from – this book represents a small selection, especially if variations are taken into account. So it is not realistic to expect to know them all. However it is realistic to be aware of the kinds of tools there are, and what they achieve. In this book we use an Affinity Diagram to show our view of how group the tools group together.

Statistical Quality Control tools
These are for collecting and analysing quantitative information about processes. They are derived from manufacturing, but are now increasingly applied to service industries as well. The core tools in this category are known as Statistical Process Control.

Planning tools
These select out all the information relevant to particular activities, and organise it so that it can be understood, analysed and changed as necessary.

Change Management tools
These introduce new ways of thinking and acting.

Quality Management System tools
These are tools which are built into the system, to make sure management processes and procedures work properly.

Graphic tools
These are tools of all kinds which use graphic presentation to show dimensions of the information which aren't otherwise evident or visible.

Strategy tools
These tools are designed to affect the way the whole organisation thinks and feels, and the direction in which it's moving. This group includes the most sophisticated of the tools.

Cost management tools
These work with the principles behind accounting methods, so that financial reporting supports what the business is trying to achieve.

Problem solving tools
These identify key characteristics of problems, and their implications. They help to focus energy on particular issues, one at a time.

Data capture tools
Capturing data is the first step to understanding and controlling selected aspects of the organisation. These tools identify what information is important for particular purposes, and set up appropriate ways of collecting it.

Prioritisation tools
Prioritisation is an essential aspect of many of the tools. When there is a lot of information to deal with, it is important to prioritise it in order to simplify the problem without distorting it.

Consensus tools
These deal with the difficulties involved in reconciling different viewpoints and provide rational ways of reaching agreement.

Product and Process Design tools
These help to ensure that, particularly in manufacturing organisations, processes are designed logically to deliver the right products in the right way.

The forms tools take

Management tools use a number of forms to achieve their purpose. These include:

Graphic forms
The majority of the tools in this book use a graphic form either for a part or for the whole of the tool. Graphic forms include diagrams, tables, forms, questionnaires and lists. They are particularly important for data capture and for showing relationships.

Templates
These are organisational patterns or designs which can be used to organise or reorganise activities. Strategic tools often take this form.

Philosophies
Sometimes the tool is a philosophy – a set of ideas and beliefs which helps to interpret and shape the data.

Processes
Tools can be processes – fixed sequences of activities which can be introduced into the organisation.

Teams
Teamwork is particularly associated with TQM. At their best, teams provide a way of moving beyond individual capacity.

Physical organisation
A small number of tools work through physically reorganising the environment in which people are working, in order to highlight or differentiate activities.

Implementing the tools

For the most part, the business of understanding the tools, and deciding which ones to use and how, forms part of what is thought of as a hard approach to management; a tinkering with the mechanics of management and organisation. However the tools are implemented in a complex organisational framework where the softer aspects of management are extremely important – issues of motivation, culture, management style, leadership and communication will have a direct bearing on how successfully the tools can be used.

The culture of the organisation
People can't be expected to adapt to the tools straight away. Even simple tools can seem unnatural and unwieldy the first time round. Often the tools ask people to think in ways which are strange to them, and which impose a discipline which they may resent. Typical reactions are to ignore or sabotage the tool, proving it wasn't any good anyway.

Cultures where management tools are effective are cultures where results are more important than politics, and where staff are sure that management wants to know the truth, and not just an acceptable version of it. Cultures don't change overnight, of course, but if they are given a chance, tools can help the process. The effectiveness with which they can solve problems, or improve quality, or improve communications, is very compelling once it gets underway.

Facilitation
Facilitation is an important concept for implementing tools – so much so that we've actually called it a tool. Facilitation is a skilful and demanding role, which can often be taken by an outside consultant. Facilitators not only provide the hard support – knowledge of the tool, the equipment for making it work and so on – but also control the softer implementation issues, making sure the saboteurs are identified and kept at bay, for example.

Training
Training can take various forms – sometimes practice is all that's needed, or reading a book. For other tools, extensive training will be needed, and it might be best to use specialist consultants rather than trying to go it alone.

How to use this book

This book is a Swiss army knife of tools. We've given enough detail to show the size and shape of the tool, and instructions which are enough to use the simpler tools (in Swiss army knife terms, to open bottles.) However this book is entirely inadequate as a guide to performing more complex operations – no precision engineering with the Swiss army knife. The references point to follow-up material. Or the next step might be to call in the experts – trainers or consultants.

What we hope you will get from the book is the bigger picture – knowledge of what tools are available, a sensitivity to when they should be used, and above all an understanding of how tools help to understand and control aspects of the organisation which are otherwise intractable.

Whether you use the material here directly, or as a jumping off point, we hope that you will find these tools interesting and empowering in the daily battle to manage the organisation.

Acknowledgements

Thanks to Clive Richards at Coventry University and David Lewis, Roger Stotesbury and Rob Waller at Information Design Unit for their support in making this book happen.

And special thanks to the Wünderkinder, Anna Brennan and Susy McKeever, who spent a long hot summer in pursuit of editorial and typographic excellence.

Impact chart of TQM tools

Each tool is classified by what it will achieve for the organisation and not by how easy or difficult it is to implement.

So, for example, the tools on the left (●) aren't necessarily the easiest to carry out. It is just that by themselves they won't analyse or change the organisation.

●

Tools which gather or communicate information

Action Plans
Attitude Survey
Brainstorming
Checklist
Checksheet
Customer needs analysis
Customer Satisfaction Assessment
Delphi Technique
Error Cause Removal
Focus Group
Interviewing
Meeting Checklist
Questionnaire
Suggestion Schemes
Supplier Survey
Team Briefing

Tools which involve a simple level of analysis

Affinity Diagram
Band Graph
Bar Graph
Clean Sheet Analysis
Concentration Diagram
Critical Success Factors
Endpoint State Analysis
Flowcharts
Force Field Analysis
Histogram
Lateral Thinking
Line Graph
Paired Comparisons
Pareto Analysis
Pie Chart
Problem Analysis
Quality Objectives
Radar Chart
Rating Sheet
Relations Diagram
Responsibility Matrix
Scatter Diagram
Scenario Writing
Spider Diagram
Thinking Hats
Trend Chart

● ● ●

Tools which include a more complex level of analysis

Acceptance Sampling
Activity Analysis
Arrow Diagram
Attributes Analysis
Audit
Barrier Analysis
Block Diagram
Break-even Chart
c chart
Cause and Effect Diagram
Classification of Defects
Control Chart
Corrective Action
Cost Benefit Analysis
Cost of Quality
Critical Path Analysis
Cusum Chart
Data Flow Diagram
Decision Analysis
Design Review
Design of Experiments
Design-To-Cost
Facilitation
Fagan Inspection – Documents
Fagan Inspection – Software
Failure Mode Effect and Criticality Analysis
Fault Tree Analysis
Fishbowl Meeting
Gantt Chart
Gap Analysis
Inspection
Loss Function Analysis
Matrix Diagram
Multi-vari Chart
Nominal Group Technique
np chart
p chart
Performance Evaluation Review Technique
Performance Metrics
PRE-Control
Process Analysis
Process Capability Analysis
Process Definition
Process Failure Analysis
Process Model
Quality Function Deployment
R chart
Regression Analysis
Relevance Tree
Reliability Prediction and Analysis
Root Cause Evaluation Matrix
Solution Effect Analysis
Stratification
Training Needs Analysis
Tree Diagram
u chart
$\bar{x}$ chart
Z chart

● ● ● ●

Tools which lead to changes to part of the organisation

Activity-Based Accounting
Benchmarking
Company Wide Quality Improvement
Cross Functional Teams
Family Teams
Feedback Loop
Hoshin
Job Re-design
Management by Objectives
Poka Yoke
Preventative Maintenance
Quality Circle
Quality Council
Quality Improvement Team
Self-inspection
Statistical Process Control
Total Productive Maintenance
Zero Based Budgeting

● ● ● ● ●

Tools which lead to major changes in how the whole organisation works

Business Process Re-engineering
Business Simplification
Departmental Purpose Analysis
Just-In-Time
Kaizen
Mission Statement
Zero Defects

Affinity Diagram of TQM tools

Here we group the tools together by type. This chart is useful if you are fairly clear about what you want to do, and need to know what tools can help you.

Some tools appear in more than one group, because they share characteristics with more than one type. For example, a matrix diagram is a Graphic tool, and also a Prioritisation tool.

Statistical quality control

Acceptance Sampling
c Chart
Control Chart
Cusum Chart
Design of Experiments
Multi-Vari Chart
np Chart
p Chart
PRE-Control
Process Capability Analysis
R Chart
Regression Analysis
Reliability Prediction and Analysis
Scatter Diagram
Statistical Process Control
Stratification
Trend chart
u chart
x̄ chart

Planning

Action plans
Arrow Diagram
Critical Path Analysis
Gantt Chart
Meeting Checklist
PERT
Responsibility Matrix
Scenario Writing

Change management

Activity Analysis
Barrier Analysis
Cross Functional Teams
Endpoint State Analysis
Facilitation
Family Teams
Fishbowl Meeting
Focus Group

Quality management system

Audit
Company Wide Quality improvement
Corrective Action
Fagan Inspection – Documents
Fagan Inspection – Software
Feedback Loop
Inspection
Quality Improvement Team
Quality Objectives
Self-Inspection

Graphic tools

Band Graph
Bar Chart
Block Diagram
Concentration Diagram
Data Flow Diagram
Fault Tree Analysis
Flowcharts
Gantt Chart
Histogram
Line graph
Matrix Diagram
Pie Chart
Process Model
Quality Function Deployment
Radar Chart
Relations Diagram
Relevance Tree
Spider Diagram
Tree Diagram
Z Chart

Strategy

Benchmarking
Business Process Re-engineering
Business Simplification
Departmental Purpose Analysis
Hoshin
Job Re-Design
Just-In-Time
Kaizen
Management by Objectives
Mission Statement
Preventative Maintenance
Quality Circle
Quality Council
Team Briefing
Total Productive Maintenance
Training Needs Analysis
Zero Defects

Cost management

Activity-Based Accounting
Break-even Chart
Cost Benefit Analysis
Cost of Quality
Design-To-Cost
Life-Cycle Costing
Zero Based Budgeting

Problem solving

Affinity Diagram
Attributes Analysis
Cause and Effect Diagram
Clean Sheet Analysis
Decision Analysis
Fault Tree Analysis
Force Field Analysis
Gap Analysis
Lateral Thinking
Spider Diagram
Problem Analysis
Process Analysis
Process Definition
Process Failure Analysis
Relations Diagram
Relevance Tree
Root Cause Evaluation Matrix
Solution Effect Analysis
Thinking Hats
Tree Diagram

Data capture

Attitude Survey
Benchmarking
Brainstorming
Checklist
Checksheet
Concentration Diagram
Customer Needs Analysis
Customer Satisfaction
    Assessment
Error Cause Removal
Interviewing
Performance Metrics
Questionnaire
Suggestion Schemes
Supplier Survey

Prioritisation

Classification of Defects
Critical Success Factors
Matrix Diagram
Pareto Analysis
Quality Function Deployment
Rating Sheet

Consensus

Delphi Technique
Nominal Group Technique
Paired Comparisons

Product and process design

Design Review
Failure Mode Effect and
    Criticality Analysis
Kanban
Loss Function Analysis
Poka Yoke
Process Analysis

The tools

Acceptance Sampling

Tool to judge if products are up to standard, without having to inspect each one.

Affinity group: Statistical Quality Control

Classification • • •

When to use it
Usually for inspecting large volume production where 100% inspection is too expensive. Low volume production may not provide such an accurate sample.

What you'll achieve
Economic alternative to inspecting everything: provides important manufacturing information, and prevents subcontracting disasters.

When not to use it
Don't use Acceptance Sampling when everything has to be right, for example in parts of a safety-critical process: use 100%, 200% or 300% inspection instead. Don't inspect samples together from batches produced at different times. And use only where the underlying process is under control.

And be careful
Always the risk of accepting bad lots and rejecting good ones: people often aren't happy about rejecting whole batches based on a sample. And consider whether any level of defects is acceptable, and whether inspecting at the end is really as good as controlling the process all the way through.

Training
People will need fundamental statistical knowledge as well as knowledge of standard plans (ie sample sizes and acceptance criteria). Software available.

Where to find out more
BS6001: Sampling procedures for inspection by attributes, British Standards Institute, 1991

Quality Control Handbook, Juran J, McGraw Hill, 1988

Total Quality Control, Feigenbaum A V, McGraw Hill, 1983

Process flowchart

Calculate necessary sample size for various batch sizes

Calculate criteria for acceptance – the Acceptable Quality Level (AQL) per sample. Use BS6001.

Inspect sample and analyse data

Accept or reject batch

Analyse reasons for rejected products and take preventative action as necessary

Based on results, vary and adapt sampling as part of acceptance control programme

Acceptance Sampling can be used for internal interfaces or between manufacturers and external suppliers.

A large ringbinder wholesaler uses an Acceptance Sampling plan with the manufacturers of the folders. Sampling criteria are the alignment of the rings and their fit. If there are more than a certain number of defective folders in the sample taken from each delivery, the batch is rejected. The inspector uses a fitness for purpose judgement.

This method of quality control does not guarantee that all the ringbinders will be of exactly the same standard, or indeed that they will all be fit for purpose.

On one occasion the company supplied customised folders to a major corporation for a senior management briefing document. Executives whose folders didn't work demanded replacements. In this case, because the company were supplying a premium customised product, they should have carried out 100% inspection.

Acceptance Sampling in a ringbinder wholesaling business

Batch size
Ringbinders are made up in different batch sizes to fulfil particular orders.

Sample size
For each batch, a sample size is calculated. BS6001 contains look-up tables for this. Here, the sample size is the number of folders from the batch which will be examined.

Reject number
This is the number of defective folders found in the sample which will lead to the whole batch being rejected. Again, BS6001 contains look-up tables for this.

(The table below shows indicative numbers only – don't use this as a substitute for the proper tables!).

Batch size	Sample size	Reject number
50 - 100	10	2
100 - 200	15	3
200 - 400	20	4
400 - 1000	30	5

Action Plans

Tool for breaking down objectives into tasks and deciding who will do what and when.

Affinity group: Planning

Classification •

When to use it
Particularly useful for planning initiatives where tasks fall outside the normal pattern of people's responsibilities.

When not to use it
Don't use when the project is sizeable, with action points well into double figures. Use a more formalised approach such as Critical Path Analysis or Gantt Charts.

Training
Explanation and simulation are useful preparations, but technique can be understood from books.

What you'll achieve
A way of planning how best to use people to achieve particular objectives. Makes sure people know exactly what their responsibilities are, and in what order.

And be careful
Just allocating tasks won't necessarily make them happen, particularly when they fall outside normal job routines. Check on memory, motivation and progress. Keep the plan simple and keep it up to date.

Where to find out more
Benchmarking, Camp R, ASQC Quality Press and Quality Resources, 1989

How to Develop and Present Staff Training Courses, Sheal P R, Kogan Page, 1989

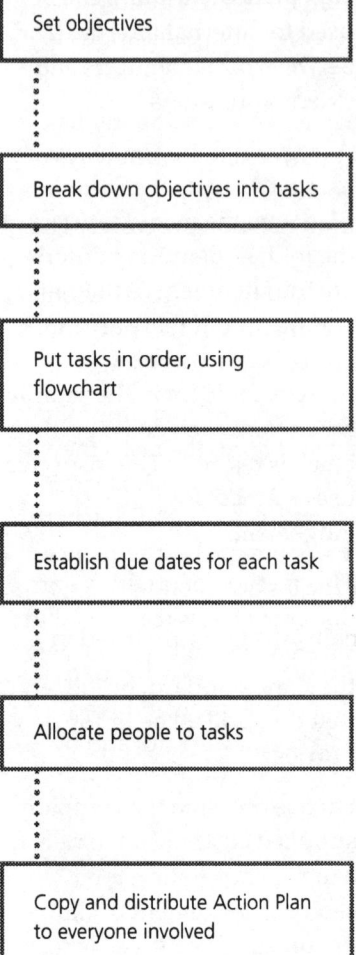

Process flowchart

- Set objectives
- Break down objectives into tasks
- Put tasks in order, using flowchart
- Establish due dates for each task
- Allocate people to tasks
- Copy and distribute Action Plan to everyone involved

Example

Action Plans are a good discipline for organisations to adopt.

An engineering company has set up a team to look at ways of rationalising its communication processes. The team consists of representatives from different departments who do not normally work together.

At their first meeting, the team brainstorms all the tasks they have to do. The project leader then creates a rough flowchart to work out the best sequence for the tasks.

Finally, the tasks are listed in an Action Plan which makes it clear for everyone involved what they have to do, and by when.

Action Plan
Forms Management Team 7.3.96

Action	Start Date	Finish Date	Who	How
Collect forms	8.3	29.3	All	Ask heads of Departments
List forms	29.3	5.4	JG	Database
Check duplication	29.3	5.4	TW	Manual check
Book room for next meeting	8.3	12.4	TW	
Research forms design	8.3	5.4	GA	Library
Research forms management systems	8.3	5.4	BW /JG	Library, software catalogues
Circulate agenda	10.4		AB	

Activity Analysis

When business or management processes are changing, a tool to check which activities will still be appropriate.

Affinity group: Change Management

Classification • • •

When to use it
Use Activity Analysis when your organisation is changing processes within or across departments, perhaps because of computerisation or new software.

What you'll achieve
Activity Analysis is a planning tool which prevents you from ending up with a muddle of old and new activities when processes change. In particular prevents redundant activities surviving.

When not to use it
Don't start Activity Analysis too early in the change cycle: wait until it's fairly clear what's going to happen

And be careful
Not a good idea to change everything all at once: concentrate on activities which matter most.

Training
Understanding of objective setting, definition of activities and the principles of process definition will be useful.

Where to find out more
Benchmarking, Camp R, ASQC Quality Press and Quality Resources, 1989

Process flowchart

Identify objective of the new process

List all activities which make up present process

Divide present activities into three categories:
- those which fit in with new outcomes
- those which don't
- those which can realistically be changed to fit

Create revised list of activities to match the new process

Example

Activity Analysis is important when automated systems are being introduced, otherwise people may continue with tasks which have lost their point.

In the example, a small firm of architects has operated a manual office system since the company began. This has caused problems with records and invoicing, with clients complaining and project managers blaming the office for getting it wrong.

So the company is introducing an automated invoicing system. At first there is little difference in the way things work. The office still sends out hard copy invoice sheets, for example.

It takes a new office manager to realise that the system and the process don't match, and to carry out an activity analysis which takes advantage of the new technology.

Activity Analysis
Objective: to improve efficiency, accuracy and recall of invoicing

Original invoicing process activities	Activity Analysis
1. Every month office sends to all architects: • printed copy of current jobs • batch of pro-forma invoice sheets • yellow sticky with a note to say that invoicing is due.	**Modify** Office sends jobs list and invoice forms on line.
2. Project manager looks up details in project file.	**Keep** No plan to put project records on line.
3. Project manager fills in proforma invoice sheets, writing comments and notes over it as necessary.	**Modify** Project manager fills in actual invoice.
4. Office types up invoice.	**Remove**
5. Office sends invoice back to project manager for sign-off.	**Remove**
6. Office sends invoice to client.	**Keep**
7. Office files copy of invoice by date.	**Modify** Stores computer file.
8. Office ticks copy of invoice in red when payment arrives.	**Remove** Automatic record when payment is entered on the system.

Activities making up the new process

1. Office sends electronic jobs list and invoicing forms to project managers.

2. Project manager looks up details in project file.

3. Project manager fills in invoice details electronically and sends to office.

4. Office prints out invoice and sends to client.

Activity-Based Accounting

Accounting method for determining the true cost of activities.

Affinity group: Cost Management

Classification • • • •

Identify all the key areas of cost which make up different activities in the business

Instead of averaging areas of cost across a number of different activities, identify the measurements needed to establish the true cost of each activity

Set up accounting systems to collect these measurements

Use Activity-Based Accounting information to make decisions about the relative efficiency and quality of each different activity

When to use it
When the balance of activities in an organisation is changing and previous overhead calculations are no longer accurate.

What you'll achieve
Knowledge of the precise cost structure of particular activities: much more sensitive information which will probably have a significant effect on decision-making.

When not to use it
Don't introduce this in isolation: if you're not going to use the new information to change the way things are done, it's a waste of time.

And be careful
Means a major shake-up in accounting. May take time, training and consultancy. Make sure the resources are there to support the change.

Training
Even experienced accounts staff may need training as ABA is different from traditional management accounting.

Where to find out more
Relevance Lost: The Rise and Fall of Management Accounting, Thomas Johnson H and Kaplan S, Harvard Business School Press, 1986

Fast Focus on TQM, Barrett D, Productivity Press, 1994

Example

Activity Based Accounting is important for organisations with different product lines and different cost structures for each.

An example which illustrates this is a record company which wants to achieve growth by moving into retailing as well as maintaining its core wholesaling business.

Before the retail operation developed, warehouse activity was evenly balanced between bulk orders and those which had to be specially picked and pulled. So warehousing costs were averaged out and charged at a flat rate per item.

As the retailing side of the business developed, the ratio of picked and pulled items began to increase dramatically. As a result, the flat rate charge no longer covered costs.

It was time to cost the two different kinds of activity separately by introducing activity accounting.

Calculations for a record company's warehousing rates

Costs (£)	Old	New
Per unit		
Bulk orders	.06	.06
Picked and pulled orders	.10	.10
Mix		
Average 1 million units		
50% Bulk	30,000	
30% Bulk		18,000
50% Pick and Pull	50,000	
70% Pick and Pull		70,000
Total operating costs	80,000	88,000
The Rate		
Charge per unit flat rate	.08	.08
Profit per million units	Break-even	(8,000)

Affinity Diagram

Tool which brings ideas together to form coherent themes.

Affinity group: Problem Solving

Classification • •

Identify problem and phrase neutrally

Brainstorm ideas and impressions individually, and record on file cards

Sort cards into groups. Discard those with no affinity

Label groups and organise cards under them to form chart

Present chart

Analyse results and plan action points

When to use it
For gaining insight into complex problems where opinions and views vary and there are no easy answers.

What you'll achieve
Method of bringing together different viewpoints and sorting them out constructively. Significantly increased chance of gaining insights into how to deal with the problem.

When not to use it
Don't use for minor problems, for those with obvious answers, for situations where outcomes are predetermined, or in cultures where openness is not appreciated.

And be careful
Can need experienced facilitator to turn sceptics used to relying on their own judgement into productive participators who see the benefits of working together.

Training
Training necessary for facilitator, preferably by another more experienced facilitator.

Where to find out more
The Memory Jogger, Brassard M and Ritter D, GOAL/QPC, 1994

Handbook of Quality Tools, Ozeki K and Asaka T, Productivity Press, 1990

Using a tool such as an Affinity Diagram is often an effective way of concentrating on 'soft' issues, before introducing 'hard' procedures.

One computer sales and repair company had something of a poor reputation for product quality and for quality of service. In response, senior management introduced quality control procedures. Three months into the quality programme, all the indications were that it was not working well.

Using an outside facilitator, the company set up an affinity session with their staff to find out why.

The session proved to be very revealing. Management could see what people were thinking, and start to change priorities and attitudes.

What's getting in the way of the quality programme?

1 No Rewards

Nobody notices if you carry out the procedures or not
Doesn't affect sales commission
Not paid to do it
No rewards

2 No Need for it

Customers always complain
We're no worse than anyone else
We're still in business – what's the problem?
We've got a great quality record
I've never had a complaint

3 No Ownership

We don't really know what we're supposed to be doing
Who's responsible? Isn't it their fault?
No one else is going to do it
Not my responsibility
Not sure we can do it

4 Resistance to Change

It won't help
We all know how to do our jobs
It might not work
Haven't had the training

5 Gets in the way of Our Work

Good idea but not a priority
Too many meetings
Won't help reach targets
Makes more work
Too Busy

Arrow Diagram

Scheduling tool to show order of daily operations and their relationship to each other.

Affinity group: Planning

Classification: • • •

When to use it
In production, as part of day-to-day operations management. Can also be useful for planning projects. Simpler version of Critical Path Analysis.

What you'll achieve
Easy-to-follow map of what happens when in the daily cycle. Shows what daily critical path is, and impact of delay in one area on others.

When not to use it
Don't try to use for systems or processes when operations don't have fixed relationships.

And be careful
Make sure you unwrap processes as far as possible: only one main connection between operations, and no complicated loops.

Training
Familiarity with Critical Path Analysis will help. Short course appropriate to learn conventions.

Where to find out more
Handbook of Quality Tools, Ozeki K, and Asaka T, Productivity Press, 1990

The Seven New QC Tools Made Easy, ed The Seven New QC Tools Research Group, JUSE Press Ltd, 1984

Process flowchart

List all operations in daily schedule

Create operation card for each one

On large sheet of paper, arrange cards in time order, left to right

Create Arrow Diagram using conventions

Write time for operation under arrow leading from it

Use for monitoring and evaluating process

12

Example

The Arrow Diagram is a simplified kind of Critical Path Analysis, specially developed for scheduling internal operations.

In this example, the company assembles fans from imported components. There are five different models of fan, each requiring a different set of parts.

The assembly process is straightforward, but production quality has been variable.

The operations manager constructs an Arrow Diagram to clarify what the production cycle for each fan should be. He can then monitor the progress of actual jobs against the diagram, and identify the critical path.

From the diagram, it emerges that the problem lies with low inventory, causing a shortage of parts. The solutions to be considered might include standardising parts further, increasing inventory, or ordering critical parts earlier.

Wider issues might involve closer relationships with marketing and suppliers to handle peaks and troughs.

Arrow Diagram for assembling fans

Symbols

◯ node or connection point   ➤ operation

ⓧ node number   ⁃➤ dummy operation

◇ decision box

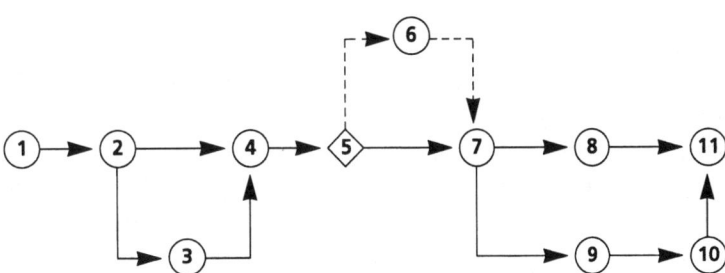

	Activity	Duration (days)
①➤②	Receive production schedule	0.5
②➤③	As necessary create drawings	3.0
③➤④	As necessary create bill of material	1.0
②➤④	Raise work order	0.5
④➤⑤	Decide schedule	0.25
⑤⁃➤⑥	Computer updates schedule	0
⑤➤⑦	Assemble kit parts	1.0
⑦➤⑨	Raise shortage report	0.25
⑨➤⑩	Chase shortages	1.0
⑦➤⑧	Load assembly	0.5
⑧➤⑪	Assemble parts	5.0

Attitude Survey

Tool for sampling opinion about changes or particular initiatives.

Affinity group: Data Capture

Classification •

Process flowchart

Identify issues about which you'd like to know staff views

Prepare questionnaire, using guidelines

Analyse results and carry out any improvements

Repeat Attitude Survey to assess effectiveness of improvements

When to use it
Use in times of organisational change when co-operation and commitment are very important.

What you'll achieve
Information about how people perceive the changes, and a way of assuring them that their opinions are important.

When not to use it
Don't carry out a formal Attitude Survey if you can't promise to respond positively: the exercise will only breed cynicism if nothing happens, along the lines of 'they ask our opinion and then don't want to know'.

And be careful
Structure the questionnaire carefully around specific issues, otherwise it'll just be an opportunity for a general moan.

Training
Knowing the dos and don'ts of questionnaire writing is important.

Where to find out more
Total Quality Management, Pera International, Chapman Hall, 1991

Example

Using an Attitude Survey is a public and positive way of signalling that something important is about to happen.

A technology company is considering ISO 9000. They feel they are discriminated against for major contracts because they are not registered and have on occasion not been eligible to tender at all.

Before starting out, they decide to carry out an Attitude Survey to judge the level of awareness about ISO 9000, and the level of enthusiasm.

Some managers argue against the survey because they feel the decision is theirs, whatever staff feel. They feel it will not be helpful if the questionnaires reveal problems.

However the Managing Director believes that if the survey shows up problems, the company should start an awareness programme and postpone plans until a majority of staff supports them. This is the reason behind the last question.

ISO 9000 Attitude Survey

To all staff
This questionnaire is to find out what you think about ISO 9000 and whether you think we should try for it. Please be honest in your answers. The information will be confidential and we have not asked for your name.

1. Summarise briefly what you know about ISO 9000

   ....

   ....

2. Do you know anyone whose company has achieved it?
   ❏ Yes   ❏ No

3. Do you think certification will require from you:
   ❏ a lot of effort   ❏ average amount of effort
   ❏ too much effort   ❏ no effort at all
   ❏ not much effort

4. How would you rate the quality of management procedures in your area?
   ❏ very good   ❏ poor
   ❏ good   ❏ very poor
   ❏ average

5. What is the single most important thing you feel should be done to improve performance within your work area?

   ....

6. How well do you feel your internal suppliers support you?
   ❏ very well   ❏ poorly
   ❏ well   ❏ very poorly
   ❏ average

7. How well do you feel you support your internal customers?
   ❏ very well   ❏ very poorly
   ❏ well   ❏ in an average way
   ❏ poorly

8. Would improvements in your area benefit external customers?
   ❏ Yes   ❏ No
   if yes, say how ....

   ....

9. Do you think we should aim to achieve ISO 9000?
   ❏ Yes   ❏ No

Attributes Analysis

Tool for selecting the right people for key roles in project teams.

Affinity group: Problem Solving

Classification • • •

When to use it

For key appointments in project teams, or elsewhere in the organisation, when there are a number of likely candidates and you're not sure who'll do the best job.

When not to use it

Don't bother to use it if you need someone's expertise anyway, or if there are no real contenders.

Training

Training in listing attributes useful.

What you'll achieve

An objective way of assessing who will do the best job, irrespective of seniority, political alliances and so on.

And be careful

Attributes Analysis is a broad-brush approach. It shouldn't override individual judgements which may be much more finely tuned to the circumstances.

Where to find out more

The Quality Toolkit, Marsh J, IFS Publications, 1992

List all attributes which are relevant for the role

Rank attributes
1 Unimportant   3 Desirable
2 Useful   4 Essential

Create attributes form, listing Desirable and Essential attributes

Rank candidates
1 Weak   3 Strong
2 Average   4 Very strong

Select candidate with the highest score

16

Example

Using Attributes Analysis makes sure that the reasons behind decisions about appointments are understood and agreed.

One secondary school wants to put together a team to look at the problems of the most able students. They are not sure who to select as project leader however. Some feel experience is the most important criterion, and support Mr Jones who has been on a course. Others feel that it should go to one of the Deputies. Yet another group feel that personal leadership characteristics are most important and support Mrs Davies who can work with even the most difficult staff and students.

To solve the problem, the Principal and his senior staff agree a list of attributes they are looking for, and priorities. They then score the candidates. Although Mrs Davies is only one point ahead of Mr Bailey, it is clear that her strengths are in the Essential attributes, whereas Mr Bailey's are more in the Desirable category.

Attributes Analysis for a project leader

Essential Attributes	Mr Jones	Mrs Davies	Mr Bailey
Ability to work with others	3	4	3
Understanding of the issues	4	3	4
Problem solving ability	3	3	4
Communication skills	2	4	3
Good judgement	2	4	4
Enthusiasm	4	4	2
Commitment	4	4	2
Persuasiveness	1	4	3
Desirable Attributes			
Experience of the issues	4	2	2
Ability to make presentations	2	3	4
Ability to write reports	3	3	3
Good organisational skills	2	2	4
Good time management	2	3	4
Total Score	36	43	42

Audit

Formal assessment tool to make sure standards are maintained.

Affinity group: Quality Management System

Classification • • •

When to use it
As fact-finding initiative at the start of change process, regularly as part of a quality management system, or as a one-off exercise in a particular area to find out what's happening.

When not to use it
Generally best to avoid an initial audit until you're fairly sure procedures are being followed. Otherwise results will be very negative.

Training
Training is necessary and valuable. Specialist audit training and certification courses available.

What you'll achieve
An independent assessment of how closely procedures are being followed. Opportunity to review procedures and standards, and change as necessary.

And be careful
Auditors need perspective and must have tact: they can seem fussy and unsympathetic, and miss important issues if they don't communicate well. On the other hand, they need to be wise to evasion.

Where to find out more
Management Audits, Sayle A J, McGraw Hill, 1981

Process flowchart

Compile checklists of points of conformance audit is looking for

Warn people you are auditing so they have information ready

Interview and check documentation. List evidence of non-conformances

Analyse non-conformances and agree better controls or changes in procedures, as appropriate

Prepare audit report with analysis and action points

Example

Audit can be used as a starting point for a quality management system, or as an important part of maintaining it.

A shelving company which is registered for ISO 9000 receives orders by phone for particular combinations of components, which are then assembled from the warehouse and transported to the customer.

This process is recorded by a series of forms which have to be filled in for each order. The forms are then filed under the order number in the general office.

As part of the audit, the auditor picks a random sample of orders and checks that all the forms have been filled in and filed correctly.

By checking on what people actually do, the audit exercise is able to show that one procedure – involving the form A021 – should be changed, and some adjustments made to improve conformance.

Audit sample of jobs 352, 428, 440, 518

Forms	352	428	440	518
A006 Job specification	✓	✓	✓	✗ (1)
B12 Progress docket	✓	✓	✓	✓
A021 Request to warehouse	✗	✗	✗	✗ (2)
A032 Job completion	✓	✓	✓	✓
A125 Transport docket	✓	✓	✓	✓
A125 (a) Arrivals notification	✗ (3)	✓	✓	✓

Discrepancies and explanations
1. Job specified orally – couldn't find forms.
2. A021 not used. Copy of job specification used instead.
3. Has been seen but missing from file.

Recommendations
- Amend A006 to show when forwarded to warehouse.
- Discontinue A021.
- Make sure supplies of forms are freely available.

Band Graph

Graphic tool for showing how quantitative information is made up and for comparison.

Affinity group: Graphic Tool

Classification • •

When to use it
As an alternative to Pie Charts or Bar Charts, when you need to show both how a given quantity is made up, and how it compares with others.

What you'll achieve
A single Bar Chart shows the breakdown of the components in a given quantity. Placing two or more Band Graphs in parallel means you can compare them, as you could with a segmented Bar Chart.

When not to use it
Don't use for precision. Band Graphs are for creating strong general impressions only.

And be careful
Comparing Band Graphs is not actually very easy visually, and reading from the scale almost impossible after the first graph. So label segments clearly.

Training
None for the concept. Training in using graphics software might be necessary.

Where to find out more
Handbook of Quality Tools, Ozeki K, and Asaka T, Productivity Press, 1990

Process flowchart

Collect data and set out in measurements table

Add column to table showing percentage proportion of each measurement

Draw axis for Band Graph – a horizontal line divided into %

Draw band and divide into percentage proportions, following measurements table. Label sections

Place subsequent graphs underneath. Sections between graphs can be linked with dotted lines

Example

The Band Graph is one of the graphic tools to consider for presenting information clearly.

A senior manager in a multinational company is compiling a report comparing the company's divisions world-wide. All divisions have the same budgets and the same performance targets. But by analysing expenditure, the company hopes to uncover good practice and possible efficiencies. So the important part of the report is the breakdown of expenditure for each division and, most importantly of all, how the divisions compare.

The manager has a graphics package on his PC. He likes the way Pie Charts show the distribution of expenditure in each division, but is frustrated because Pie Charts can't be directly compared. He feels he is closer with a segmented Bar Chart, with different shadings for each performance category, but finds having to refer back to the key for the different shadings awkward.

Finally he creates a Band Graph, which allows him to show clearly both how the total expenditure is made up and how this compares between divisions.

Cross divisional comparisons of expenditure

☐ Sales and Advertising

▧ Production

■ Distribution

■ Overheads

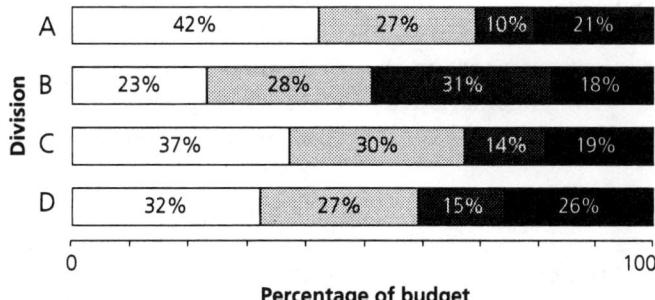

Percentage of budget

Bar Chart

Graphic tool for showing how quantitative values compare.

Affinity group: Graphic Tool

Classification • •

When to use it
For showing how values of a number of items compare and contrast – a straight alternative to the Pie Chart.

What you'll achieve
Effective way of showing comparisons: people are very good at interpreting comparative differences in height.

When not to use it
Don't use when you can't find a suitable scale. The vertical scale should show contrasts clearly, and the horizontal axis should not have more than 10 bars.

And be careful
Don't stack bars for comparing a number of items : comparative heights can't be judged across the graph without a common base-line. Group bars instead, or use Band Graph.

Training
None for the concept. Training in graphics software could be useful.

Where to find out more
The Quality Toolkit, J Marsh, IFS Ltd, 1992

Handbook of Quality Tools, Ozeki K and Asaka T, Productivity Press, 1990

Process flowchart

Collect data and set out in table

Create chart

Vertical axis:
From table, Identify maximum and minimum values and calculate total range by subtracting minimum from maximum

Horizontal axis:
One bar for each data category

Work out scale to suit space available and values

Count up occurrences within each bar and plot on vertical axis

Draw Bar Chart

Example

Bar Charts are good for making clear comparisons between collections of data.

As part of its quality drive, Company D, which sells telephones, has sets up a Helpline for customers who are experiencing problems with particular products. The Helpline records the calls on a Checksheet. When a Bar Chart has been created from the figures, it is possible to make clear general comparisons between the different products. The chart highlights two main problems, products B and D. The results will be analysed in more detail by both the product design and product support departments responsible for products B and D.

Bar Chart showing problems with telecommunications equipment

TALLY SHEET

Product	Tally	Total
A	11111 11111 11	12
B	11111 11111 11111 11111 11111 11111 111	33
C	11111 11111 11111 11111 1	21
D	11111 11111 11111 11111 11111 11111 11111 111	38
E	11111	5
F	11111 11111 11111 1	16
G	11111 11111 111	13
H	11111 111	8
		145

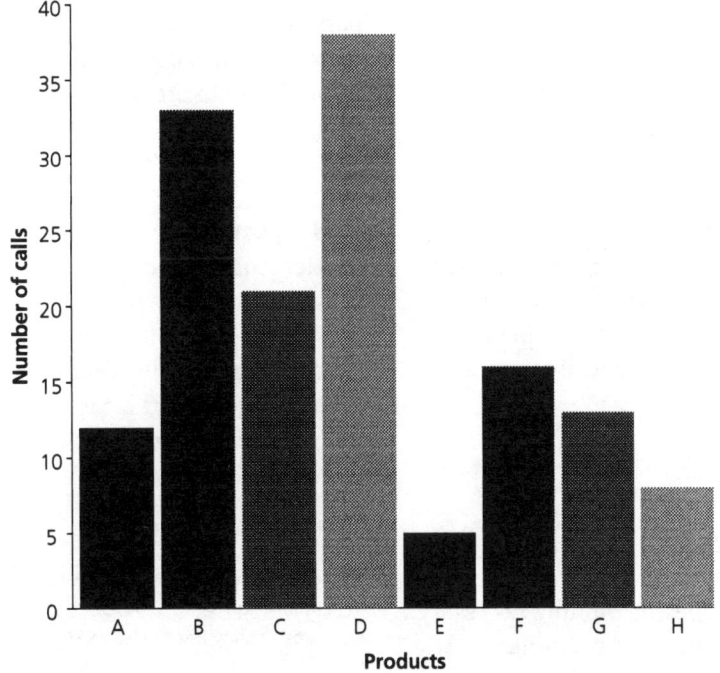

Results of the first quarter of the Customer Product Helpline

Barrier Analysis

Tool for identifying barriers to change within organisation.

Affinity group: Change Management

Classification •••

When to use it
When you want to make sure that a particular project or change initiative you're contemplating has at least a reasonable chance of success.

What you'll achieve
Using Barrier Analysis significantly reduces likelihood of an initiative being sabotaged by major unforeseen barriers of attitude or resources. Also provides information to prepare the ground.

When not to use it
Don't rely on Barrier Analysis when you don't know the situation or the people well enough to identify the real barriers.

And be careful
Barrier Analysis needs to be done realistically – both pessimism and optimism can cause difficulties. If using with broad range of staff rather than management group, consider using a facilitator.

Training
No specific training necessary. Useful to see examples.

Where to find out more
Benchmarking, Camp C, ASQC Quality Press and Quality Resources, 1989

Process flowchart

Define change being considered

Brainstorm potential and actual barriers to change

Group barriers into themes

Check that majority of barriers can be overcome. If not, abandon project

List actions to remove barriers

Barrier Analysis is very often used as a prelude to change.

One car hire company which wants to improve its place in the national rankings has carried out an extensive benchmarking exercise among its competitors focussing on, among other things, levels of customer service. This exercise has shown that it has a long way to go in matching the quality of service delivered by the top 5 companies.

Senior management meet to consider how to go about improving standards and performance.

They draw up a Barrier Analysis which shows that many barriers can be overcome but that it will take a lot of effort to change attitudes and incentivise staff.

A minority of the senior management group feel that the company's inability to improve the quality of its cars is a critical barrier. The group agrees to look further at this problem.

Barrier Analysis
Objective: to improve levels of customer service to match the top 5 car hire companies

Barriers to change	Can they be overcome?	Action Plan
Management attitude		
Complacency	Yes	Share results of benchmarking report
Don't understand problem	Yes	Training about customers
Don't know what's really happening	Yes	Introduce Management by Walking Around
Lack of incentives	Yes	Change bonus scheme to include customer service targets
Staff		
Under Pressure	No	Provide stress training
Not right calibre	Not always	Improve selection methods
Poor attitude	Yes	Training
Apathetic	Yes	Incentives
Financial		
Staff not paid enough	Partly	Change way pay is made up
Poor quality of cars	No	Needs further analysis
Poor servicing of cars	Yes	Change sub-contractor

Benchmarking

Establishing standards of comparison between similar activities in different organisations.

Affinity group: Strategy

Classification • • • •

When to use it
For making sure you're reaching the same standards as your competitors. Particularly feasible if you can find relevant collaborators, perhaps in quality departments, who can share information without revealing commercial secrets.

When not to use it
Don't embark on a lengthy Benchmarking exercise if customers and stakeholders are happy with the way things are. Watching what others are doing is important, but customers are more important than competitors.

Training
Short course on principles, methods and case studies, would be very useful for those leading the exercise.

What you'll achieve
You'll gain an understanding of the standards and targets you can realistically set – because others have achieved them – and which, at the very least, your customers will expect.

And be careful
Competitor information is often hard to get and consequently is not always reliable. And it's often hard to be certain what exactly the competition is. All organisations have unique features which can make comparisons treacherous.

Where to find out more
Benchmarking, Robert C Camp, ASQC Quality Press and Quality Resources, 1989

Strategic Benchmarking, Watson G H, Wiley, 1993

Process flowchart

```
┌─────────────────────────────┐
│ Identify the key products or │
│ processes you want to        │
│ Benchmark                    │
└─────────────────────────────┘
              ┆
┌─────────────────────────────┐
│ Identify competitors         │
└─────────────────────────────┘
              ┆
┌─────────────────────────────┐
│ Identify possible            │
│ collaborators –              │
│ organisations doing similar  │
│ things who aren't competitors│
└─────────────────────────────┘
              ┆
┌─────────────────────────────┐
│ Brainstorm sources of        │
│ information:                 │
│ • libraries                  │
│ • government statistics      │
│ • business databases         │
│ • journals and reports       │
│ • company reports            │
└─────────────────────────────┘
              ┆
┌─────────────────────────────┐
│ Gather and analyse           │
│ information regularly        │
└─────────────────────────────┘
              ┆
┌─────────────────────────────┐
│ Establish strategies to      │
│ close any gaps               │
└─────────────────────────────┘
```

Example

Often posing as a customer will reveal valuable Benchmarking information, particularly in a service-led industry.

A clothing manufacturer wants to set up a mail order operation. However they are conscious of the problems that can afflict mail order – jammed telephone lines, limited payment methods, mistakes in orders, shortages of stock. In order to familiarise themselves with what customers expect, they carry out a Benchmarking exercise by posing as customers.

The results of the survey give them a baseline for what they must achieve. In fact they are quite reassured and feel they can do better than many of their competitors.

Benchmarking in the mail order clothing trade

Ordering	Competitor organisations					
	1	2	3	4	5	6
Times available	8-8	8-10	24hrs	8-6	8-10	8-11
Stock availability check	✓	✓	✓	✓	✓	✓
Re-order if out of stock	✓	✓	✗	✗	✗	✓
Information required from - old customer	Number	Number Name	Name	Name Address	Name	Number Name Address
Information required from - new customer	Name Address D.O.B.	Name Address	Name Address D.O.B. Occup.	Name Address D.O.B. Occup.	Name Address	Name Address
Payment						
With order	✓	✓	✓	✓	✗	✓
On delivery	✗	✗	✗	✗	✗	✗
Invoiced after delivery	✗	✗	✗	✗	✓	✗
Visa	✗	✗	✓	✓	✓	✓
Switch	✓	✓	✓	✓	✓	✓
Delivery						
Average (days)	6	5	4	4	3	2
Guaranteed (days)	7	5	7	5	3	2
By post	✓	✓	✓	✓	✗	✗
By courier	✗	✗	✗	✗	✓	✓
Returns						
Collected	✗	✗	✗	✗	✗	✓
By post	✓	✓	✓	✓	✓	✗
Money refunded (days)	14	14	30	7	28	14
Postage paid	✓	✓	✗	✗	✗	✗

Block Diagram

Graphic tool to show key elements of processes and their owners.

Affinity group: Graphic Tool

Classification • • •

When to use it
As a first step in defining interdepartmental processes. Works at a higher level than flowcharting.

When not to use it
Not so relevant for processes which don't move through departments.

Training
Straightforward tool. Necessary rules can come from books.Software available.

What you'll achieve
Overview of how processes relate to different departments, and who's responsible for them at each stage. Provides a basis for analysing or redesigning them.

And be careful
Keep at overview level: add further detail in departmental flowcharts. Too much detail makes the diagram difficult to interpret.

Where to find out more
The Quality Toolkit, Marsh J, IFS Ltd, 1992

Process flowchart

Define start and end points of the process

Work out which departments the process goes through

Create process chart with blocks for parts of the process, and columns for departments

Add any other details of information flows and work activities

Check validity of the diagram with the departments concerned

Block Diagrams are the obvious starting point for describing complex processes. They make a significant difference to how people understand their work.

A chemicals company needed to make efficiency gains. It processed radioactive materials and therefore had inspection and security requirements to fulfil. But the resulting paperwork transactions could take up to 5 days before chemicals were even booked on the computer, and another 2/3 days before the materials were finally in store.

The company started its review by charting its acceptance process at the Block Diagram level. This showed how the process moved constantly back and forwards between operations, inspection and security.

The next stage was to question whether all these activities were necessary. Perhaps inspection and security could be performed by the same person. Maybe someone outside administration could have access to the computer. Maybe a paperless system could be possible.

Block Diagram for a chemical acceptance and storage process

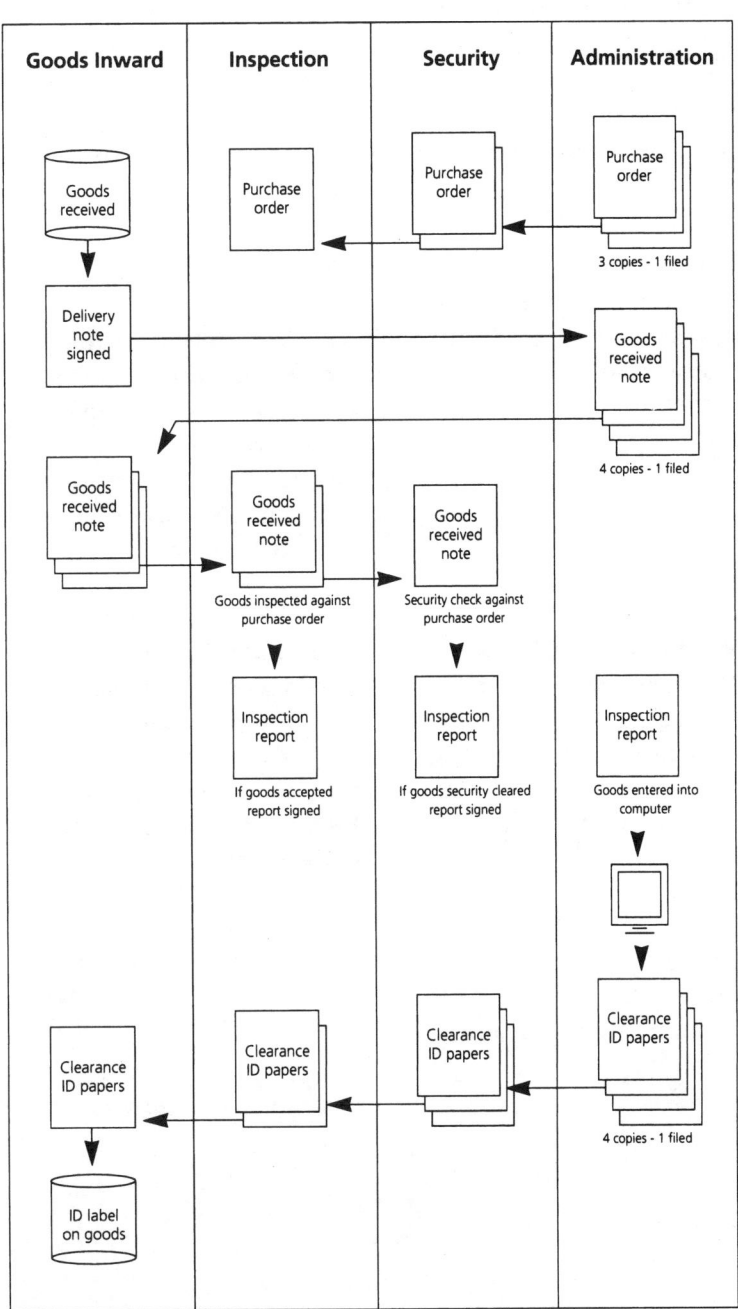

Brainstorming

Tool for maximising group's creativity and problem solving abilities.

Affinity group: Problem Solving

Classification •

When to use it
When you need plenty of good ideas about solving difficult or unusual problems.

What you'll achieve
Many more times (approximately three times, it is claimed) the number of ideas you'd have from the same people working separately. People stimulate each other's thinking. Also ideas likely to be more creative.

When not to use it
Don't use when you don't have a clear idea of what the problem actually is, or when there is one right answer you can derive from a logical thinking process.

And be careful
Needs good facilitating. Too casual, and criticisms of people's ideas will start. Too firm, and creativity stops. Facilitator must create a fun, hothouse atmosphere.

Training
Concept straightforward. Training for the facilitator desirable.

Where to find out more
Creative Thinking and Brainstorming, Rawlinson J G, Wildwood House, 1981

The Memory Jogger, Brassard M, and Ritter D, GOAL QPC, 1981

Process flowchart

Facilitator defines subject of brainstorm

Everyone has 15 minutes to write down all ideas they can think of. Alternatively, everyone in turn gives an idea (or says 'pass')

Facilitator records all ideas without comment or criticism

Facilitator asks group for more ideas until ideas run out

Group discusses, selects and prioritizes the best ideas

Example

Brainstorming is well recognised in creative industries, but it can also help when people aren't used to generating ideas.

A computer consultancy who had developed a software design methodology wanted to find an image for their product which was lively and interesting, but not too slick.

Using their personnel manager as facilitator, they brainstormed the problem and came up with the suggestions listed opposite. Although it was obvious that ideas such as snowflakes or the leaping lion were not appropriate, the group didn't comment or criticise till all the ideas were written down.

The ideas provoked a lively discussion. In the end, the group agreed on the tessellated tiles image, which, conveyed the concept of creativity combined with order – just right for the product.

IMAGES TO DESCRIBE A SOFTWARE DESIGN METHODOLOGY

MAP

ROAD WITH SIGNPOSTS

DATA FLOW DIAGRAM

FLOW CHART

MAGNIFYING GLASS

MOTORWAY SIGN

STEPPING STONES ACROSS MARSH

JET PLANE THROUGH CLOUDS

ARCHITECT'S BLUEPRINT

BUILDING PLAN

STARSHIP

TRAIL BLAZING THROUGH CLOUDS

BUILDING A HOUSE

SNOWFLAKE PATTERNS

NESTED BOXES

TESSELLATED TILES

PATH THROUGH BUILDING SITE

TREE WITH BRANCHES

RIVER

LEAPING LION

GEOMETRY SET

PENCILS, RUBBERS, CRAYONS

Break-even Chart

Graphic method of showing relationship between costs and profits.

Affinity group: Cost Management

Classification • • •

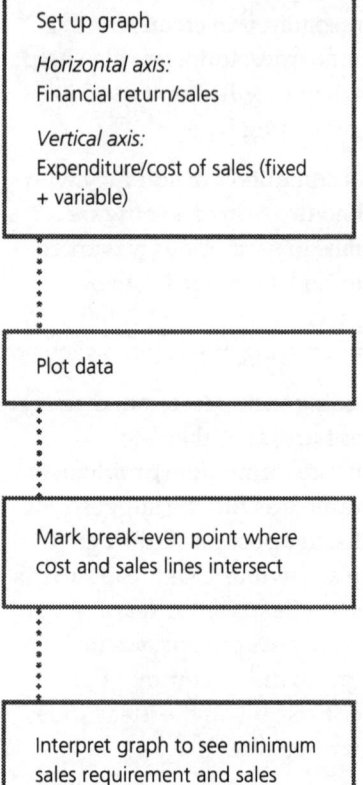

Process flowchart

Set up graph

Horizontal axis:
Financial return/sales

Vertical axis:
Expenditure/cost of sales (fixed + variable)

Plot data

Mark break-even point where cost and sales lines intersect

Interpret graph to see minimum sales requirement and sales figure for optimum profit

When to use it
For comparing an expenditure to an economic return. Can be used to justify projects and investment expenditure, or to set sales targets.

What you'll achieve
A focus on profit rather than turnover: an understanding of how increasing the existing sales levels brings more profit than developing new products.

When not to use it
Don't use break-even calculations without reliable information on variable costs (related to volume) and fixed costs.

And be careful
Remember you can't just extend the cost line indefinitely: at a certain capacity, costs will hit a step change when major new investment is needed to produce more. Profits won't actually hit the roof.

Training
Some expert advice is necessary – calculating costs will need help from the accountancy department.

Where to find out more
Quality Control Handbook, Juran J, McGraw Hill, 1988

Example

Break-even Charts are an important part of sales and profit calculations.

A reproduction furniture company has developed a new gothic cupboard. They can either sell wholesale or direct to the public, by advertising in the national press.

The company is divided about which route to take. To help to resolve the issue, the finance department is asked to prepare some figures, which it presents as the Break-even Chart opposite.

The figures show that the break-even point for selling wholesale is 100 units. The break-even point for selling direct, taking into account advertising costs of £8,000, is 120 units.

The company must consider whether they can increase the price for direct sales to compensate for the extra fixed costs (eg advertising).

Break-even Chart – wholesale

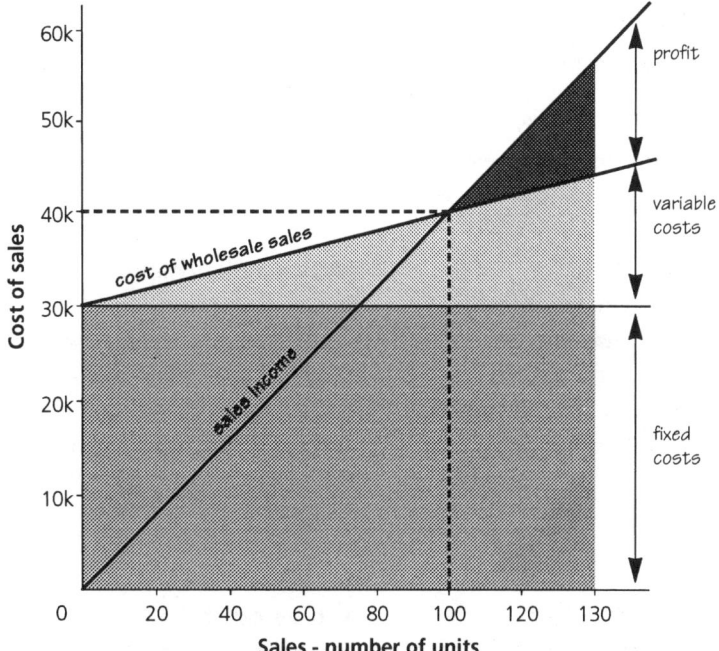

Break-even Chart – direct sales

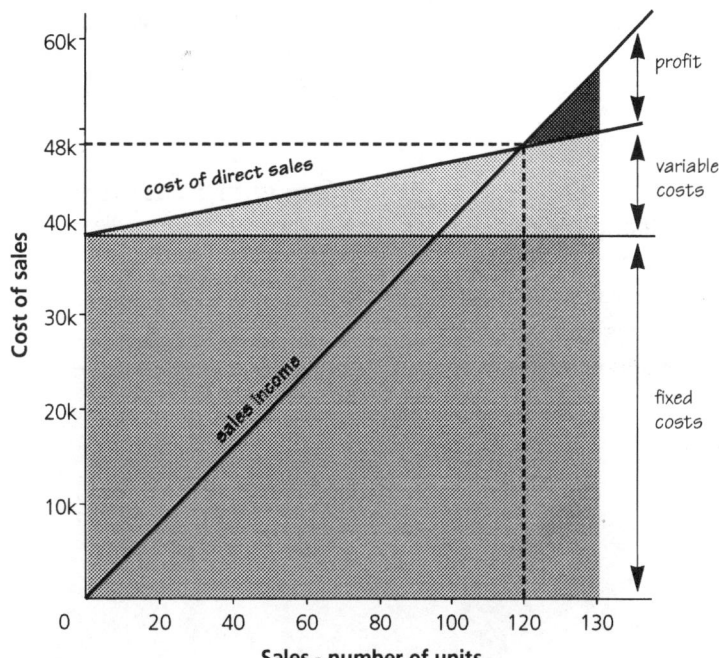

Business Process Re-engineering (BPR)

Tool for radical overhaul of business processes.

Affinity group: Strategy

Classification • • • • •

When to use it
When facing fundamental change, perhaps because of technology or competition, and you have to do something radical to survive. Or for start-ups, to provide a competitive advantage.

When not to use it
Don't use this approach unless significant change is necessary – certainly not just because it's popular.

Training
This is a tool you would expect to be used by experienced management consultants. Needs extensive research to consider and justify concepts.

What you'll achieve
Successful projects claim significant improvements in efficiency and customer service, often by doing things in ways no-one had thought of. Survival of the company may be at stake.

And be careful
Takes massive amounts of time and resources to make significant changes. Consider key activities first: wholesale change may damage organisation.

Where to find out more
Re-engineering the Corporation, Hammer M, and Champy J, Nicholas Brealey Publishing, 1993

Business Process Re-engineering, A Handbook for Executives, Towers S, Stanley Thornes, 1994

Process flowchart

Identify need for fundamental change in efficiency or customer service

Identify what customers want

Design new, logical, cross-functional processes to serve customers' needs

Build or adapt Information Technology systems to support new processes

Implement changes and measure improvements

Example

Obvious examples of BPR are when companies decide to do things differently in ways which are visible to customers.

A Canadian DIY manufacturer had moved into retailing and was among the first to establish out-of-town sites. However falling sales and profit levels were causing concern.

The company decided to take out the link in the value chain from warehousing to retailing, so reducing costs. And staff would be trained to give product support and so increase customer service.

These changes meant a radical overhaul of supplier relationships, moving to a more Just-In-Time relationship. The inventory management system had to be computerised to provide on-line, real-time stock information. Then there was an extensive building programme, adding retail areas to warehouses. Existing retail sites were closed and staff extensively re-trained.

The gamble paid off however and the company is for the moment comfortably ahead of the competition.

BPR in DIY retailing

Original value chain - before BPR

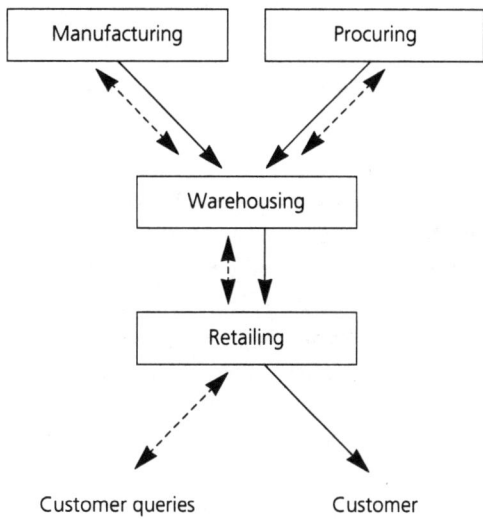

After BPR Lower costs - better customer service

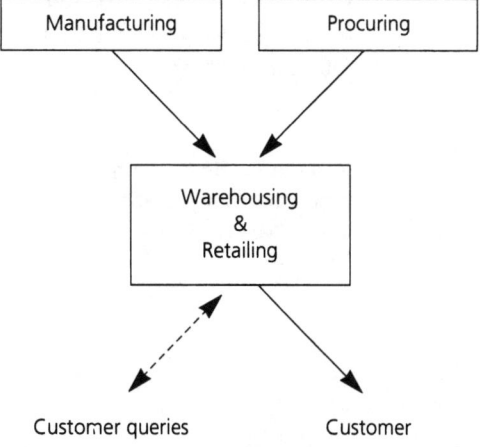

Business Simplification

Tool for streamlining business operations for maximum efficiency.

Affinity group: Strategy

Classification • • • • •

List customer requirements

Create flowchart of existing processes which deliver them

Select activities directly needed for customer requirements

Redesign so that essential activities are carried out in simplest, most controllable way

Measure new performance levels

When to use it
To rationalise and simplify the way things are done. Can be introduced gradually over time to specific parts of the business.

What you'll achieve
A more logical, streamlined version of your existing business. It's a way of improving processes without causing major disruption.

When not to use it
Don't use for radical change or where global change is necessary – use Business Process Re-engineering instead.

And be careful
Don't go too far with eliminating activities: you'll only have to reintroduce complexity. And if you use consultants, make sure staff are fully involved – it's their jobs that'll change .

Training
Probably not a tool for amateurs: best carried out in conjunction with industry consultants.

Where to find out more
Benchmarking, Camp Robert C, ASQC Quality Press and Quality Resources, 1989

Example

Administrative systems are often prime targets for simplification.

A manufacturing company offered a mail order kitchen door and shelf service. It offered a full exchange or refund if the doors or shelves didn't fit – even if the fault was the customer's. This offer represented a unique level of customer service.

Exchanges represented about 20% of orders, and were dealt with quickly. However to get a refund, staff had to go through an elaborate process of checking and confirmation.

Customers started to complain about the time it took to get a refund, so the company brought in consultants to devise a simpler and quicker process.

Three months later the number of refunds had risen but was more than offset by savings in staff time. In addition customer relations improved and sales staff were able to concentrate more on selling and less on processing paperwork.

Business Simplification of a refunds process

Before Business Simplification

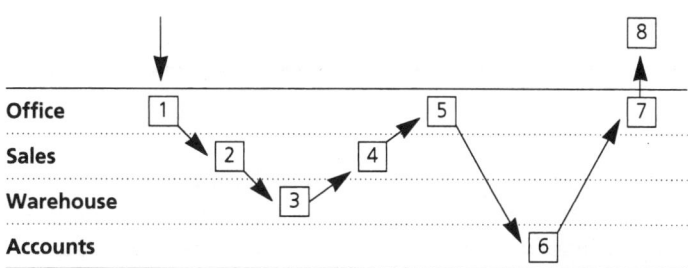

➤ 1 Request for refund comes to office
➤ 2 Office verifies order with sales staff
➤ 3 Warehouse checks to see if item is returned – if not, refund put on hold until it is
➤ 4 Sales staff confirm customer doesn't want alternative
➤ 5 Sales staff report to office
➤ 6 Office requests cheque from Accounts
➤ 7 Accounts sends cheque to office for approval
➤ 8 Office sends cheque to customer

After Business Simplification

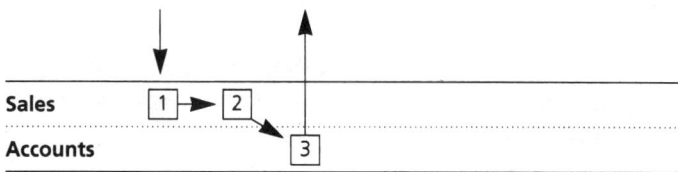

➤ 1 Request for refund comes to office
➤ 2 Office verifies order with sales staff
➤ 3 Office asks Accounts to send refund cheque to customer

c Chart

Control chart for monitoring the number of defects in a particular unit of production.

Affinity group: Statistical Quality Control

Classification • • •

Process flowchart

Set sample size

Collect data about defects and calculate average number of defects per sample

Calculate probabilities (using probability tables) and set upper warning and action limits

Set up chart and monitor the number of defects per unit in relation to average

When to use it
Use the c Chart for processes making individual units, which could each have a number of faults in a number of different places.

What you'll achieve
Indication of when the average number of defects in the units being produced goes outside acceptable limits. Also information about the process which may lead to quality improvement ideas.

When not to use it
Don't use c Charts for controlling products which have to meet specifications – they only show relative performance. c Charts are for attributes, not variables.

And be careful
Make sure samples consist of identical products – any variations will skew the results.

Training
Training in Statistical Process Control is essential to set up charts like this– once they're running, in-house training is needed to use them.

Where to find out more
Quality Control Handbook, Juran J, McGraw Hill, 1988

A Practical Approach to Quality Control, Caplan R H, Hutchinson Publishing Group, 1978

Example

c Charts can be used to monitor the quality of things like:

- painted doors (for scratches and flaws)

- painted coachwork (for irregularities)

- windscreens (for bubbles in the glass)

- furniture with a polished finish (for scratches and flaws).

The c Chart does not monitor whether things are the right size, or whether they will fit with something else – in other words, conformance to specification. Rather it monitors faults which can occur randomly within each product, showing how the number compares to an acceptable average.

c Chart for monitoring the number of bubbles in blown glass vases

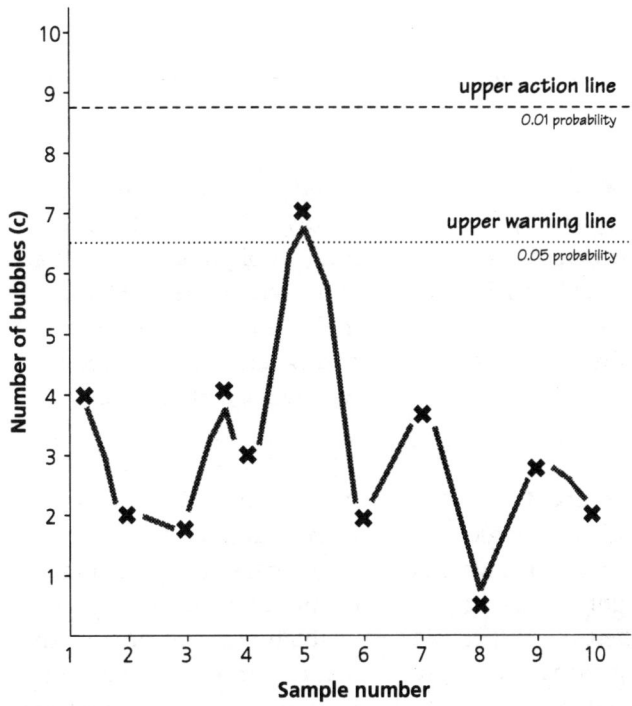

Cause and Effect Diagram

Problem solving tool to uncover the reasons behind problems.

Affinity group: Problem Solving

Classification • • •

When to use it
When there is a fairly large-scale problem, perhaps involving a number of people and activities, which could have a number of causes.

What you'll achieve
A way of finding which of a number of potential causes are at the root of the problem, making use of the experience and expertise of the people who work with it.

When not to use it
Not appropriate for logical, puzzle-type problems which have one right answer, or in cultures where it is difficult for people to be open about what they think and feel.

And be careful
Identifying causes can degenerate into spreading blame. This tool needs good facilitation to prevent this and to move group members on from any preconceptions they may have.

Training
A straight-forward tool. But training and experience both important for facilitator.

Where to find out more
The Guide to Quality Control, Ishikawa K, Asian Productivity Centre, 1982

The Memory Jogger, Brassard M and Ritter D, GOAL/QPC, 1994

Process flowchart

Define problem and put on right of diagram, at the end of a horizontal line

Identify main causes and join to horizontal line by sloping lines

Brainstorm subordinate causes and attach to main cause lines

Look for root causes by identifying causes which occur more than once or which are related

Propose solutions to root causes

Example

Cause and Effect Diagrams can be used for abstract problems or to trace physical causes.

A small, semi-industrial pottery used the tool to solve a problem with glazes. The pottery used distinctive brightly coloured glazes, applied mechanically and decorated by hand.

The pottery had faced a spate of quality problems with its base glazes. An increasingly high percentage had to be rejected because they were cracked, and the hand painters complained of the rough and uneven texture of many of the others.

The pottery brought everyone together to discuss the problem. A facilitator started a Cause and Effect Diagram on the flipchart at the front of the room. As the meeting progressed, the diagram was gradually filled in.

Two themes emerged. As the company expanded, it was taking on new operators who didn't understand the process fully. And its machinery was wearing out and needed improved maintenance or replacement.

Hartscombe pottery

Problem: the quality of glazes is falling

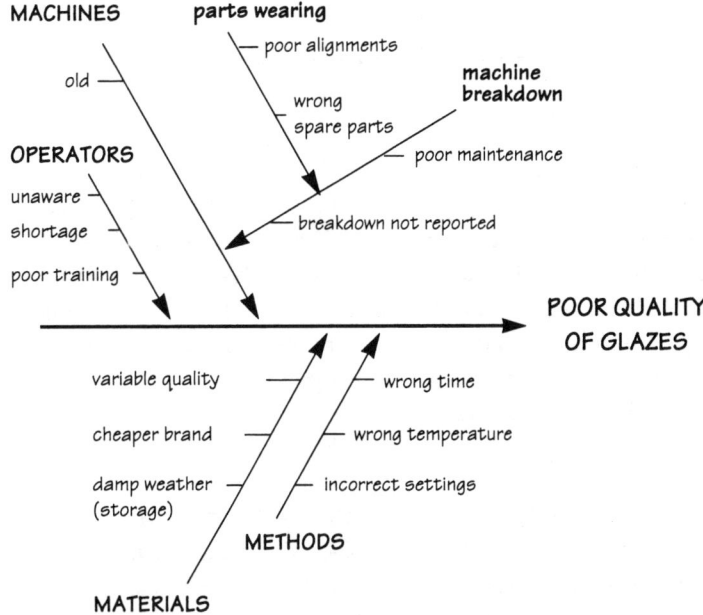

Checklist

A list of things to be routinely done, remembered or checked.

Affinity group: Data Capture

Classification •

Identify points in processes or procedures where checklists are needed

List all the things that have to be checked

Construct checklist – a tickbox followed by things which need to be checked

Make copies of checklists and have them available at the point of use

Tick off points as they're dealt with, and sign completed list

When to use it
As part of a quality management system, to support the standardisation of tasks. Can be used as a one-off prompt, for individual tasks, but makes most difference as a way of defining routine tasks.

What you'll achieve
Reduced stress and increased efficiency, as people don't have to rely on unreliable short-term memories to make sure tasks are carried out properly.

When not to use it
Don't use for complicated instructions – checklists support procedures, but don't replace them.

And be careful
Keep descriptions of things to check short and clear. Remember to tick things off as they're done, otherwise you'll forget what's been done and what hasn't.

Training
No training needed.

Where to find out more
Quality Control Handbook, Juran J, McGraw Hill, 1988

Example

Without the security of a checklist even routine operations can go wrong if someone forgets a vital detail.

A design agency had been having a bad run of luck with print. One job took over a fortnight to dry, because there was a mismatch between the density of the ink and the absorbency of the paper. Another job went well over budget because the accounts manager assumed that the cost of film was included in the print quote, when it wasn't.

The agency staff agreed to tighten up on print specification procedures. They listed all the questions that needed to be asked, and produced a checklist. All the boxes on the checklist had to be ticked, and the checklist signed, before the printer could accept a print order.

The checklist made everyone much more comfortable, especially junior staff, who knew that any mistakes could cost the company a lot of money.

Print Specification Checklist

- [ ] Printing process specified
- [ ] Printer capability checked
- [ ] Delivery cost included
- [ ] Level of quality specified
- [ ] Film supplied
- [ ] Any part of job subcontracted
- [ ] Repro specification agreed
- [ ] Paper specification agreed
- [ ] Time to pass proofs agreed
- [ ] Proof type specified
- [ ] Appropriate binding system specified
- [ ] Imposition follows binding method
- [ ] Best folding method agreed
- [ ] Ink colours agreed
- [ ] Dummies wanted
- [ ] Number in print run specified
- [ ] Delivery address specified
- [ ] Delivery dates agreed
- [ ] Out-of-hours contact agreed
- [ ] Person to sign off print specified
- [ ] Date:
- [ ] Signed by:

Checksheet

For recording numbers of occurrences at regular intervals.

Affinity group: Data Capture

Classification •

Define what to observe, measure and record

Set observation intervals

Make checksheet with things to measure down the left, and measurement intervals along the top

Collect data

Present results in an appropriate graphic format

When to use it
For collecting data over time to show trends and recurring patterns which need to be understood and controlled.

What you'll achieve
Checksheets set up a system for collecting hard data to confirm or refute beliefs or impressions.

When not to use it
Checksheets won't explain one-off incidents or random sequences. And only use when you have some idea of the root cause.

And be careful
Sometimes it can take longer to collect the data than fix the problem in the first place – think about ways of simplifying the task, perhaps using an automated system. And where possible, let people collect their own data – then they'll trust it.

Training
No training needed to record observations.

Where to find out more
Handbook of Quality Tools, Ozeki K and Asaka T, Productivity Press, 1990

The Memory Jogger, Brassard M and Ritter D, GOAL/QPC, 1994

Example

Collecting data can be the only way of resolving serious differences of opinion.

A hospital was experiencing friction between its consultants and its medical secretaries. The system of allocating one secretary to each consultant had been changed, with all work going into a central pool to be carried out by whoever was free. The doctors said that, ever since, their reports had taken longer to complete and were full of mistakes.

Both sides agreed to record the length of time it took reports to go through the system, and to monitor how many mistakes there were in each. In addition, the secretaries would record:

• delays due to words they couldn't read, or

• delays because parts of the report was missing.

The figures collected over a four-week period seemed to suggest that the typing pool had a capacity limit of somewhere around 30 reports per week. Over that number, there were serious bottlenecks and higher error rates.

CHECKSHEET

MONITORING PRODUCTION OF DOCTOR'S REPORTS

REPORTS	WEEK 1	WEEK 2	WEEK 3	WEEK 4
TOTAL REPORTS TYPED	32	24	21	46
REPORTS DELAYED - 5 DAYS FROM DELIVERY	21	8	5	26
NEED RETYPING - SPELLING MISTAKES	7	4	2	12
DELAYED - BY QUERIES	8	2	3	6
DELAYED - BY SOMETHING MISSING	6	2	0	8

Classification of Defects

For classifying quality problems by their level of seriousness.

Affinity group: Prioritization

Classification • • •

When to use it
When a number of opportunities to improve products or services present themselves, and you need to decide which ones to pursue.

What you'll achieve
Guidelines for prioritizing resources to support improvements which really matter to customers – not just the ones that are easiest to carry out.

When not to use it
Don't use as an alternative to common sense. Often priorities are intuitively clear. The process of defining and classifying defects can be very time-consuming.

And be careful
Good definitions of levels of problems make classification easier. And make sure to update priorities as legislation and/or customer expectations change.

Training
A training day will be needed to become familiar with defect classification systems.

Where to find out more
Quality Control Handbook, Juran J, McGraw Hill, 1988

Process flowchart

Make a list of all the defects in a process or organisation

Decide on how many levels of seriousness to use for the classification

Define each level of seriousness

Classify each defect

Target quality effort on the most serious defects

Example

The toy industry has to enforce rigorous quality standards as defects can harm children and make manufacturers and retailers liable to prosecution.

A toy company wants to import a range of small, cheap toys. It wants its suppliers to improve both the perceived quality of the toys – their design and presentation – and their conformance to British safety standards. However they accept that some compromises will have to be made if the deal is to remain economically viable.

The company uses the Classification of Defects tool to resolve this issue. The supplier will make all Level A improvements right away, and introduce Level B improvements gradually over the next two years. Level C and D improvements will be considered during this period if the line generates a high enough level of sales and profit.

CLASSIFICATION OF DEFECTS FOR IMPORTED TOYS

CLASSIFICATION LEVELS

AFFECTS	LEVEL A	LEVEL B	LEVEL C	LEVEL D
DANGER TO CHILD	Yes	Unlikely	No	No
USABILITY	Signifi- cantly	Limited	Limited	Very little
BUYING DECISION	Will lose customers	May lose customers	Unlikely to lose customers	Unlikely
CONFORMANCE TO REGULATIONS	Fails on safety	Borderline on safety	Minor non conformances	Conforms fully

CLASSIFICATION OF DEFECTS

LEVEL A
- Sharp edges on mouldings
- Inflammable paint used for detailing
- Moving parts jam
- Poor branding on packaging
- Moving parts not covered
- Instructions left out

LEVEL B
- Tastes bad in mouth
- Flimsy – assembly falls apart
- Plastic too brittle – breaks easily
- Unoriginal product design (follower, not leader)
- Poor instructions

LEVEL C
- Packaging overpromises
- Colours sometimes uneven
- Lack of distinctive product characteristics
- Overdesigned (use too much material)

LEVEL D
- Inconsistencies between products
- Faces not realistic
- Too much packaging
- Difficult to assemble

Clean Sheet Analysis

For developing alternative ways of operating, to achieve better results.

Affinity group: Strategy

Classification • •

When to use it
When the demands on your business are changing, and there is an opportunity to think again about how things are done.

What you'll achieve
Using Clean Sheet Analysis gives you a chance to start afresh and work out logically how it would be best to do things. You can have surprising insights by ignoring the usual constraints.

When not to use it
Don't use such a radical approach if improving or modifying your present operations will bring the improvements you need.

And be careful
Clean Sheet Analysis can be just a distraction if in reality things can't be changed.

Training
Training is needed for industry-specific benchmarking.

Where to find out more
Benchmarking, Camp R, ASQC Quality Press, 1989

Process flowchart

Specify operation under review

Collect all possible objective data about it, using benchmarking techniques

Brainstorm ways to change to meet new goals

Create new model of operations, to meet standards set by benchmarking data

Either implement new model, or use to improve existing operations

Example

An established consultancy company realised it was in a mature market place. And in a situation where there was fierce competition and lower day rates. A major review was necessary, so they decided to use Clean Sheet Analysis and Benchmarking exercises. These tools established that technological fields were promising, as there was a niche of clients accessible, and the cost of entering this field was no longer prohibitively high.

Clean Sheet Analysis created a new model of what was needed: a different type of consultant, and lower overheads. For the first they would need to be of a higher calibre and therefore would only be afforded on an associate basis. Secondly the company would release it's head office and use the Internet instead, to link consultants. Secretaries were replaced by part-time support and marketing and telesales were sub-contracted on a 'no results - no fee' basis.

The company was now poised for the new age. Thinking outside the boundary – Clean Sheet Analysis – is sometimes a question of survival.

Clean Sheet analysis for reinventing a management consultancy company

Brainstorm

Overheads too high

Wrong type of work

Wrong type of consultants

Not flexible enough

Not up to date with technology

Missing new markets

Sales process outdated

Not using sales specialist

Employing staff – not networking

Administration distributed to consultants

Not using technology

Company Wide Quality Improvement

Tool for improving internal company processes by setting up a chain of internal customer-supplier relationships.

Affinity group: Quality Management System

Classification ••••

Create project management structure and appropriate project teams

Make a flowchart of the process under review

Identify customer-supplier relationships throughout the process

Find ways of improving customer-supplier interfaces

Introduce a recognition or reward system for improvements

When to use it
As part of a long-term programme to improve internal processes. Especially useful in large organisations and where consensus is the only way forward.

What you'll achieve
Small changes which combine to increase efficiency and improve morale, without causing major upsets or disruption.

When not to use it
Don't use this tool if what you need is radical or instant change. Doesn't suit some cultures or smaller less bureaucratic organisations.

And be careful
Because it's slow and steady, it can fizzle out due to the inertia of organisations. Needs constant management support.

Training
Training in flowcharting and analysis will be necessary.

Where to find out more
The Quality Management Library, CCTA, HMSO, 1992

Example

As part of a Company Wide Quality Improvement programme, a company examined the relationship between its IT unit and the rest of the organisation. Informal reports had suggested some frustration on both sides.

Problem management was a good example of this. If users had a problem, they rang the help desk. However, it was only manned between 10am and 3pm. When users did speak to the help desk, it logged the problem and passed it on to the relevant maintenance engineer. But sometimes no-one would take responsibility for the problem.

The maintenance engineers were supposed to tell the help desk when they had finished. Often they did not, however, particularly when their work was carried out after hours. So sometimes no-one knew if the problem had been dealt with or not.

By analysing these problems in terms of the customer-supplier interface, a programme of gradual but significant improvements emerged.

Help desk analysis

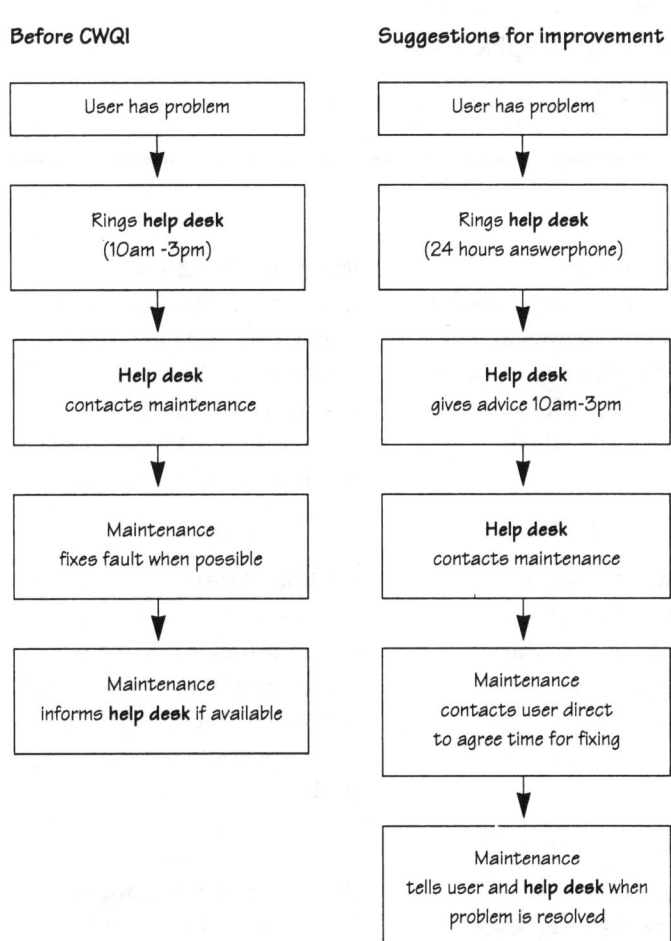

Before CWQI

| User has problem |
| Rings **help desk** (10am -3pm) |
| **Help desk** contacts maintenance |
| Maintenance fixes fault when possible |
| Maintenance informs **help desk** if available |

Suggestions for improvement

| User has problem |
| Rings **help desk** (24 hours answerphone) |
| **Help desk** gives advice 10am-3pm |
| **Help desk** contacts maintenance |
| Maintenance contacts user direct to agree time for fixing |
| Maintenance tells user and **help desk** when problem is resolved |

Concentration Diagram

Graphic method of recording where problems occur, to gain insight into what's causing them.

Affinity group: Graphic Tool

Classification • •

When to use it
As one of a number of tools to find out what's causing problems in the way products or processes work, and so to see how to solve them.

When not to use it
Don't use as the first diagnostic tool, or the only one.

Training
No formal training needed.

What you'll achieve
Insight into where problems are located and what this might mean. This is the only way to make this connection: you can't see it by looking at traditional tables of data.

And be careful
Concentration Diagrams are only one tool for finding causes of problems: often best to combine them with other tools to see all aspects of the problem.

Where to find out more
The Memory Jogger, Brassard M and Ritter D, GOAL/QPC, 1994

Quality Control Handbook, Juran J, McGraw Hill, 1988

Process flowchart

Define problem

Set up diagram as a visual representation of the product or process under review

Plot data on diagram

Check for connections between the location of problems and their causes

Example

Concentration Diagrams have been used in a wide variety of ways, from plotting cholera epidemics and archeological finds, to diagnosing faults on equipment or filling in forms. It is a very powerful tool because, uniquely, it uncovers spatial relationships between data.

One organisation used a Concentration Diagram to help solve its problems with the photocopier. The machine was constantly in use, and consequently always running hot and experiencing feed problems. In addition the quality of copies was variable and the machine was the most hated in the building.

The maintenance engineers became very frustrated by the level of hostility directed at them, and decided to use a Concentration Diagram to help them to diagnose the problems exactly.

They put a large diagram of the machine on the wall beside it, and asked users to mark down any problems they experienced. This not only gave the engineers the information they needed, but made the users feel better.

Concentration Diagram for recording faults with a photocopier

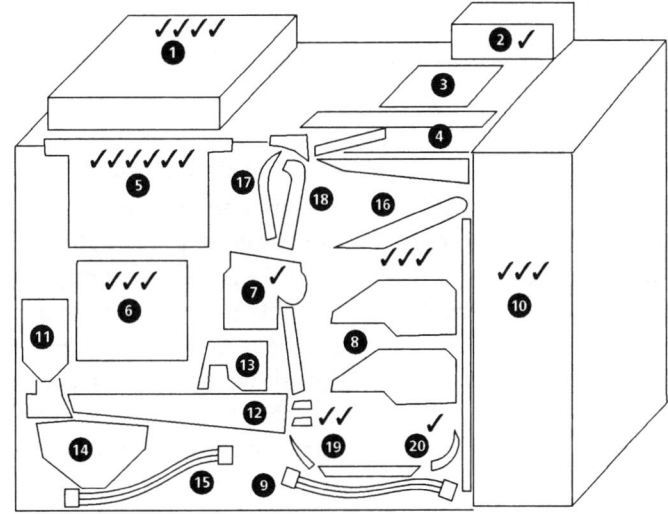

Control Chart

Tool which supports Statistical Process Control in monitoring process performance.

Affinity group: Statistical Quality Control

Classification • • •

Set up appropriate Control Chart
Vertical axis:
Measurement
Horizontal axis:
Time

Set as appropriate:
• upper and lower conrol limits
• warning line
• average value

Plot measurements or data

Analyse results

Take immediate actions and introduce quality improvement strategies, as necessary

When to use it

For monitoring and controlling how a manufacturing process is performing over time – from small batch to large production run. To stop problems before they develop too far.

What you'll achieve

Information on when the process is slipping out of control – gives shop floor visibility to movement in the process, and signals when it is outside acceptable limits. Also insight into quality improvement strategies.

When not to use it

Don't use for random processes or when data has no relationship over time, for example in project-based work.

And be careful

Make sure you know what you want the chart to reveal: that you've chosen the right things to measure, and the right type of chart to analyse them. The wrong tool means the wrong conclusions.

Training

Training in Statistical Process Control is essential for setting up charts and calculating the various control lines. Once established, all operators can be trained to maintain them.

Where to find out more

The Economic Control of Manufacturing Quality, Shewart W, Dover Press, 1936

Quality Control Handbook, Juran J, McGraw Hill, 1988

Control Charts, Murdoch J, MacMillan, 1979

Control Charts are the visible tools of Statistical Process Control. They provide the window through which the performance of the process can be viewed. By providing a control at the point of manufacture, processes can be kept with tolerance at all times. Quality is built-in – not inspected-in.

Control Charts are an essential part of the car industry's achievement in improving quality and reducing cost. Systems such as Ford's Q1 quality specifications ensure that all parts of the car subassemblies from a wide range of suppliers fit together. Other engineering industries which rely on Control Charts for controlling parts specifications are aerospace and indeed space technology. It could probably be argued that without Control Charts there wouldn't be a man on the moon.

A generic Control Chart

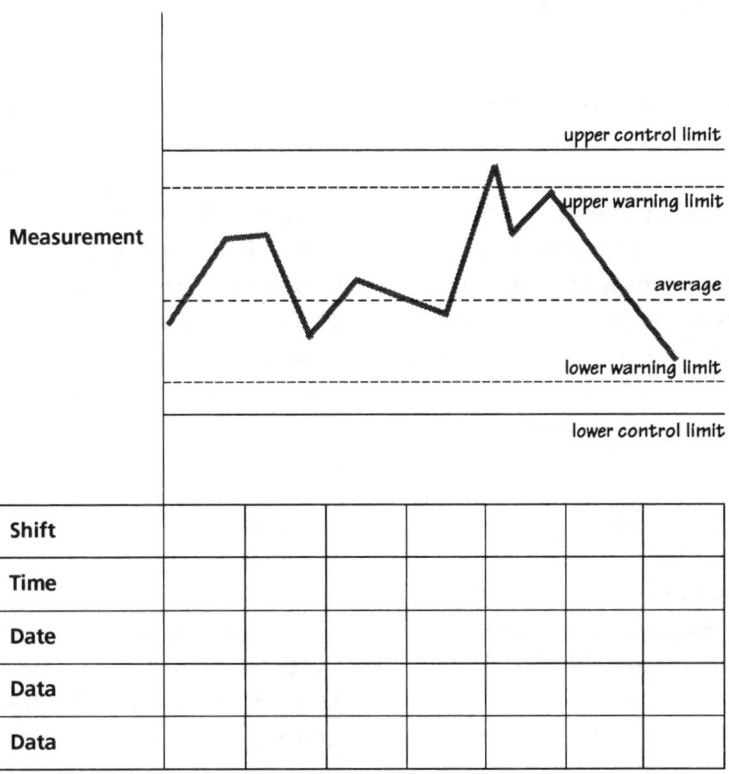

Corrective Action

Tool for focusing on root causes of problems.

Affinity group: Quality Management System

Classification • • •

Identify most significant problems from data or from audit

Form team to analyse problem and find the root cause

Develop and implement solutions in consultation with those involved

Monitor results

When to use it
For solving underlying problems which consistently result in poor quality products or processes. Particularly good as a way of responding to customer complaints.

What you'll achieve
Corrective Action will lead to long-term solutions to problems which otherwise would continue to deteriorate and cause trouble over time.

When not to use it
Don't use the Corrective Action mechanism for occasional or not-very-important problems.

And be careful
There are cultural issues involved in the concept of Corrective Action: people can feel threatened and criticised. Management should take the lead and initial responsibility, and then delegate.

Training
Part of training for implementing quality management systems.

Where to find out more
Total Quality Management, Pera International, Chapman and Hall, 1991

Total Quality Control, Feigenbaum A V, McGraw Hill, 1983

Managing for Total Quality, The Industrial Society

Example

Corrective Action can be used in the early stages of quality improvement, to deal with immediate problems.

A storage systems company used it in this way. Although they had started a quality management initiative, they felt they could not wait for it to be in place before starting to deal with customer complaints. So a file was set up to record customer complaints and to detail the corrective action needed to make sure the problem wouldn't recur. Only when action had been taken was the file considered closed for that complaint.

Senior management took a direct interest in the complaints file, providing resources for solving problems as they arose, and monitoring progress. This gave the complaints file a high priority in the company which also helped to get things done.

In the meantime, work to set up a complete quality management system continued in parallel.

Complaints file

Corrective Action for a storage systems company

Number of types of problem in the period Jan.89 - Mar. 90

Storage systems	SL	I	A	SD	SP	Par	PID	Other	Total
Short delivery	96	152	53	08	40	04	02	65	420
Damaged	26	43	08	01	00	05	57	02	142
Wrong goods	37	70	21	06	00	12	89	14	249
Late	14	08	13	07	04	09	08	02	65
Wrong discount	32	17	12	03	01	13	35	38	151
Cancellation	03	03	00	00	00	03	01	02	12
Early delivery	01	02	00	00	00	01	00	00	04
Balance problem	05	07	01	01	01	35	01	06	57
Total	214	302	108	26	46	82	193	129	1100

Cost Benefit Analysis

Tool for comparing costs of investments with benefits they'll bring.

Affinity group: Cost Management

Classification • • •

Process flowchart

Decide on time and activities Cost Benefit Analysis will cover

Brainstorm all factors incurring costs or bringing benefits, including hidden costs and intangible benefits such as customer service

Where possible, allocate money value to factors and divide into cost/benefit lists

Compare the results and analyse reasons

When to use it
When you're trying to decide if a particular investment will be worthwhile, or if there are better ways to do what you want to do.

What you'll achieve
A rational way of assessing and prioritising proposed investments: choose those which bring the most benefits.

When not to use it
Don't try developing a detailed Cost Benefit Analysis if intangible and unquantifiable factors form the major part of the decision.

And be careful
Money is usually not the only consideration, take other factors into account.And use the accounting principle of conservatism: underestimate benefits, and estimate costs high.

Training
Anyone can do simple analyses. More complex ones need some training, in costing and accounting principles and methods.

Where to find out more
Cost Benefit Analysis, Layard R, Penguin, 1972

Total Quality Management, Pera International, Chapman and Hall, 1991

58

Example

Investment decisions at any level can be supported by cost benefit calculations.

One small manufacturing company had relied on the same accounts and secretarial support for the last twenty years. But work had increased in volume and their secretary was thinking of working part time or retiring altogether in the not too distant future.

The logical thing to do seemed to be to buy a PC with accounts and wordprocessing packages. However it did seem like a big investment.

To convince them, the secretary put together a Cost Benefit Analysis which showed that the PC would bring considerable savings, particularly if she could work fewer hours, as she wanted. Break-even would come in year 2. In addition the company would have more timely profit and loss accounts, better cash flow, and a regular balance sheet (which wasn't possible with a manual system).

Cost Benefit Analysis for buying a PC

Costs (£)	Year 1	Year 2	Year 3	Year 4	Total
PC machine	2500	000	000	000	2500
Maintenance contract	000	150	150	150	450
Training	600	200	200	200	1200
Software accounts	500	000	200	000	700
Software wordprocessing	200	000	000	000	200
Total annual costs	3800	350	550	350	5050
Cumulative cost	3800	4150	4700	5050	

Benefits (£)	Year 1	Year 2	Year 3	Year 4	Total
Staff salary saved	2000	2500	2500	2750	9750
Fewer consumables	100	100	100	100	400
Reduced book-keeping fees	800	850	900	900	3450
Total annual benefit	2900	3450	3500	3750	13600
Cumulative benefit	2900	6350	9850	13600	

Cost of Quality

Way of calculating the costs involved in quality improvements.

Affinity group: Cost Management

Classification • • •

When to use it
When you're planning a quality improvement programme, and need to plan and justify resources.

When not to use it
Don't try to make Cost of Quality calculations when you don't have the information to estimate or calculate costs at this level of detail. The calculations won't be credible.

What you'll achieve
There can be significant cost benefits, particularly in large volume manufacturing where rework is reduced. The analysis prevents spending on improvements which won't help the business.

And be careful
Costs are only one part of quality equation. You may have to override Cost of Quality to keep customers happy: 'it's not worth it' isn't a good response to a complaining customer.

Training
Training in costing principles and methods is essential.

Where to find out more
Quality Management Library, CCTA, HMSO, 1991

Total Quality Management, Feigenbaum A V, McGraw Hill, 1983

Set up process flowchart and list activities and outputs

For each activity or output, calculate costs of conformance, ie what it costs to get things right. These are costs of appraisal and prevention

Calculate costs of non-conformance, ie how much mistakes cost, in time and materials. These are costs of failure

Using Pareto, identify where mistakes matter most and cost most: concentrate improvement efforts there

Example

The Cost of Quality is often very tangible in the service sector.

The new manager of a particular hotel soon realised that room-cleaning needed to be improved. The cleaning manager argued that higher standards would cost too much. So the new manager undertook a Cost of Quality study.

He kept careful records over the next three months of the total cost of cleaning the hotel. He then broke this down into costs of conformance – which are legitimate – and costs of non-conformance, which can be eliminated or improved.

As a result, he identified two areas where improvements could be made – in managing the way staff work, and in improving the quality of their work.

Unfortunately his cleaning manager was upset by these results and resigned, but she was soon replaced by a more efficient manager who was able to make the improvements the new manager wanted.

Cleaning a Hotel: The Cost of Quality

The Process	Cost of conformance	Cost of non-conformance
Plan and order cleaning supplies	Management time	Stockholding for extra supplies. Expensive alternatives for undersupply.
Train staff	Staff and management time	Staff overtime to re-do work.
Manage staff	Management time	Staff overtime for understaffing. Wasted hours for overstaffing.
Cleaning	Labour and materials	Rework costs. Extra materials.
Customer complaints		Management time. Loss of customer goodwill. Loss of business.

Cost of Quality July - September

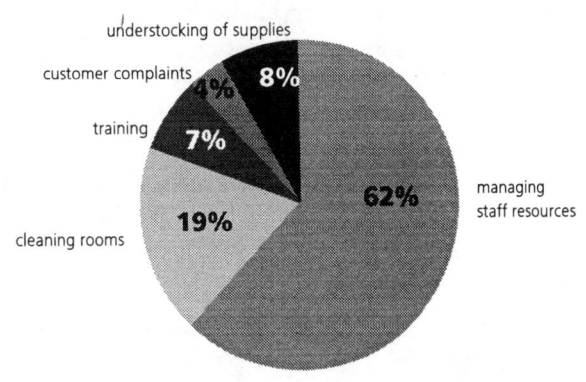

Critical Path Analysis

Project planning tool showing interrelationships between activities and timings, and particularly the activities critical to the total time.

Affinity group: Planning

Classification • • •

When to use it
For planning projects made up of a number of interdependent activities, where completion dates are vital. Assumes previous experience of timing and cost for each event.

When not to use it
Not worthwhile for projects with simple sequential dependencies. Use PERT when reliable estimates of time can't be made.

Training
Some training will be needed, perhaps from a textbook. Computer tools are now available that make calculations and produce charts.

What you'll achieve
An understanding of which activities you will have to push through, and which are less critical. Shows consequences of any one delay. Allows resources to be moved to areas where they will have the most impact.

And be careful
The vulnerability of all planning tools is that you may leave something out. And be realistic, not optimistic, in allocating time and resources to activities.

Where to find out more
Critical Path Construction and Analysis, Morris L N Morris, Pergamon Press, 1967

Management and Organisation, Sisk HL, South Western Publishing Co, 1973

The Quality Toolkit, Marsh J, IFS Ltd, 1992

Process flowchart

List all project events

Create file cards or boxes for each event showing estimated time and cost

Arrange events in order, showing which ones precede or constrain others

Put earliest start date on top left of first event and finish date on top right

Work forward through all events

Identify activities whose finish times affect completion date: mark as critical path to determine overall finish time of project

62

Example

Critical Path Analysis is best used for repeat projects with a predictable pattern of cause and effect, and where reliable estimates are available from previous projects.

In the example, the activities which make up the Critical Path take 2, 3 and 4 days. There is little opportunity to improve these times. However the last event takes 10 days, and any delay in brickwork will delay the finish date. The slack occurs with the plumbing and basement. What can be done to speed up the drying of the plaster?

Key:

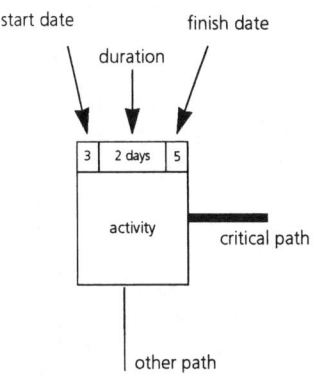

A Critical Path Analysis from the construction industry

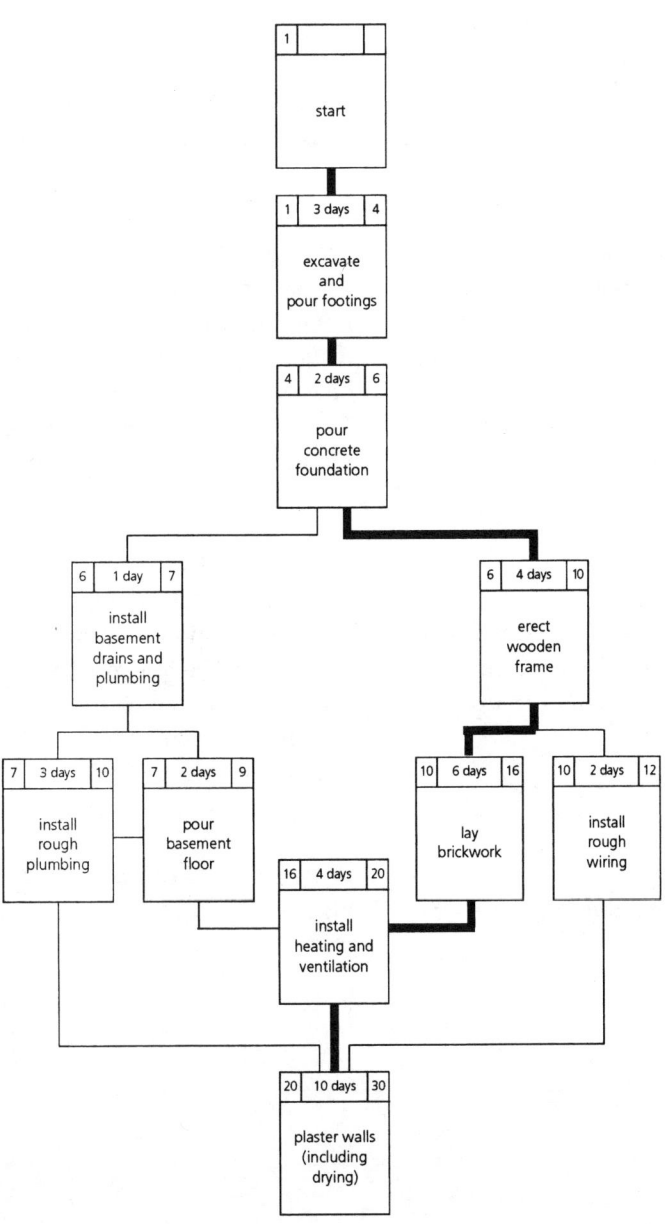

Critical Success Factors

Way of identifying really important issues which will affect the success of a particular enterprise.

Affinity group: Prioritisation

Classification • •

When to use it
Use at a strategic level, when you need to pick out the really important trees in the wood. Particularly relevant for new enterprises and in change situations.

When not to use it
Don't use in situations where there is already consensus about what's important.

What you'll achieve
An understanding of what issues will cause most difficulty, and which need to be monitored and controlled. This shows how to concentrate efforts and prioritise resources.

And be careful
All issues will seem important to someone and you'll have to be selective. People must at times be prepared to accept that their particular interests have to take second place.

Training
No formal training necessary.

Where to find out more
The Quality Toolkit, Marsh J, IFS Ltd, 1992

List all possible issues which could affect the success of the enterprise

Group the issues into categories or affinity groups

Decide whether or not each category affects the overall success of the activity

Select important categories and identify as Critical Success Factors (not more than 8)

Example

Particularly when an enterprise is new and unfamiliar, it is possible to miss one or two Critical Success Factors. So it's important to identify them early.

In this example, a university department is launching a new course combining communication theory, design and writing. Constructing the course is a complex process involving a number of compromises with the curriculum and with staffing. In order to guide these decisions, the course team develop a list of eight Critical Success Factors. They can assess the impact of their decisions by considering whether they support or damage the CSFs.

For example, opinions are divided about what to call the course. By interviewing actual and potential students, they discover that the most preferred name isn't very attractive to students. Since making the course attractive to students is one of the CSFs, they decide to change it.

Critical Success Factors for a new course

1. Attractiveness to students
   Without enough students, the course will suffer. So decisions about curriculum must bear this in mind.

2. Coherent and comprehensive curriculum
   To be accepted by the college, the curriculum has to be solidly constructed.

3. Attractiveness to employers
   This will have a direct effect on how employable students are.

4. Economy of delivery
   The course has to be delivered within college resources – which may mean sacrificing some good ideas.

5. Quality of delivery
   Staff will need time to prepare new course materials.

6. Ability to attract external funding
   Must be seen to be relevant and innovative to attract support.

7. Effective marketing
   Scarce resources will have to be used to promote the course.

8. Effective management
   The success of the course will depend on the effective management of resources.

Cross-Functional Teams

For using expertise from different work areas to solve particular problems.

Affinity group: Change Management

Classification • • • •

When to use it
Use Cross-Functional Teams for problems or projects which affect more than one department, cutting across the way work groups are organised at present.

What you'll achieve
In the short term, you'll achieve solutions to particular problems which take a range of opinions and perspectives into account. In the longer term, using Cross-Functional Teams will improve relations between different departments in the organisation.

When not to use it
Don't use Cross-Functional Teams unnecessarily, when the problem can be solved more simply, or where the culture of the organisation doesn't support team decision making.

And be careful
Cross-Functional Teams won't feel as if they belong anywhere in particular and can drift. They must be given responsibility and authority to resolve the particular problem.

Training
Training in team working is important.

Where to find out more
Implementing Quality, Griffiths D N, ASQC Quality Press, 1990

Process flowchart

Define problem or project for cross-functional team to solve

Select team members (based on experience and expertise), and appoint a leader and a facilitator

Work out project plan to investigate problem

When problem is solved, close team and copy report to managers of all departments concerned

Example

One large manufacturing company had made significant progress in introducing a quality culture into its organisation. However they were finding it difficult to introduce an appropriate and equitable way of rewarding staff for their efforts and achievements. The personnel department had researched some possible schemes, but there were always objections from one group or other who felt they wouldn't benefit as much as their colleagues.

The company solved the problem by forming a Cross-Functional Team to build on the personnel department's research and talk to all the different interest groups in the organisation. The team had a list of objectives and reporting dates. Otherwise, management implied, there might not be an awards scheme at all.

And not surprisingly the team delivered the goods.

```
Cross-Functional Team recommendations
for a new rewards system

The team agreed on the following approaches:

1. A company-wide profit-sharing scheme
   approved by the Inland Revenue.
   This would recognise the overall achievement
   of the business.

2. An individual award scheme
   based on money-saving suggestions.
   The accounts department would calculate the size
   of the award in proportion to the amount saved.

3. Discretionary awards
   decided by the Quality Steering Committee
   from an annual budget.
```

Customer Needs Analysis

Structured approach for ensuring customer needs are met.

Affinity group: Data Capture

Classification •

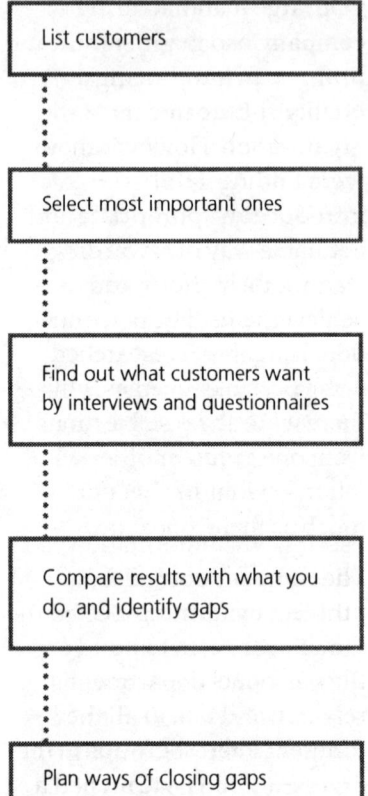

Process flowchart

List customers

Select most important ones

Find out what customers want by interviews and questionnaires

Compare results with what you do, and identify gaps

Plan ways of closing gaps

When to use it
Use as part of your customer service programme, to find out what your customers actually want. Works for internal and external customers.

What you'll achieve
The analysis will provide real insights into what customers are thinking and saying about your business. The results can provide powerful arguments for change in the organisation.

When not to use it
Don't survey customers when you won't be able to respond to their comments: customers will expect to see some results from your enquiries.

And be careful
There'll be surprises: things you thought important won't be mentioned, perhaps. Take time to analyse and explain results: take action only when you're sure you've interpreted comments correctly.

Training
Reading about the technique and looking at examples would be useful.

Where to find out more
Implementing Quality, Griffiths D N, ASCQ Quality Press, 1990

Example

During its Company Wide Quality Improvement programme the accounts department of a large multinational decided to find out what its internal customers really wanted from it. It identified its main customers as Administration, IS and Sales. It asked these departments to fill in a questionnaire and used the results as a basis for further discussion and negotiation.

The biggest surprise lay in seeing what information each department wanted from them. In part this reflected the impact of the Quality Improvement Programme, as departments needed to analyse their performance in an increasing amount of detail.

Accounts Department
Customer Needs Analysis Questionnaire

Please fill in this questionnaire to give us a clearer understanding of the service you need from us. Answers will be treated with complete confidentiality.

1. What financial information do you need from us?
   ....
   ....

2. What other services do you need from us?
   ....
   ....

3. What response time to your queries would you find acceptable?
   ....

4. Do we provide information you do not use?
   ❐ Yes   ❐ No

5. Do your staff understand our role?
   ❐ Yes   ❐ No

6. Could your staff make use of any basic training in accountancy?
   ❐ Yes   ❐ No

7. What gaps are there in the service we offer?
   ....
   ....

8. Do we present information in the most readable way?
   ❐ Yes   ❐ No

9. Are there any ways in which we could improve?
   ❐ Yes   ❐ No
   If Yes, say how ....
   ....

10. How could we improve to meet your needs more exactly?
   ....
   ....
   ....

Customer Satisfaction Assessment

For monitoring levels of customer satisfaction.

Affinity group: Data Capture

Classification •

Brainstorm ways of measuring customer satisfaction:
- number of complaints
- meetings with key customers
- comments book
- focus group meetings with staff who deal direct with customers
- customer satisfaction questionnaires
- following up lost sales
- using market research organisations

When to use it
As part of customer service programme, to find out how happy customers actually are. Applies to internal and external customers.

What you'll achieve
Up-to-date insights into what customers are actually thinking and saying about you.

When not to use it
Be wary of collecting customer satisfaction data when you're not in a position to change: otherwise it will be very demoralising.

And be careful
Don't just hear the good news: remember that for every complaint six people are unhappy and don't tell you. If you're getting bland feedback, it's worth digging deeper.

Chart measurements over time

Plan strategies to solve any problems the analysis reveals

Training
Reading about the technique and looking at examples will be useful.

Where to find out more
Total Quality Management, Pera International, Chapman and Hall, 1991

Implementing Quality, Griffiths D N, ASCQ Quality Press, 1990

Total Quality Control, Feigenbaum A V, McGraw Hill, 1983

Example

The accounts department of a large multinational had conducted a Customer Needs Analysis to find out what information and services their internal customers required. After six months of concerted effort the department felt pleased with its progress and was confident that its customers would have nothing left to complain about.

However the accounts manager felt that they should measure their success more professionally. So they carried out a further survey, this time to see how well they had understood and reacted to the needs of their customers.

And there were some surprises. Customers still felt they wanted more information about a number of costs and charges. The accounts department had to learn that customer needs and expectations are not static, and have to be managed.

Accounts Department
Customer Satisfaction Assessment

Following our questionnaire about what you wanted from us, we would like to know how well we are succeeding in meeting your needs. Please answer these questions using the scale. **1 is the worst score and 5 the best.**
Answers will be treated with complete confidentiality.

1. How well do we communicate with you? 1 2 3 4 5

2. Do we give you the information you need? 1 2 3 4 5

3. Do we answer your queries promptly? 1 2 3 4 5

4. Do we answer your queries politely? 1 2 3 4 5

5. Do we respond positively to your suggestions? 1 2 3 4 5

6. Do you feel we have a concern for quality? 1 2 3 4 5

7. Do we anticipate your needs, or do we always seem to be one step behind? 1 2 3 4 5

8. Have we increased your understanding of accounts? 1 2 3 4 5

9. Do we work with you as a team? 1 2 3 4 5

10. Any other comments

....
....
....

Cusum Chart

Control chart for attributes or variables which highlights small deviations from normal performance.

Affinity group: Statistical Quality Control

Classification • • •

When to use it
For products or processes where small variations are important.

What you'll achieve
Trends will be highlighted. Cusum Chart magnifies small changes and is sensitive even to marginal shifts which would be very difficult to see otherwise.

When not to use it
Don't use when small variations aren't important.

And be careful
Cusum Charts aren't as easy to interpret as other kinds of control charts: remember that the slope is the important thing, not the height of the line.

Training
Knowledge of statistics needed to calculate and interpret charts: software available.

Where to find out more
The Economic Control of Manufacturing Quality, W Shewart, Dover Press, 1936

A Practical Approach to Quality Control, Caplen R H, Hutchinson Publishing Group, 1978

Process flowchart

Establish average or reference values for the process or product

Set up chart
Vertical axis:
Cumulative difference from reference value
Horizontal axis:
Measurements or observations

Analyse gradient: steep gradient means greater rate of change

Take action, as necessary

Example

Cusum Charts are useful in the chemical industry, where small variations in the concentration of chemicals may be very significant. Without the chart, the importance of these variations is much more difficult to interpret. Observations on the chart are plotted cumulatively, and a trend line drawn to establish the gradient. In this example, the rate of change is clearly increasing, and the process needs attention.

Cusum Chart showing changes in chemical concentration

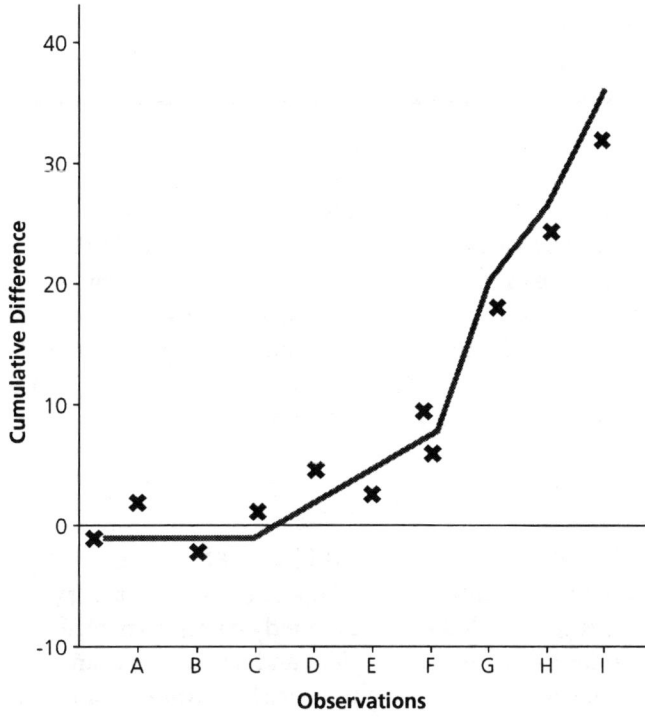

Data Flow Diagram

Graphic technique used in software industry for showing where data comes from, how it's used, how it's processed, and where it goes.

Affinity group: Graphic Tool

Classification • • •

When to use it
Data Flow Diagrams are used in the design phase of information systems development, to specify the data flow. Once they're agreed, the specification of the system can begin.

What you'll achieve
Accurate representation of data flows which specialists, managers and users can all understand. Diagrams provide a way of seeing the change and its consequences.

When not to use it
Don't use Data Flow Diagrams as a general process modelling tool: they're specifically for information flows.

And be careful
Diagrams can become very unwieldy – keep structure clear and remember primary purpose is comprehension and communication: if they confuse, they're failing.

Training
Software developers will know how to use them.

Where to find out more
Quality Control Handbook, Juran J, McGraw Hill, 1988

System Analysis and Design: a Foundation for the 80s (ed W M Coterman et al), Elsevier Science Publishing Co, 1981

Process flowchart

Write out in narrative form what the data flows are for a particular part of business process

⋮

Create diagram using data flow notation

⋮

Break down diagram into further levels of detail as necessary

⋮

Repeat for all parts of business process

⋮

Group diagrams to show whole process

Example

Notation for Data Flow Diagrams can vary, but essentially there are four elements.

Data sources ▭

Data flows ➤

Processing nodes ○

Data stores ▬

Data Flow Diagrams can be used both to make clear how systems are working at present, and to show how things could or should be changed in the future.

The example shows a top-level diagram for a software development project which will integrate the organisation's ordering and delivery processes. The diagram is similar to a process flow model, except that it is exclusively concerned with what happens to information.

Data Flow Diagram of an ordering and delivery system

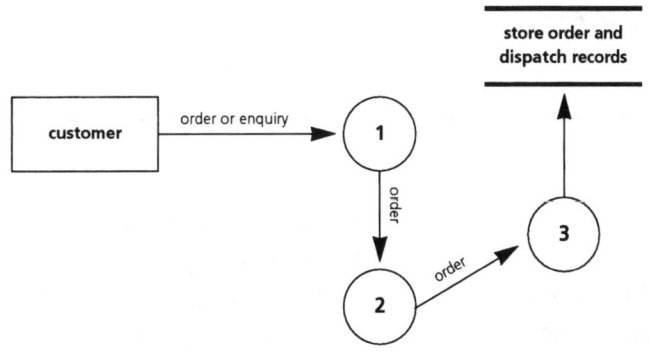

Symbols

① log into sales

② log into stores

③ log into dispatch

Decision Analysis

Structured approach to making decisions.

Affinity group: Problem Solving

Classification • • •

When to use it
Decision Analysis is good for choosing between the attributes of things such as equipment or materials where each option is clearly defined.

What you'll achieve
The tool provides a logical analysis of facts to support the decision, ie good for persuading budget holders you're making the right choice. The process involves all levels of expertise in the decision in a very visible way.

When not to use it
Don't use Decision Analysis for abstract decisions: use problem solving or consensus tools instead.

And be careful
It is also necessary to consider the adverse consequences of choices: some choices look good but are actually high risk and may not be appropriate. Use Solution Effect Analysis.

Training
Some training in using ratings may be needed.

Where to find out more
Total Quality Management, TQM International Ltd, 1992

Process flowchart

Define decision statement

List criteria to consider in making the decision

Divide criteria into 'musts' and 'wants'

Brainstorm options to satisfy the decision statement

Check options against 'must' criteria

Compare options which fulfil 'must' criteria against 'want' criteria, using weighted ratings

Present results as a table and select option with highest score

Example

One area where decision making is difficult, and where Decision Analysis is very appropriate, is in IT. Faced with a bewildering array of hardware and software products, all developing rapidly, and all being aggressively marketed, it is important to start the decision-making process with a carefully worded decision statement which clearly defines the parameters of the choice.

A good example might be the decision faced by hospitals in choosing electronic nursing systems. Conflicting views of suppliers, technical experts, managers at local and national levels, and clinicians, will make it difficult for nursing management to know how to evaluate the different systems. Here, a Decision Analysis exercise will approach the problem logically and shows clearly how a particular decision has been made.

Choosing a computer system for nurses

Decision statement

Select a computer system which will capture all the data needed by nursing management

Decision criteria

Musts

- be compatible with existing hospital admissions system
- include all nursing management functions
- come with adequate training and support
- have at least one site or extensive simulation up and running

Wants

- attractive screen design
- easy to use
- good price relative to other products
- approved by RHA
- provide real time data

Selecting options

Musts	A	B	C	D	E
Compatibility	✓	✓	✗	✓	✓
Functionality	✓	✓	✓	✓	✓
Training and support	✓	✓	✓	✓	✓
Track record	✓	✓	✗	✓	✓

Classification of remaining options

Wants	Weight factor	A	B	D	E	Maximum score
Attractiveness	4	32	28	24	32	40
Easy to use	6	30	30	24	42	60
Price	5	50	30	35	10	50
RHA approved	2	08	10	14	04	20
Real time	8	00	00	00	80	80
Total		120	98	111	168	250

Conclusion

The clear leader is option E, because it gives real time data. In this example, the clinicians' preference gives this a weight factor of 8, which outweighs the RHAs approval (weight factor 2).

Delphi Technique

Tool for forecasting long-term future developments.

Affinity group: Consensus

Classification •

When to use it
When future developments, for example in communications, politics or technology, will be of vital concern to your business.

What you'll achieve
A snapshot of expert opinion without the distortions of group conflict such as: dominant characters, social pressures, personal disagreements etc. Therefore provides a chance to make up your own mind.

When not to use it
Don't use for predictions about broad social change: the technique works best in fields of specialised study where the experts have hard knowledge on which to base their predictions.

And be careful
It won't always be possible to make experts agree, if developments are genuinely uncertain or controversial. In that case, use your judgement.

Training
Reading about it will usually provide enough information.

Where to find out more
Tools for Thought, Waddington C H, Jonathan Cape, 1977

Design and Marketing of New Products, Urban G, and Hauser J, Prentice Hall, 1980

Process flowchart

Create questionnaire about future developments in particular industry

Send to selected experts

Collate replies and send back complete list of developments to experts

Ask experts for a percentage probability for each development

Plot results to show range of opinions and send back to experts

Ask experts to revise opinions until a consensus is reached

Example

Questions about the Internet are beginning to trouble many businesses, and there is much debate about the impact future developments will have on a range of business activities, from banking to publishing. Answers depend on both technology and strategy.

Using the Delphi Technique a business such as publishing can gain insights into the nature of the threat it faces, and likely timescales.

Future developments on the Internet

Thank you for agreeing to take part in our prediction exercise on developments on the Internet.
Please answer the questions as specifically as you can.

1. How long before books are routinely published on the Internet?
   - ❑ 1 Year
   - ❑ 2 Years
   - ❑ 5 Years
   - ❑ 10 Years

2. How can publishers make money out of publishing on the Internet?
   ....
   ....

3. Who will be in control of the Internet
   - in 2 Years' time ....
   - in 5 Years' time ....
   - in 10 Years' time ....

4. When is provision for security of transactions, for example with credit cards, likely to become a reality?
   - ❑ 1 Year
   - ❑ 2 Years
   - ❑ 5 Years
   - ❑ 10 Years
   - ❑ Never

5. When is a system for preventing unauthorised access to information on the Internet likely to be developed?
   - ❑ 1 Year
   - ❑ 2 Years
   - ❑ 5 Years
   - ❑ 10 Years
   - ❑ Never

6. What are the implications for the banking community of the possibility of using the Internet for transactions?
   ....
   ....

7. When are we likely to see a policy on censorship of materials published on Internet?
   - ❑ 1 Year
   - ❑ 2 Years
   - ❑ 5 Years
   - ❑ 10 Years
   - ❑ Never

Thank you for your co-operation.
We will send you the results of our survey for your further comments when these are available.

Departmental Purpose Analysis

For departments to improve their standards of performance.

Affinity group: Strategy

Classification • • • • •

Analyse tasks in department in relation to company's overall objectives

When to use it
Use this tool as part of a wider programme of change and improvement throughout the organisation. Tends to be of most use in larger, more complex organisations.

What you'll achieve
Each department has the opportunity to take a fresh look at what it's doing and how things might be improved. Better than having an outsider impose new performance standards.

Assess how well skills and resources are being used to carry out tasks

Revise tasks and responsibilities in the light of these analyses

When not to use it
The analysis may not be appropriate when more radical change is being considered and the very existence of the department is under question.

And be careful
DPA doesn't automatically work across departmental boundaries. Be careful departments don't start to make their own way, without regard for what others are doing, thus creating departmental barons with their individual serfdoms.

Make best-guess judgement about the performance of similar competitor departments

Set performance measures

Training
Familiarity needed with task analysis, performance targets and review procedures. Personnel department may be able to train or advise.

Where to find out more
Total Quality Management, Pera International, Chapman and Hall, 1992

Review departmental performance and set improvement targets

Example

Departmental managers in a large corporation have been told to report on their efficiency and draw up improvement plans. They have not been given specific targets: departments are to argue their individual cases.

Each department puts together a DPA team chaired by a senior manager. The team includes representatives from the department itself, personnel, internal suppliers, internal customers and finance.

The team works out the resources coming into the department. It then identifies the tasks it carries out and what resources these involve. Members of the team use the three checklists opposite, both to focus their own thinking, and to structure interviews with other people outside the department.

The team produces a report with recommendations which will act as an implementation plan. Reaching new standards will not be easy, but after this exercise, at least everyone in the department is confident it can be done.

Departmental Purpose Analysis Checklists

1. Evaluating What We Do

☐ What is our department's purpose?

☐ Who are our suppliers?

☐ Who are our customers?

☐ What do our customers want from us?

☐ Are we doing the right things to satisfy our customers?

☐ Do we have a reason for each of the tasks we do?

☐ Do all our tasks add value to the organisation? If not, why not?

2. Evaluating How Well We Do Things

☐ Are there any measurable standards for our department?

☐ What would a world-class standard of performance be?

☐ How far away from that are we?

☐ What is the most important problem we know we have?

☐ How does it affect our customers?

☐ What are the root causes of the problem?

☐ Is there a solution?

☐ How can we stop it happening again in the future?

☐ What is the next most important problem?

3. About Continuous Improvement

☐ What extra services can we offer our customers?

☐ How can we become more efficient?

☐ What targets are we setting for increased effectiveness and efficiency?

☐ What skills and training are needed to make this happen?

Design of Experiments

Way of improving processes by optimising process variables.

Affinity group: Statistical Quality Control

Classification • • •

When to use it
For investigating and improving processes, either at the design stage or as part of quality improvement.

What you'll achieve
You'll actually improve your processes over time, as opposed to simply controlling or monitoring them, to make sure they don't break down. All variable factors will be optimised.

When not to use it
Don't use without cultural commitment to quality as continual improvement.

And be careful
Results from individual experiments can be inconclusive or, from a number, contradictory: important to interpret them sensibly. Make sure you've asked the right question.

Training
The level of technical and statistical know-how needed depends on the situation – some experiments are common sense – but in general a good grasp of the basics of statistics is essential.

Where to find out more
System of Experimental Design, Taguchi G, Quality Resources, White Plains, NY, 1987

Quality Control Handbook, Juran J, McGraw Hill, 1988

Designing for Quality, Lockner R, and Matar J, Chapman and Hall, 1990

Process flowchart

Define objectives of the process

Brainstorm factors affecting performance

Decide how to measure noise factors, ie uncontrollable effects

Design experiments to see how other factors and their interactions affect the process

Analyse and interpret results

Adjust the relevant factors and run confirmation experiment

Example

An example of the common sense approach to the Design of Experiments is supplied by a small, semi-industrial knitting business in Italy; part of the 'garage' textile economy.

The quality problem concerned the number of breaks in the knitting yarn which the machine operators experienced. Breaks were expensive, not only because the machines had to be re-threaded (since they were not sophisticated enough to have back-up threading), but also because the garment piece had to be started again, wasting yarn and production time.

Operators noticed considerable variation in the frequency of breakages, so they set up a number of experiments to try to find out what effected the phenomenon, and what they could do about it.

Using a combination of measurements and common sense, the business managed to virtually eliminate breakages altogether.

Experiments to reduce the number of knitting yarn breakages

Objective: To reduce the average rate of breakages (daily count) from 82 per 1000 metres

Variable factors	Rate of breakage per 1000 metres
Machine oiling interval reduced from 4 to 2 hours	74
Wool oiled	60
Tension down 1	86
Better quality yarn	18
Size of motor on machine	78
Room temperature up	46
Humidity down (using fans)	33

Seven possible factors were chosen as a basis for experimentation. One factor at a time was altered, with the others kept constant.

The average results showed that 4 factors had a dramatic effect, namely:

• better quality yarn
• lower humidity
• higher room temperature
• oiled wool

Conclusion:
Machine maintenance and motor size had some impact, while reducing tension made the problem worse.

Design Review

Project management technique for making sure designs meet customer requirements at each stage of development.

Affinity group: Product and Process Design

Classification • • •

When to use it
As part of the monitoring and control of technical development projects, to make sure the development work is going in the right direction.

What you'll achieve
The opportunity to pick up mistakes or problems early in the project when they can be put right with comparative ease. Helps control design drift, with suggestions and additions being adopted piecemeal.

When not to use it
Don't use for projects which don't have some kind of technical design component. And don't introduce Design Review too late in the day, when most of the work has been done.

And be careful
People carrying out the Design Review must be qualified to judge: not all clients or colleagues will necessarily know what to look for. Make sure it's done properly: don't let the design team experts turn the review into a whitewash.

Training
Training advisable in teamwork and negotiation for managing the Design Review – they don't have a good record of success.

Where to find out more
Quality Management Library, CCTA, HMSO, 1992

Quality Control Handbook, Juran J, McGraw Hill, 1988

Total Quality Control, Feigenbaum A V, McGraw Hill, 1983

Process flowchart

Design Review points fixed as part of project plan

Deliverables at Design Review points specified

Review team evaluates deliverables against standards and specifications

Review team produces reports with recommendations for improvements, as necessary

Example

Design Reviews are used extensively in the software development industry, in an attempt to prevent projects from joining the ranks of some of the more spectacular IS system failures of recent years.

During reviews designers may try to brush aside the comments of the reviewers by saying that all problems will be sorted out in the end. The review team has to judge when this is true, and when the problems are more fundamental.

In a recent example, a Design Review Team picked up a capacity problem in a system that was designed to provide an emergency service. Although the design team had been working to a 'reasonable' average capacity of requests, it was clear to the review team, who included customers of the new system, that the system would be overloaded for over 20% of the time. Resolving the problem meant changing the technological basis of the design, but it avoided yet another expensive IS disaster.

Software Design Review Checklist

- ☐ Performance to date meets requirements specification
- ☐ Design appears stable
- ☐ Code checked for errors
- ☐ Designers' assumptions checked
- ☐ Work complete for this stage
- ☐ Work method efficient
- ☐ No unwelcome maintenance implications
- ☐ Risk level acceptable
- ☐ Design strategy traceable
- ☐ Development records up-to-date

Design-To-Cost

Design method which takes cost into account as major constraint.

Affinity group: Cost Management

Classification • • •

Process flowchart

Calculate overall cost target, using Life-Cycle Costing approach

State in general terms what project is to achieve

Develop alternative designs and evaluate with cost targets in mind

Select preferred design and monitor and adjust throughout development, to meet cost targets

When to use it
For development projects where there's more than one way to get the required result.

What you'll achieve
Reduced risk of costs running out of control and then being justified by design requirements. Ensures that if features are to be added, the full cost will be taken into account. And avoids the over-engineering syndrome.

When not to use it
Don't use Design-To-Cost when accurate overall cost estimates are very difficult to judge – cost constraints could be harmful if set too low.

And be careful
Always analyse effects of design changes on the final product: don't risk losing essential functionality.

Training
Calculating and adjusting cost parameters for large projects requires costing training and expertise. Software exists for calculating Life-Cycle Costs for specific and complex products.

Where to find out more
Quality Control Handbook, Juran J, McGraw Hill 1988

Total Quality Control, Feigenbaum A V, McGraw Hill, 1983

Example

The garment industry uses Design-To-Cost extensively. Any given style of garment can always be made up in a number of ways, using different fabrics and manufacturing techniques. While the designer may always want the best fabrics and techniques, cost constraints are dictated by how much the customer will pay.

The skill in Designing To Cost in this way, lies in knowing what cost-cutting will affect the customer's perception of the garment, and what won't matter so much. This equation is different for different market sectors: young people, for example, are not so sensitive to whether fabrics are 100% natural fibres or not.

The example opposite shows careful judgement by the design team. Intended as a mid-price garment for older customers, it keeps its attractiveness in fit and overall appearance, and compromises on details which will not be noticed.

Design-To-Cost for an evening dress
Aim: To produce an evening dress for no more than £50 wholesale.

Original costs (£)

Design	62.00

High cost elements

Silk fabric (compared with silk blend)	8.00
Inset zip	0.50
French seams	1.50
Bias cut	4.00
Exclusive trim	1.50
Full lining	3.00

Element	Effect on appearance	Effect on performance	Effect on fit
Silk fabric	Medium	Medium	Low
Inset zip	Low	Low	Low
French seams	Low	Medium	Low
Bias cut	High	Medium	High
Exclusive trim	High	Medium	Low
Lining	Medium	Medium	Low

The designer decides to keep the bias cut and the exclusive trim, and leave out the other options, which are desirable but too expensive.
This brings the garment into the target price range.

Endpoint State Analysis

Method of deciding direction by defining a desirable endpoint.

Affinity group: Change Management

Classification • •

Select topic which is subject of change or quality management initiative

Brainstorm descriptions of the present state of awareness or achievement in topic

Develop statements of the desired endpoint for each description

Develop action plans to achieve desired endpoints

When to use it

When things are changing and it's important to understand what new objectives are, and how to reach them.

What you'll achieve

This tool provides a compelling combination of realism and positive action: plans originate from where the organisation is now, and take it where it wants to go.

When not to use it

Don't use where there isn't yet agreement about what changes and where the organisation is going: these issues need to be largely resolved before positive planning can start.

And be careful

The desirable has to be balanced with the realistic: if they are too visionary, endpoints will lose credibility.

Training

No special training required.

Where to find out more

Benchmarking, Camp R, ASQC Quality Press, 1989

Example

Endpoint State Analysis is useful for pulling together plans and actions which result from change initiatives, to make sure these activities are coherent.

For example, a university department needs to make significant efficiency gains, which include an increase in student numbers from 22 to 30. This has major implications for recruitment and for resourcing the course. Staff need to be sure about what their new priorities are.

Listing the areas which will be affected by the change, quantifying them, and finding solutions, represents a positive approach to meeting the demand for increased efficiency, and helps to set the department's new strategy.

ENDPOINT STATE ANALYSIS FOR A UNIVERSITY DEPARTMENT

Area of change	Present state	Endpoint state	How to get there . . .
Number of applications	53	75	Careers events, visits to 6th forms, enhance reputation of department.
Entry qualifications	DE	CD	As above.
Number of staff	4.5	6	Attract research grants to fund post graduates who teach.
Number of computers	18	30	Apply to central university funds.
Access to internet	Partial	Total	Enlist Dean to lobby computer services.

Error Cause Removal

Tool for people to communicate their problems to management.

Affinity group: Data Capture

Classification •

Appoint an ECR administrator

Supply people with forms on which they write down any problems they've observed

Administrator formally acknowledges problems, preferably within 24 hours

Administrator selects appropriate problems for further work by an improvement team

When to use it

Use for maintaining the vitality of an improvement programme, to consolidate a culture of improvement.

What you'll achieve

You'll hear about some new problems you weren't aware of, and people will feel they're being listened to – that their problems matter.

When not to use it

Don't use ECR at the start of an improvement programme when everyone knows what the problems are and there is a danger of creating a bottleneck.

And be careful

Make sure of senior management commitment and the ability of the organisation to respond. ECR will die quickly without clear signals that ideas are taken seriously and pursued.

Training

No training needed for setting up and running the scheme.

Where to find out more

Quality Control Handbook, Juran, J, McGraw Hill, 1988

Quality is Free, Crosby P B, McGraw Hill, 1979

Error Cause Removal schemes can identify all kinds of problems, from the apparently trivial to the obviously significant. However the principle of the tool is that all problems are important, even – or especially – if they can be easily resolved. Anything that's a problem to someone will have a negative effect on the quality of their work.

The first time a management consultancy tried the scheme, their clients were sceptical, since so many of the problems seemed trivial – things that could be sorted out overnight. However they were surprised by the improvement in morale that dealing with these apparently simple problems brought.

However, the process highlighted some more fundamental issues also.

Error Cause Removal – sample problems

My computer runs out of memory every time I want to use a diagramming application . . .

The main photocopier is always running out of paper.

I can never find the travel claim forms, and I can't fill them in when I do !

My job role has never been properly defined . . .

The paging system keeps interrupting my phone calls . . .

No-one can use the binding machine properly – all our reports look awful.

We don't have a standard format for proposals: how do I know which approach is most likely to be successful ?

The client database is unreliable and seems to lose entries I'm sure I've asked to be put on . . .

Can we have better coffee?

We don't see each other enough socially.

Facilitation

Key role for getting groups to work together successfully.

Affinity group: Change Management

Classification • • •

Process flowchart

Become familiar with the issue team is dealing with

Discuss with leader what a good result from meeting would be

Make sure team understands and keeps to any rules of discussion, decision-making etc

Arrange to provide any further information needed

Summarise and report back ideas to team throughout meeting, and at the end

When to use it
Use Facilitation when groups of people who don't usually work together have to solve a particular problem or make a decision.

What you'll achieve
It's a way of keeping control of the process (as opposed to content) of meetings. Often the essential ingredient in successfully introducing new tools and techniques.

When not to use it
Probably best not to use a facilitator from inside the organisation if it's early days and group culture is likely to be difficult to manage.

And be careful
Facilitation is a demanding role: needs firmness and empathy, organisation and flexibility. Not everyone can handle it.

Training
Formal training in facilitation is a good investment: experience is important too.

Where to find out more
Total Quality Management, Pera International, Chapman and Hall, 1992

Example

The role of the Facilitator is not always understood by organisations new to the kind of co-operative tools and techniques which are typical of TQM.

One organisation employed a Human Resource Management consultancy to help in identifying staff problems, developing new job roles and restructuring reward packages. A key part of this process was to gain the agreement of the Trade Unions.

On the recommendation of the consultants, management called a meeting with the unions early on. However they did not want the consultants to be present, feeling that the presence of outsiders would be intrusive.

The meeting broke up after 15 minutes. Apparently the manager organising the brainstorm had started off listing management comments on the top right of the chart, and Union comments on the bottom left, signalling that the old divisions remained.

Facilitation skills

The facilitator should be familiar with:

- group dynamics
- roles in meetings
- skills transfer
- decision-making styles
- group behaviour patterns
- techniques for managing disruptive behaviour
- techniques for identifying differences between group members

Fagan Inspection – Documents

Applies Inspection method to document production.

Affinity group: Quality Management System

Classification • • •

When to use it
For developing documents with a technical or instructional content, where the information has to be right.

When not to use it
Don't use in hierarchical cultures where organisational status will override roles.

Training
Moderator should be trained in teambuilding and in the method. Team members need training in error recognition by being given samples to analyse.

What you'll achieve
More accurate documents and a quicker, more controlled document development process. People working together spot many more errors than people working individually.

And be careful
Defining errors in documents can be subjective – use checklists, and spend time emphasising the different roles people are using.

Where to find out more
Applying the Fagan Inspection Technique, Reeve J T, Quality Forum vol 17, No 1, March 1991

Process flowchart

Assemble inspection team:
Moderator – team leader
Author
Inspectors
Reworker
Data analyst

Author presents document to team in half-hour walkthrough

Team members inspect document individually, using checklists

Whole team carries out inspection. Errors noted and categorised

Moderator produces written report of inspection and analyses detection data

Reworker makes corrections for moderator's approval

Example

Fagan Inspection is an efficient way of checking the accuracy and content of technical publications. Often review and checking processes are carried out by peer review, with drafts passing round a number of individuals who don't consult with each other and who can have different perceptions of the document's purpose.

One organisation calculated that it was spending over £14,000 on internal review processes for each of its technical documents. Senior staff spent several hours editing and commenting on all aspects of the drafts, including proof-reading. Since there was no communication between commenters and the author, the author had no opportunity to argue for aspects of the documents which caused comment, with the result that the final versions were extremely bland.

Fagan Inspection rationalised this process and resulted in more interesting and coherent documents produced at a substantially lower cost.

Error Checklists for Fagan Inspection Documents

---

1. Contents check for:

- ☐ Factual errors
- ☐ Gaps in content
- ☐ References to other materials
- ☐ Opinions presented as facts
- ☐ Errors of emphasis

2. User-friendliness make judgements about:

- ☐ Tone
- ☐ User access to the information
- ☐ Where diagrams would help make content easier
- ☐ Lists instead of continuous prose

3. Style comment on:

- ☐ Spelling
- ☐ Grammar
- ☐ Punctuation
- ☐ Ambiguity
- ☐ Inconsistency in the use of terms
- ☐ Use of the passive voice
- ☐ Use of jargon
- ☐ Inconsistency of tone

4. Structure check for:

- ☐ Contents list
- ☐ Heading working as a set
- ☐ Correct heading hierarchy
- ☐ Index
- ☐ Text logically connected at sentence, paragraph, section and chapter levels

Fagan Inspection – Software

Inspection method for software design and code to catch errors early.

Affinity group: Quality Management Systems

Classification • • •

When to use it
For controlling software design and programming projects, to catch errors as early as possible in the development cycle.

When not to use it
Don't use in cultures where there are likely to be conflicts, tensions and power struggles between team members. Can't be imposed from above.

Training
Moderator needs training in teambuilding and in the method. Team members need training in error recognition by being given samples to analyse.

What you'll achieve
Tests at IBM showed a 23% increase in coding productivity. Individual programmers receive feedback on the type of errors they're prone to make.

And be careful
It's essential to have common understanding of definition of error as being deviation from specification. Use checklists and error specifications to focus attention.

Where to find out more
Design and Code Inspections to Reduce Errors in Program Development, Fagan M E, IBM Systems Journal, 1976

Process flowchart

Assemble inspection team:
Moderator – team leader
Program designer
Program coder
Tester

Designer presents overview of project and own area of responsibility in detail

Team members familiarise themselves with project and detect errors individually

Whole team carries out inspection as a group. Errors noted and categorised

Moderator produces written report of inspection and analyses detection data

Errors are reworked by designer or coder

Example

Fagan inspection was developed by IBM to address the problem of catching errors in software design and programming early. The cost of fixing errors rises in relation to how late in the process they are discovered. The idea behind inspection was to carry out rigorous checking early on in the process.

For his study sample Fagan took a sample of software development involving three designers and thirteen coders. Normal review procedures consisted of a series of walkthroughs. The inspected sample was compared with a similar sample checked in this way.

Results showed a very significant increase of 38% in error identification. In addition coding productivity increased by 23%.

The Inspection method was also applied to Application Development, with similar results. As the method becomes familiar, results could be even better for organisations who adopt it.

Fagan Inspection - software
Example of inspection checksheet for software design

Name of designer

Types of problems	Missing	Wrong	Extra		Errors	Total % errors
Definition	16	02	00	=	18	4.1
Usage	18	17	01	=	36	8.1
Logic	126	57	24	=	207	46.6
Higher Lvl Docu.	01	00	01	=	02	0.05
More Detail	24	06	02	=	32	7.2
Maintainability	08	05	03	=	16	3.6
Other	15	10	10	=	35	7.9
Performance	01	02	03	=	06	1.4
Prologue	44	38	07	=	89	20
Register Usage	01	02	00	=	03	0.07
Standards	00	00	00	=	00	00
Total	254	139	051	=	444	

Failure Mode Effect and Criticality Analysis

For anticipating errors in a product or process, and finding ways of preventing them

Affinity group: Product and Process Design

Classification • • •

List all the activities in the project or process you're planning

---

When to use it
Use FMECA at the planning stage of products or processes to focus attention on avoiding problems. Applies to manufacturing and service industries.

What you'll achieve
The confidence of taking a proactive approach to avoiding mistakes. Provides a safety net to make sure you haven't overlooked any obvious problems.

Identify the things that could go wrong with each activity

When not to use it
Don't use if you need a Quality Improvement Tool: FMECA is about avoidance, not active improvement.

And be careful
Like all predictive tools, it isn't foolproof. You can spend a lot of time predicting things that won't happen, and missing the things that will.

Identify the effects of these errors

Estimate the probability and seriousness of each error

Training
Some training or experience in ranking probability and criticality will be useful.

Where to find out more
Quality Control Handbook, Juran J, McGraw Hill 1988

Quality Management Library, CCTA, HMSO, 1992

Total Quality Management, Pera International. Chapman and Hall, 1992

Produce plans to prevent most important problems, or mitigate others

Example

Although FMECA applies in production and manufacturing, it can also be used in service processes.

A small company planned to send out an advertising mailshot for an information product they had developed. In order to make sure things went smoothly, they worked out a simple FMECA and took action to prevent the problems they had anticipated.

In spite of this the mailshot was not successful, because the mailing list was out of date and had mismatched names and organisations. The company received irate phone calls from those who had been misaddressed.

The company now knows that bought-in databases have to be extensively verified, but the FMECA was obviously no substitute here for experience.

FMECA for an advertising mailshot

Item	What could go wrong	Probability 1 - 10	Criticality 1- 10	Effect	Prevention
Mailshot concept	Won't communicate well to the public	5	10	Reduce returns on the mailshot	Use PR company, read PO guidelines, evaluate other direct mail (benchmarking)
Mailshot design	Won't fit all constraints	7	4	Cost time to put it right	Make a physical dummy, including envelope
Database	Some names missing	10	5	Some letters will start Dear + address	Put a title instead of the name
Printing letters	Print quality not very good: smudges	6	3	Some letters won't look very smart	Print in batches of 50 can catch any problems early on
Posting	Post codes incomplete	10	1	Cost more to send	Add in £20 extra to the budget for the job.

Family Teams

An approach to solving problems within one particular work area.

Affinity group: Change Management

Classification • • • •

Process flowchart

Define issue for Family Team to investigate

↓

Set up Team with leader and facilitator

↓

Carry out Action Plans to investigate issue

↓

Report results to management and rest of 'family'

When to use it
As part of quality improvement programme, so that people who work in the same functional area can work together to examine particular quality issues.

What you'll achieve
Particular improvements, and a general improvement in communication and co-operation within the work group.

When not to use it
Don't use Family Teams for problems which are more broadly-based, or when the 'family' culture isn't right for co-operative working.

And be careful
Family Teams can be too cosy: they're not just chat shops. A clear direction and sense of purpose is needed, as well as deadlines and an audience for the results of the work.

Training
Training in teamwork and facilitation will be useful.

Where to find out more
Implementing Quality, Griffiths D N, ASQC Quality Press, 1989

Example

During a Departmental Purpose Analysis exercise in a major utility, a Family Team was put together to investigate the department's customers.

The Family Team gave themselves a tight timescale to prevent the project from drifting. They agreed to commit themselves to presenting a report to senior management in just over two months.

The sense of urgency generated by this deadline, along with a precise objective, gave the group a sense of purpose and the project went well.

Following on from the report, new Family Teams were formed to tackle some of the problems identified in it.

Action Plan for investigating customer needs

Team Objective: To identify our customers and investigate their needs

Date	Activity
14.2	Start-up meeting
14.2	Identify customers
21.2	Quantify relative importance of customers
25.2	Select most important customers for more detailed study
28.2	Send out customer questionnaires
14.3	Analyse results
28.3	Interview key customers
11.4	Identify key problems and draw up recommendations to restore them
25.4	Complete report to senior management

Fault Tree Analysis

Graphic method of setting out causes and origins of potential problems with product or service.

Affinity groups: Graphic Tool, Product and Process Design

Classification • • •

Process flowchart

Start with block diagram for top level description of product or process

List what could go wrong at this level

Take each failure and create a Fault Tree for it, using Fault Tree Notation

Recommend ways of limiting or preventing failures

When to use it
Fault Tree Analysis is a tool for analysing the design and performance of technical processes: can be used as a basis for Reliability Prediction.

What you'll achieve
A view of the process which concentrates on what could go wrong, showing the effect one failure has on the rest of the process. Particularly good at showing how failures interrelate.

When not to use it
Don't use Fault Tree Analysis for irregular processes: it relies on a logical structure.

And be careful
Remember to keep the diagram up to date: any changes or improvements in the process might affect the Fault Tree.

Training
Fault Tree Analysis has its own notation. Can get complex, especially if used for reliability prediction. Support software is available.

Where to find out more
Quality Control Handbook, Juran J, McGraw Hill, 1988

102

Example

An everyday example of a fault at the top level of the technical process is a car that won't start. Technical manuals typically provide car owners with some kind of a process flowchart which leads them through a series of decisions until they find a likely cause.

Fault Tree Analysis provides an overview of all causes and how they relate. So it does not so much explain how to analyse particular problems, as how the design of the ignition process works as a whole. This perspective allows the process designer or analyst to predict and defend any areas of particular weakness, rather than relying on ad hoc solutions which may have to be repeated many times before the pattern is observed.

Fault Tree Analysis: starting a car

Symbols

☐ consequence of faults

⌂ 'or' gate (this happens if one or more events take place)

○ original faults

⌂ 'and' gate (this happens if all the events below take place)

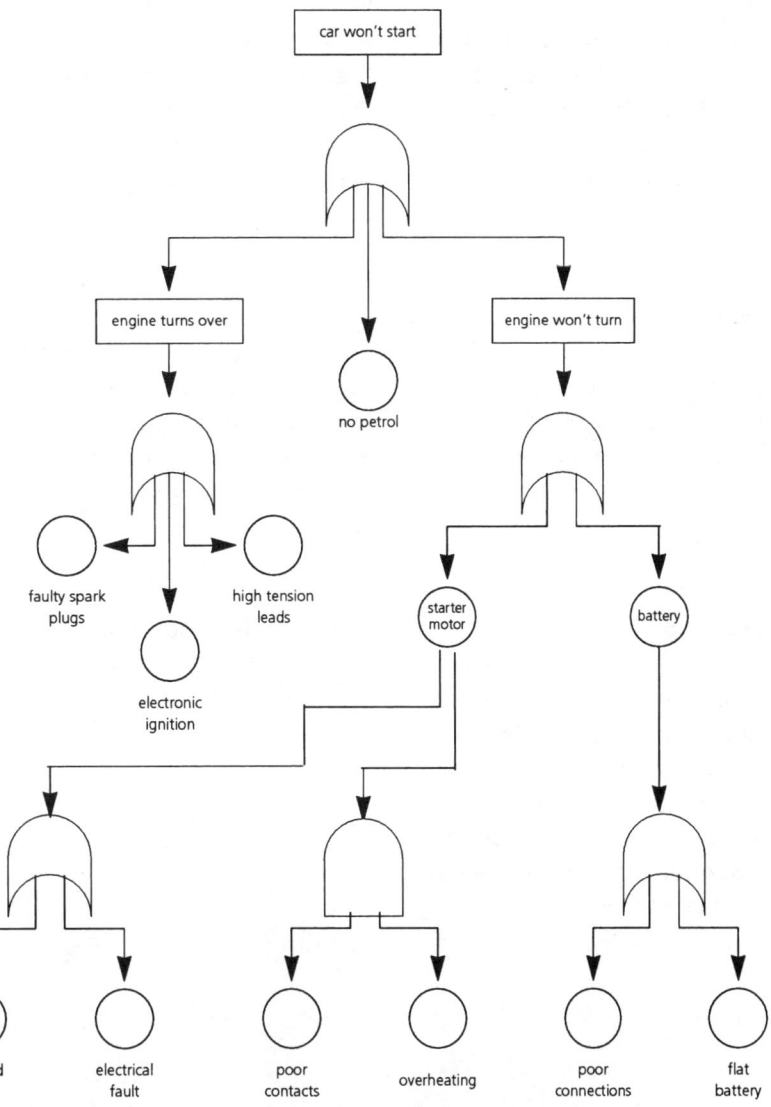

Feedback Loop

To ensure problems are noticed and put right as a matter of course.

Affinity group: Quality Management System

Classification • • • •

When to use it
Forms an essential part of a quality control system. Relates to both production processes and administrative and support processes.

What you'll achieve
A system which makes sure that problems are recognised and dealt with before people become habituated to them and they become part of the process.

When not to use it
Don't rely on the Feedback Loop for dealing with longstanding, chronic problems – use Kaizen instead.

And be careful
As with all control systems, it's important to collect data carefully and interpret intelligently. Don't overreact to changes picked up by sensors.

Training
Depends on type of work. Production Feedback Loops can be automated therefore specific training is needed to operate them. For less sophisticated systems, on-the-job training may be needed to maintain them.

Where to find out more
Quality Control Handbook, Juran J, McGraw Hill, 1988

Process flowchart

Identify goals which must be reached and therefore monitored

Establish methods of evaluating performance

Set up sensors to collect data

Analyse data for information about performance problems

Devise strategy for solving problem

Feed back necessary changes into process

Feedback Loops are an important concept in managing internal processes. An engineering company had recently brought in a new office computer system including a microfiche facility. However far from improving efficiency, the new system started to cause serious delays in processing paperwork, to the extent that suppliers threatened to cut off supplies because they were not being paid on time.

Investigation revealed that the speed of the computer system in some areas was causing bottlenecks in others. Since no-one knew how all parts of the system worked, staff couldn't help each other when this happened.

To solve the problem all staff were trained to use all parts of the system. A simple Feedback Loop was also established, consisting of a cardboard box by each machine, to hold the work to be done at each machine. When they were empty, staff moved onto something else. When they were full, extra staff came to help. Combined with training, this simple Feedback Loop solved the workflow problem.

Feedback Loop in an office department

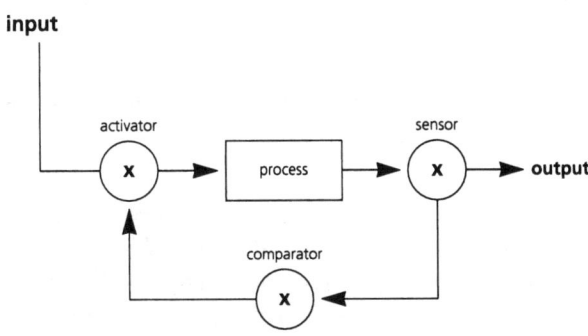

Fishbowl Meeting

Method of setting up a meeting where different groups can share opinions and information in a co-operative way.

Affinity group: Change Management

Classification • • •

When to use it
Fishbowl Meetings enable particular groups to communicate with other groups which are significant to them: customers, suppliers, managers etc.

When not to use it
Don't use when group roles can't be clearly separated in this way.

What you'll achieve
You'll gain a rapid increase in understanding: outsiders hear what insiders are trying to achieve. Misconceptions can be quickly put right.

And be careful
These meetings can be quite powerful – truths may emerge and both insiders and outsiders may feel threatened. Needs good facilitating.

Training
Training needed for the facilitator of the meeting.

Arrange participants in meeting in two circles: inner circle and outer circle

Inner circle takes active role in meeting

Outer circle observes and listens (or vice versa), and contributes information as necessary

Meeting ends with recommendations for improvements, approved by observers

Example

Fishbowl Meetings can be useful for bringing together sales departments with customer services, senior management with management consultants, and so on.

A Fishbowl Meeting was used by one Further Education college to improve understanding with local employers.

The college had sent out questionnaires to evaluate the training they were providing for students. The responses suggested that employers were not impressed.

In the Fishbowl Meeting, everyone had a copy of the results of the survey. The college sat in the inner circle, the employers on the outside. The agenda for the day allowed both sides to eavesdrop on each other's reactions before coming together to define the most pressing issues and find solutions.

Both sides found the opportunity to hear each other in this way illuminating, and improved relations considerably.

Fishbowl Meeting for college staff and employers

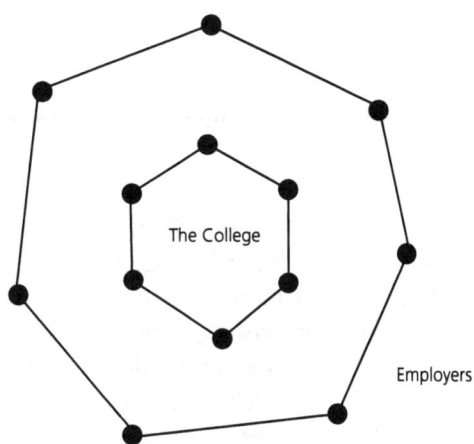

Agenda

1. Introduction from the facilitator.

2. Employers discuss results of interviewers – insiders don't comment unless they are expressly invited to do so.

3. College staff discuss results of interview in the same way.

4. Facilitator to identify concerns arising from the discussion.

5. Mixed group of employers and college staff will propose solutions to the concerns raised by the facilitator.

Flowcharts

Graphic method of representing activities and processes.

Affinity group: Graphic Tool

Classification • •

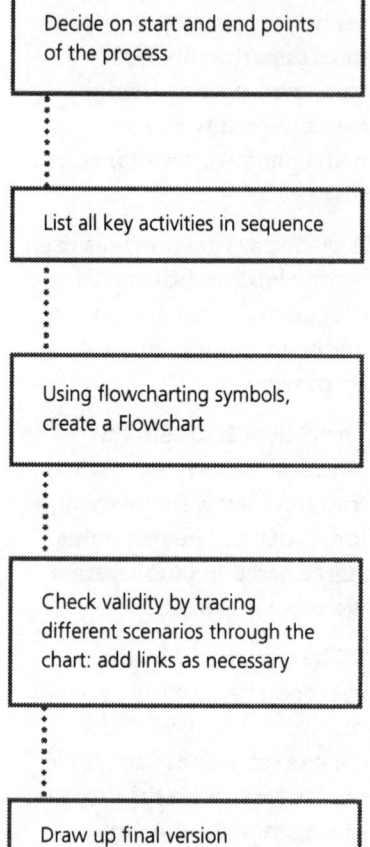

Process flowchart

Decide on start and end points of the process

List all key activities in sequence

Using flowcharting symbols, create a Flowchart

Check validity by tracing different scenarios through the chart: add links as necessary

Draw up final version

When to use it
Flowcharts are the first step in exploring and analysing how processes work. They're a very flexible tool which are appropriate for all kinds of situations.

What you'll achieve
A logical, concise way of dealing with the complexity of processes, which people can understand quickly. Making Flowcharts is a good discipline as it means looking at processes in a logical, detailed way.

When not to use it
Don't use Flowcharts when the activities in a process are very variable, or where the sequence of events isn't important.

And be careful
Keep elements of the chart at the same level of detail. And watch scale: very large process diagrams are hard to validate and control, they should be split into smaller levels.

Training
It's necessary to know relevant symbols. Software is readily available.

Where to find out more
The Memory Jogger, Brassard M and Ritter D, GOAL/QPC, 1994

Quality Control Handbook, Juran J, McGraw Hill, 1988

The Quality Toolkit, Marsh J, IFS Ltd, 1992

Example

As part of its plan to implement a quality management system, a document company produces a Flowchart displaying its management and operational processes.

The company has had some problems with proof-reading and production, with each member of staff following their own rules. The Flowchart shows where quality checklists must be used.

The circle at the top of the Flowchart signifies that this chart is part of a sequence of others.

Symbols

☐ activity

◇ decision

⬭ terminal

▱ document

➤ flowline

○ connector

Flowchart for a proof-reading and production process

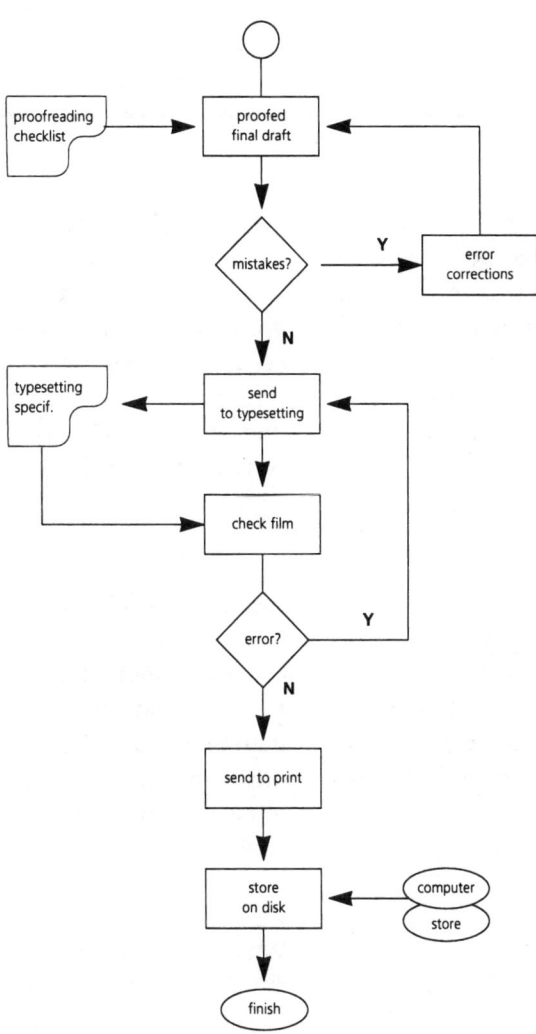

Focus Group

For particular interest groups to share information and opinions.

Affinity group: Data Capture

Classification •

Process flowchart

```
┌──────────────────────────────┐
│ Define topic for discussion  │
└──────────────────────────────┘
              ┊
┌──────────────────────────────┐
│ Prepare 5 or 6 questions     │
│ about it                     │
└──────────────────────────────┘
              ┊
┌──────────────────────────────┐
│ Bring together group of people│
│ with interest in topic       │
└──────────────────────────────┘
              ┊
┌──────────────────────────────┐
│ Set up tape recorder         │
└──────────────────────────────┘
              ┊
┌──────────────────────────────┐
│ Facilitator leads discussion │
│ structured around questions  │
└──────────────────────────────┘
              ┊
┌──────────────────────────────┐
│ Type up tape and produce     │
│ report and recommendations   │
└──────────────────────────────┘
```

When to use it

Use Focus Groups to find out opinions and perceptions –can be used by users and suppliers, experts from different organisations, or customers.

What you'll achieve

Focus Groups provide qualitative information and opinions, which are often as accurate as (and more informative than) quantitative data and facts. They provide a concentration of interest and expertise.

When not to use it

Don't use for factual information about how well people understand something for example – focus groups give impressions and opinions.

And be careful

Keep the group focussed: discuss no more than one topic at a time, and use not more than five or six related questions. Remember to interpret comments in their context.

Training

Training for the facilitator in directing the sessions might be useful, but not essential.

Where to find out more

Benchmarking, Camp R, ASQC Quality Press, 1989

Fast Focus on TQM, Barrett D, Productivity Press, 1990

Focus Groups as Qualitative Research, Morgan D L, Qualitative Research Methods;vol 16, Sage, 1988

Example

Focus Groups are an important market research tool which are widely used to test the public's response to products.

A food manufacturer and retailer carried out a series of Focus Groups with buyers and retailers to evaluate responses to their drinks, sandwiches and crisps. As is quite common with Focus Groups, there were some surprises. The target age group for the products was older than expected, in spite of young packaging. And the calorie count mattered less than taste. The Focus Groups suggested strongly that the food company should concentrate on the appearance of its products, even at the expense of nutrition.

Focus Group on drinks, sandwiches and crisps as lunchtime snacks

```
Time: 1 hour
The discussion should concentrate around the
importance of these six factors
```

1. Appearance
   How far do customers shop with their eyes?

2. Customer profile
   Sex, age.

3. Nutrition
   How concerned are customers about calorie count and healthy ingredients?

4. Taste and feel
   How important is taste, texture, crunchiness, etc?.

5. Convenience in display
   How important is the grouping of drinks, sandwiches and crisps.

6. Convenience at the checkout
   How important is speed of purchase?

Force Field Analysis

Method of analysing problems in terms of the influences that affect them.

Affinity group: Problem Solving

Classification • •

When to use it
Use Force Field Analysis for identifying and influencing the contexts which surround particular initiatives. Useful for understanding general issues of attitude and culture: can also be used to analyse market position.

What you'll achieve
Force Field Analysis has a predictive use, to estimate the likelihood of success. Also provides a way of identifying where energies should go to resolve problems, and where to leave well alone.

When not to use it
Counterproductive when you won't be able to carry out the actions you recommend.

And be careful
It's often more effective to concentrate resources on removing barriers rather than strengthening positive forces – look beyond present constraints.

Training
Some training for a facilitator would be useful.

Where to find out more
The Quality Toolkit, Marsh J, IFS Ltd, 1992

The Memory Jogger, Brassard M and Ritter D, GOAL/QPC 1994

Prepare analysis sheet with T-shaped line arrangement

Brainstorm key forces which surround the problem – positives on the left, negatives on the right

Estimate size and significance of each force – can be quantified using rating scores

Highlight important positive forces that can be strengthened

Highlight important barriers that can be weakened

Draw up a new force field analysis and a list of the actions needed to achieve it.

Example

Anyone planning to introduce a quality initiative would be well advised to carry out a Force Field Analysis first, as part of a realistic assessment of how far it is likely to be accepted.

On the positive side, people are generally proud of what they do, and happy to plan improvements. On the negative side, they will have a natural fear of change and often a suspicion of management, who they assume are acting from cost-cutting motives.

These issues will probably be common to most organisations: the balance between them will be different.

In the example, the scoring system gives negative forces an advantage of 1 point. Management may well want to prepare the ground and raise awareness further before going ahead with a detailed programme. At the moment, the analysis suggests that its success hangs in the balance.

Force Field Analysis for introducing a quality programme

Objective: To introduce a quality improvement programme into the organisation

Ⓐ Ⓑ   Ⓑ Ⓐ

Total	Significance of change	Possibility of change	Positive forces	Negative forces	Possibility of change	Significance of change	Total
7	3	4	People's desire to do well	Overworked	2	2	4
4	2	2	Acceptance of the inevitability of change	Fear of change	4	5	9
7	4	3	Benefits for customers	Suspicion of management's motives	3	3	6
7	4	3	Competitive pressures	Poor understanding of the need for change	4	3	7
25			Total	Total			26

Ⓐ How significant are the consequences of change?
Ⓑ How far is it possible to change this force?
5   very strong
4   strong
3   medium
2   low
1   weak

Gantt Chart

Graphic method of showing sequence of project tasks.

Affinity group: Planning, Graphic

Classification • • •

When to use it
Use the Gantt Chart as a project planning tool for scheduling project activities.

What you'll achieve
Gantt Charts show activities and timescales: also dependencies. Clear and unambiguous method of showing project information.

When not to use it
Don't use for small and simple projects, where a list of tasks would suffice.

And be careful
People often create elaborate charts as a defensive measure and then ignore them as soon as deadlines start to slip. Keep the chart up-to-date if you're going to use at all.

Training
For simple projects, training could consist of reading and examples. Gantt Charts are a standard feature of project planning software.

Where to find out more
The Memory Jogger, Brassard M and Ritter D, GOAL/QPC, 1994

Management and organisation, Sisk HL, South-Western publishing co, 1973

Process flowchart

Define project tasks and/or steps

Estimate time needed for each task, and start and finish dates

Create Gantt Chart
Horizontal axis: time
Vertical axis: tasks

Chart non-dependent tasks in parallel: contingent tasks in sequence

Monitor actual progress against chart

In the Family Team example, the team produced an Action Plan for their project. Since this was a small project with only a few members, an Action Plan seemed adequate.

However the Action Plan does not make clear the dependencies in the project. As things stand, team members wait for one activity to end before starting the next.

Representing the plan as a Gantt Chart shows that this isn't necessary, particularly as far as the report is concerned. Parts of the report can start before all the interviews are finished, so relieving the pressure at the end of the project.

During the project, one of the interviewers falls ill, and a key customer goes to a conference for a week. The Gantt Chart makes it possible to see how to work round these problems – in this case by extending the interview period to run parallel with initial work on identifying the problems which have emerged so far.

Gantt Chart for a Family Team project on customers

	Weeks										
	1	2	3	4	5	6	7	8	9	10	11

1. Start-up meeting
   Identify customers

2. Quantify relative
   importance of customers

3. Select most
   important customers

4. Send out questionnaires

5. Analyse results

6. Interview key customers

7. Identify problems and
   make recommendations

8. Write report

☐ Activity
■ Amendment

115

Gap Analysis

For comparing your performance with that of competitors

Affinity group: Problem Solving

Classification • • •

When to use it
Use Gap Analysis to focus on how well you compare either to competitors or to your own objectives, and why.

What you'll achieve
Gap Analysis provides a detailed breakdown of both the qualitative and quantitative aspects of the gap, showing how much your performance differs from competitors' or your own goals.

When not to use it
Don't try to use Gap Analysis without some reliable, detailed information about performance and goals.

And be careful
Don't be simplistic about the reasons for gaps: it may take much effort and experiment to close them.

Training
Training in Benchmarking is appropriate and will include Gap Analysis.

Where to find out more
Benchmarking, Camp R, ASQC Quality Press, 1989

Process flowchart

Gather data about the level of performance you're aiming at (Benchmarking)

Gather data about your own performance and compare

Identify performance gaps:
• positive
• negative
• parity

Analyse reasons for negative gaps: qualitative and quantitative

Devise Action Plan to close gap

Example

An industry newspaper owns a subsidiary company (Company A) selling database information to advertisers who want to send targeted or personalised mailshots, rather than relying on general advertising.

The databases were set up five years ago and have been profitable. However recently there have been some complaints from customers, claiming that almost every name has an error associated with it. This is resulting in considerable ill-will among potential customers.

Company A says that it is impossible to have a completely accurate database, and that their level of error is standard for the industry.

However a quick Benchmarking exercise carried out by sampling and interview reveals that Company A is falling behind the competition. It must now analyse why the gaps have occurred and take rapid steps to improve standards.

Gap Analysis for database company

Database companies	A	B	C	D	E
Negative gap					
% spelling errors	05	04	03	02	04
% attribution errors	32	10	11	06	08
% death errors	04	05	04	03	06
% gone away errors	18	16	12	6	10
% postcode errors	08	03	06	04	05
Parity					
% accuracy of mailsort	94	96	95	98	96
Delivery time (weeks)	02	03	02	02	04
Positive gap					
Cost £ per 1000 names	250	300	325	400	350

Gap Analysis

The Gap Analysis suggests that Company A is performing below the level of its competitors. This is reflected in the low cost of the database to customers. Company A now has a Cost of Quality calculation to make. At their present rate of performance, they will not be in business much longer.

Histogram

Graphic method of showing the distribution of a complete set of quantitative data.

Affinity group: Graphic Tool

Classification • •

When to use it
Use a Histogram to see the pattern of a complete set of data items, and whether or not it follows the shape of a normal distribution.

When not to use it
Don't use for analysing data items from a number of sources: use a Bar Chart instead.

Training
No training needed for how to make Histograms – and software is available on most word processors. Some understanding of statistics is necessary for collecting and interpreting data.

What you'll achieve
A very clear way of seeing how the data is distributed, whether normal or skewed in some way.

And be careful
Be careful with scale: an inappropriate vertical scale can lose or exaggerate contrasts. Keep to about 10 bars on the horizontal axis.

Where to find out more
The Quality Toolkit, J Marsh, IFS Ltd, 1992

The Memory Jogger, Brassard M and Ritter D, GOAL/QPC, 1994

Handbook of Quality Tools, Ozeki K and Asaka T, Productivity Press, 1990

Process flowchart

Collect complete set of data about particular items

For vertical axis, identify maximum and minimum values and calculate total range by subtracting minimum from maximum

For horizontal axis, identify range of items for each bar of Histogram

Count up occurrences within each bar width and plot on vertical axis

Draw Histogram

A standard use for Histograms in quality management is in looking at variances in a process. Large amounts of performance data can be given shape and coherence by Histograms, making it easy to interpret how stable the process is and how well it meets specification.

One safety-critical industry which was used to using Histograms in this way decided to apply the technique rather differently to assess safety awareness among staff. Since safety was an important part of the working environment they expected the results of their test to show a positive skew. However the results showed a negative skew with the majority falling below what the safety officers felt was an acceptable level of knowledge.

The safety officers immediately started a training programme, with the quantitative objective of achieving a normal distribution of scores around an improved average score.

Histogram of results of safety awareness tests

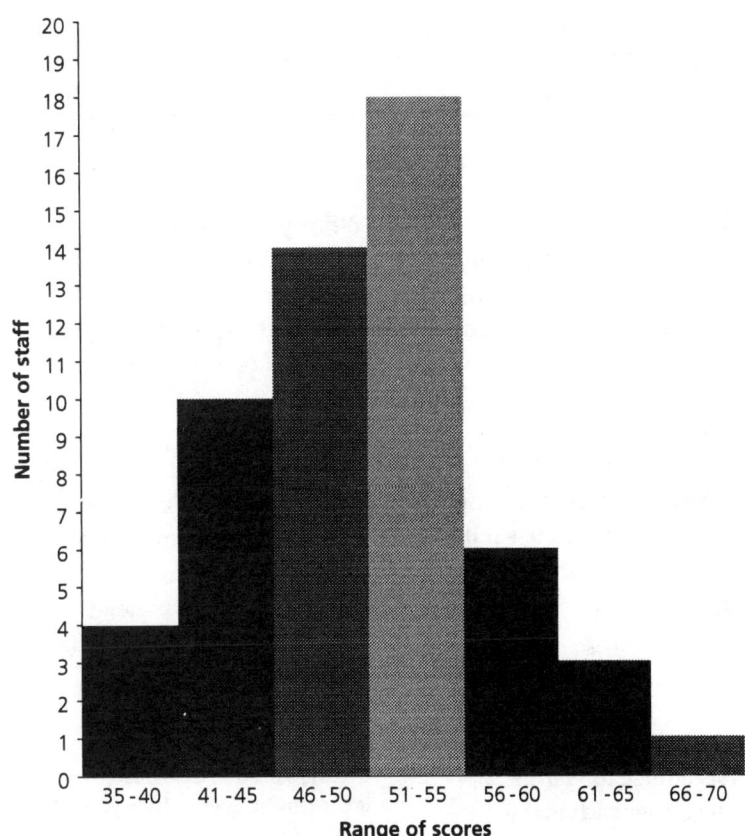

Hoshin

Also known as the Deming Cycle. A technique for achieving step change followed by incremental improvement.

Affinity group: Strategy

Classification • • • •

When to use it
For setting up a long-term structure for organisation-wide quality improvement.

What you'll achieve
Structural approach to change and improvement, viewed as a continual part of management, not just a one-off initiative.

When not to use it
Hoshin works from the top down. Don't try to use it if there isn't support from the top.

And be careful
Success depends on cultural shift towards teamwork and a co-operative focus on improvement: may need substantial groundwork first.

Training
Short course for senior management advisable.

Where to find out more
Deming's Road to Continual Improvement, Sherkenbach WW, SPC Press, 1991

Out of the Crisis, Deming WE, Cambridge University Press, 1988

Total Quality Management, Pera International, Chapman and Hall, 1992

Stage 1 Plan
Define not more than 3 issues of major importance and convert into strategies, objectives and goals

Stage 2 Do
Apply strategies and objectives top-down throughout the organisation

Stage 3 Check
Review progress at predetermined review dates, from bottom up

Stage 4 Act
Take action as necessary to keep implementation on track

Repeat process as on-going improvement programme

Example

A fast-growing high technology company with 50% of the world market had reached the stage in the UK where, if it was to exceed its £10m turnover and continue to expand sales, it would have to improve its business processes and financial controls. A disastrous inventory variance made the point clearly.

In the Plan phase, the company decided to introduce a strong customer service department to mediate between sales and manufacturing. It would handle all routine orders and prioritise them for the factory.

The Do phase involved appointing a head of department and a high quality team, who started straight away to set up a customer database.

In the Check phase, the department started to map out its processes and its relationships to other departments, to establish sound working practices.

In the Act phase, changes were made to the department as it matured and expanded, for example opening a European operation.

The Hoshin approach for setting up a new department

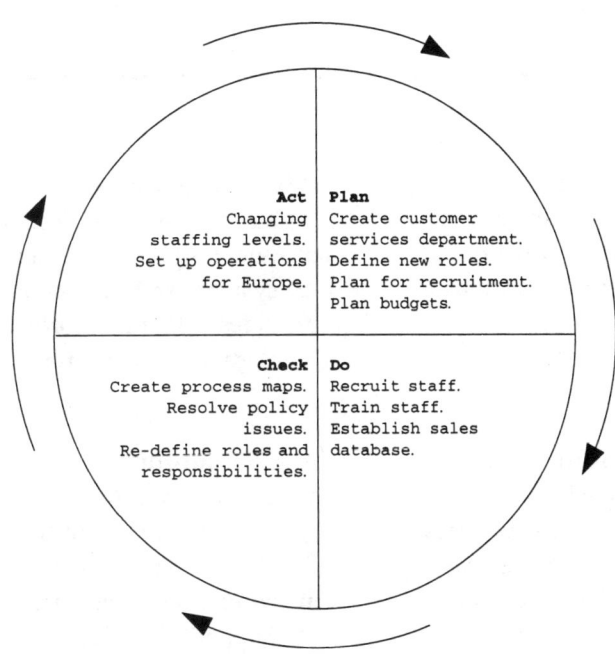

Inspection

Technique for assessing the degree of conformance of raw materials, processes and products to agreed specifications.

Affinity group: Quality Management System

Classification • • •

When to use it
As part of quality control system for production processes, to check that products conform to specification.

When not to use it
Don't use where rigorous conformance to quality is required: use Statistical Process Control techniques instead.

What you'll achieve
Reduced chance of defective product progressing through the system. And Inspection provides valuable records to highlight particular problems.

And be careful
Make sure inspectors are in agreement with each other: significant variations in interpretation of specification can happen. 100% Inspection doesn't actually guarantee quality of product.

Training
Training needed, preferably for all Inspection team members together, to keep consistency of standards.

Where to find out more
Quality Control Handbook, Juran, McGraw Hill, 1988

A Practical Approach to Quality Control, Caplen R H, Hutchinson Publishing Group, 1978

Total Quality Control, Feigenbaum, McGraw Hill, 1983

Process flowchart

Appoint Inspection team

Agree on interpretation of specification and how to measure characteristics

Judge products according to specification

Set up system for dealing with rejects

Keep Inspection records

Inspection

Example

Inspection is an important part of quality control for incoming materials. When the sampling plan has been decided, appropriate checks have to be devised and carried out, bearing in mind the use the material will be put to during the manufacturing process.

Record keeping is an important part of Inspection so that it is possible to spot suppliers who consistently send poor quality material. Suppliers who consistently cause problems should be discontinued.

The Inspection record details what checks were made, and the results.

Inspection record for incoming batch of components

Date	Number	No. in batch	No. insp.	No. faulty	% faulty	A	B	C	D	E	Misc.	Pass	Fail	Insp's initials	Return to supplier	100% test	Rectify	Senior insp's initials
03 Apr.	1131	1200	70	1	1.4	-	1	-	-	-	-	✓		MS				
12 Apr.	1197	500	60	0	0	-	-	-	-	-	-	✓		AP				
28 Apr.	1253	2500	100	0	0	-	-	-	-	-	-	✓		AP				
03 May	1304	950	70	4	5.7	-	-	4	-	-	-		✗	MS	✓			PW
15 May	1372	3000	150	0	0	-	-	-	-	-	-	✓		MS				
23 May	1419	1500	100	1	1	1	-	-	-	-	-	✓		AS				
01 Jun.	1476	2000	125	5	4	-	1	-	2	1	1		✗	AP		✓		PW
13 Jun.	1536	1700	90	0	0	-	-	-	-	-	-	✓		AS				
24 Jun.	1590	3000	150	2	1.3	-	-	-	-	2	-	✓		AS				
02 Jul.	1688	5000	200	0	0	-	-	-	-	-	-	✓		MS				
16 Jul.	1693	5000	200	4	2	-	-	-	-	-	-		✗	MS	✓			PW
31 Jul.	1730	2500	100	0	0	-	-	-	-	-	-	✓		AP				
03 Aug.	1766	3000	125	0	0	-	-	-	-	-	-	✓		AP				

Interviewing

Information gathering technique for planning and feedback.

Affinity group: Data Capture

Classification •

When to use it
For gathering information you'll need for decision making, planning or for projects. An important part of defining processes for quality management systems.

What you'll achieve
Credibility among those affected by your decisions. Insight into what people know, and what they are thinking or saying.

When not to use it
When resources are limited, or when you need information from a whole group, not just individuals.

And be careful
Unstructured interviews can quickly degenerate into polite chats or moans about the organisation. Focus on facts.

Training
Training by simulations can be very useful.

Where to find out more
Effective Interviewing, Fletcher J, Kogan Page, 1988

How to be a Good Judge of Character, Mackenzie Davey D, Kogan Page 1989

Identify key people to interview

Prepare questions in advance to structure interview

Prioritise questions by weighting responses

Schedule interviews

Interview using good practice guidelines:
• be unthreatening
• remain objective
• use open-ended questions
• use the journalist's credo: who, what, when, why and how
• summarise and feed back your impressions as you go
• take notes

Example

Interviewing is an important part of the initial stages of developing a quality management system. At this stage, the quality group is trying to establish what the organisation's main processes are, and what they look like.

Interviews have a dual purpose. They have a very important information gathering purpose, if the quality management system is to represent accurately the way people work in the organisation.

Just as important at this stage is the opportunity they provide for feedback in a safe environment. People can ask questions without being afraid of looking stupid. Or they can voice their fears and opinions and receive direct feedback from the interviewer. Also it's difficult to sustain hostility or aggression on a one-to-one basis.

So although interviewing uses a lot of time, it is usually a successful and productive tool. People like to talk about what they do and to have a receptive audience with whom to share their concerns.

Interviewing checklist for defining processes

1. Can you describe what your job involves?

2. What is your understanding of the process your department is part of?

3. What are the key procedures you follow, that should be written down?

4. How well does the system you use work at present?

5. What improvements would you like to see?

6. What is your understanding of quality management systems?

7. What are your main worries?

8. What do you think a quality management system would contribute to your job? To the work of your department?

9. What barriers do you perceive that prevent improvements?

Job Re-design

Way of improving job quality by increasing scope and level of responsibility.

Affinity group: Strategy

Classification • • • •

When to use it
When traditional roles in the organisation seem restrictive or limiting for staff. Absenteeism is often a clue to this problem.

When not to use it
Don't re-design jobs without good organisational reason: it's a major undertaking. Simpler solutions may be changes in reward systems, or better training.

Training
Not a difficult concept, but putting it into practice in a production line environment will need training.

What you'll achieve
More productive, better motivated staff. Some re-design projects cite up to 40% productivity improvements.

And be careful
Particularly with vertical enlargement, don't put people in roles they haven't the training or aptitude to fill: always consult and provide options. Otherwise can be seen as management conspiracy to get more work out of staff.

Where to find out more
Quality Control Handbook, Juran J, McGraw Hill, 1989

Process flowchart

Identify job roles that are potentially unsatisfying for staff

Investigate ways of enriching them:
• more same-level tasks (horizontal)
• more responsibilities (vertical)
• more autonomy

Discuss possible changes with managers, staff, and unions

Provide extensive training in new roles

Monitor and reward improvements in performance

Example

Job Re-design is particularly relevant to production line jobs which are repetitive and can be tiring and tedious for employees.

The garment manufacturing industry relies on production-line -type work organisation, with particular workers becoming skilled at particular parts of the garment. One company using this approach found itself facing increasing levels of absenteeism and dissatisfaction. Because of the recession it could not increase wages.

Talking to the production line workers revealed that they would find work much more interesting if they made whole garments. When the work was reorganised in this way, expanding jobs horizontally, absenteeism fell and production rates improved.

Re-designing a garment production process

The original production line

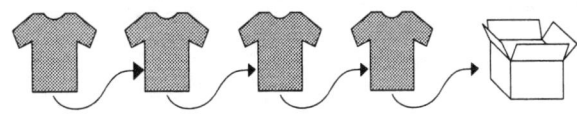

The re-designed production line

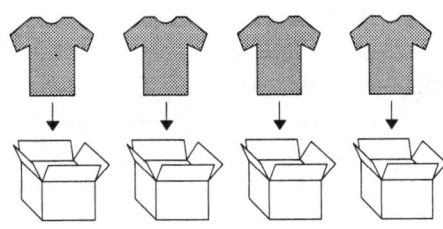

Just-In-Time

Way of organising supply chain to achieve maximum responsiveness and minimum stock holding cost

Affinity group: Strategy

Classification • • • • •

When to use it
For managing the supply chain in repetitive manufacturing, where processes are operating efficiently.

What you'll achieve
Increased responsiveness from suppliers, lower costs, and simpler processes. For industries which traditionally rely on extensive buffer stocks, savings can be enormous.

When not to use it
Don't try to use this without clear direction from the top, or without full support.

And be careful
Not easy to implement: start with pilot schemes, especially if external suppliers are involved, and build up JIT system gradually. Generally reckoned to take between 2 to 7 years to achieve. Needs full involvement and support from everyone.

Training
Training is very important, both in what can be achieved and in how to do it. Unlikely to be undertaken without consultancy.

Where to find out more
Kanban Just-In-Time at Toyota; Management Begins at the Workplace, Lu D J, Productivity Press, 1989

Japanese Manufacturing Techniques, Schonberger R, The Free Press, 1982

Process flowchart

Identify supply chain throughout production processes – internal and external links

For each internal link, identify ways of synchronising supply and demand

Work with external suppliers to achieve synchronisation

Pilot new supply arrangements as they evolve

Work internally to reduce inventory, resolving underlying problems as they emerge

Extend JIT throughout supply chain

Example

The Japanese success with JIT has created something of a mythical reputation for this tool. Just as workers stretch out their hands for the last components, so the myth goes, a lorry full of replacements draws into the unloading bay, guided either by excellent planning or telepathy.

Achieving this depends on a radical reorganisation of both supplier and internal processes. The image most used by the Japanese to explain JIT is that of the sea and the rocks. With high levels of inventory throughout the process, the rocks or problems in the business are hidden. As inventory levels fall, any underlying problems with scheduling or efficiency are uncovered and have to be dealt with. So introducing JIT has an enormous impact on the whole business.

Just-In-Time – uncovering the rocks

Before Just-In- Time
High stock levels
hide problem in the system

After Just-In- Time
Falling stock levels
expose problems in the system. It
is important to identify and solve
problems as they emerge

Kaizen

Process of slow, gradual improvement: as much an attitude as a tool.

Affinity group: Strategy

Classification •••••

Process flowchart

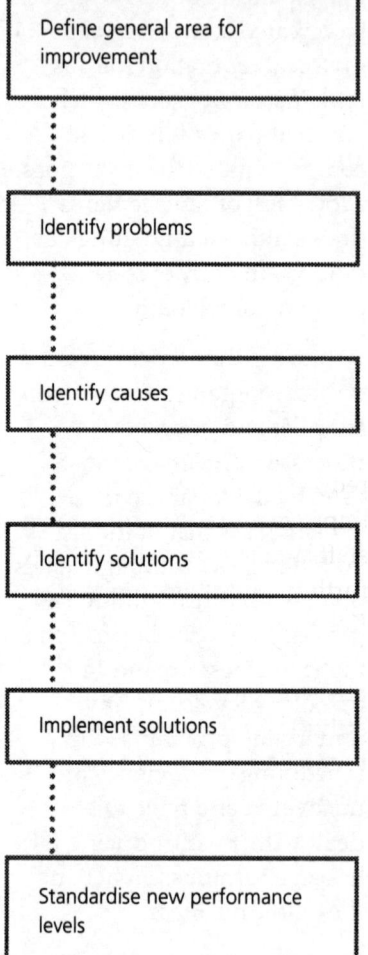

Define general area for improvement

Identify problems

Identify causes

Identify solutions

Implement solutions

Standardise new performance levels

When to use it
As part of long-term initiative to change company culture and improve quality. Helps to sustain major change by changing attitudes as well as work practices.

What you'll achieve
Slow and steady improvements in performance with minimum disruption to the organisation and a relatively low investment. Also builds a culture of co-operation and positive thinking.

When not to use it
Don't use when a radical step-change is needed to keep up with the competition.

And be careful
Kaizen is not always enough: in times of change, you're likely to face need for step change too. Kaizen can be combined with more radical measures.

Training
Training is necessary.

Where to find out more
Kaizen: The Key to Japan's Competitive Success, Imai M, McGraw Hill, 1989

Kaizen: The Understanding and Application of Continuous Improvement, Huda, Stanley Thornes, 1994

The Deming Route to Quality and Productivity, Sherkenbach WW, Mercury Press, 198

130

Kaizen provides a model for improving quality in stable times, but it can also help to normalise major change.

This is how Kaizen was used in the electricity industry.

During the government's privatisation of the electricity industry, all plants were concerned with improving efficiency. To get operating costs down, processes were re-engineered and staff numbers reduced. At the same time, to improve morale for remaining staff, and to start to build further improvements, the Kaizen philosophy was introduced. This emphasised a positive, problem solving attitude which helped people to come to terms with the new demands they faced.

Kaizen in the electricity industry

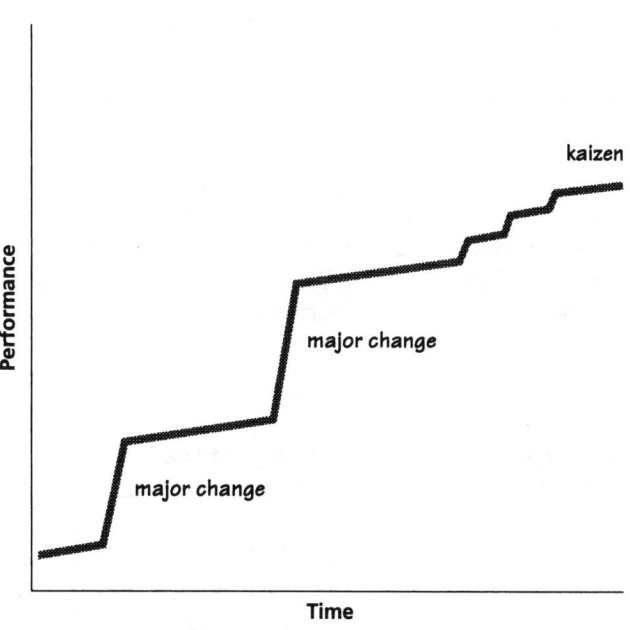

Kanban

Method of pulling materials through the production system as they're needed.

Affinity group: Product and Process Design

Classification • • • • •

When to use it
Use Kanban as a tool for introducing Just-In-Time internally into production systems.

What you'll achieve
Reduction in inventory throughout the production process.

When not to use it
Don't use in isolation: Kanban has to be part of a wider JIT reorganisation.

And be careful
Kanban requires real cultural change to work effectively. If there is no work, operators will have to find other things to do, such as Total Productive Maintenance. And accounting systems need to change – they'll probably be based on full utilisation.

Training
Extensive training needed for setting up the system. Also on-the-job training needed for operators.

Where to find out more
Kanban Just-In-Time at Toyota; Management Begins at the Workplace, Lu D J, Productivity Press, 1989

Process flowchart

Identify supply chain throughout the process

Create Kanban card (specifying the number wanted) for each component in the supply chain

Attach card to box containing components

Fill up box according to card and send to next person in the process

Wait until Kanban returns before making more components

Example

Kanban is now a well established tool in production lines using JIT. Part of its attraction lies in its visibility – anyone can see at a glance where orders are piling up or where operators are idle.

The bicycle company in the diagram uses Kanban to ensure that a steady stream of components is always ready to replace completed models which are called off to supply customer orders.

Thirty bicycles have been taken to a sales showroom and the factory now has to make 30 more. The Kanban process starts at the end of the production process with a request by the final assembly team for the parts they will need to make the 30 bikes. The operators making these parts will in turn request components from their suppliers.

If there are no more orders in the meantime, activity will stop with the completion of the 30 bicycles and only start again when there is once again a demand.

Kanban in a bicycle factory

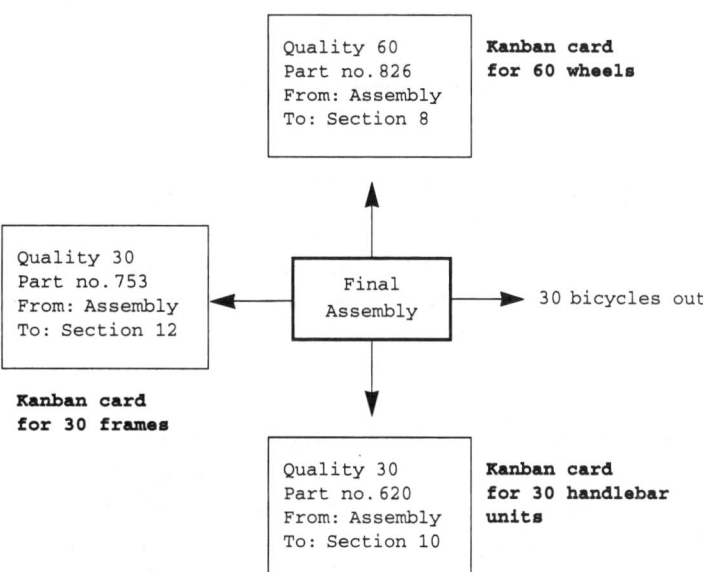

```
Quality 60
Part no. 826
From: Assembly
To: Section 8
```
Kanban card for 60 wheels

```
Quality 30
Part no. 753
From: Assembly
To: Section 12
```
Kanban card for 30 frames

```
Final
Assembly
```

30 bicycles out

```
Quality 30
Part no. 620
From: Assembly
To: Section 10
```
Kanban card for 30 handlebar units

Lateral Thinking

Tool for finding new solutions to old problems.

Affinity group: Problem Solving

Classification • • •

Define problem

Generate lateral thinking
solutions, by using:
• intermediate impossibles:
  ideas for rethinking later
• humour
• random juxtaposition
• challenging accepted outlooks
• using Thinking Hats

Work through ideas, refining
and discarding as appropriate

When to use it
For situations which need new
approaches and ideas because
the old ones no longer apply or
are no longer good enough.

What you'll achieve
New ways of thinking about
things: exciting ideas: some
viable solutions.

When not to use it
Don't use Lateral Thinking
when constraints won't allow
radical thinking to pay off.

And be careful
Needs to be supported by
traditional logical thinking: de
Bono recommends it for only
10% of the problem solving
process.

Training
Reading de Bono's book.

Where to find out more
Lateral Thinking for Management, de
Bono E, Penguin, 1982

Fast Focus on TQM, Barrett D,
Productivity Press, 1990

Example

Some striking examples of successful Lateral Thinking have come from companies whose traditional markets have disappeared and who have had to move into new ones.

A manufacturer of industrial sewing spools faced this problem in the late 70s. Their first reaction was to think traditionally about alternative uses for their product, about new markets, or new sales gimmicks. But it was soon obvious that they were fighting a losing battle and needed a much more radical solution.

The company set up a brainstorming session which set no limits on their thinking. Ideas should use existing skills and experience, but only as a jumping-off point. Lateral Thinking took them to golf balls, of which they are now a successful manufacturer. Outsiders do not often make the connection.

Lateral Thinking – sewing spools to golf balls

Traditional Thinking

Lateral Thinking

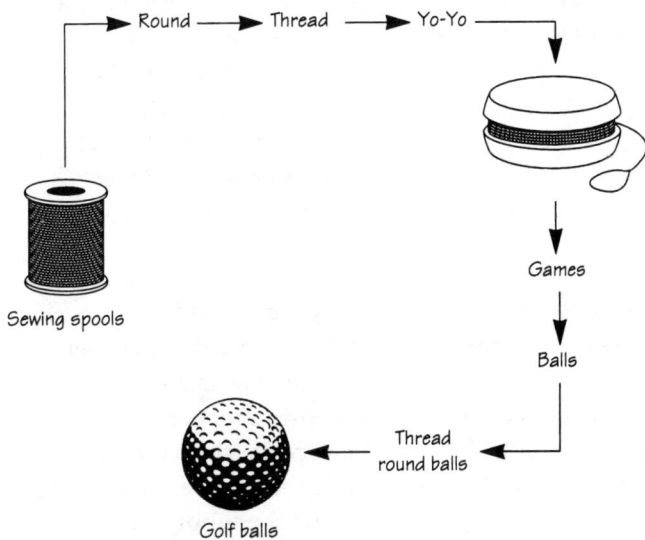

Life-Cycle Costing

Way of calculating costs over the complete life-cycle, to optimise cost for producer and customer.

Affinity group: Cost Management

Classification • • • •

Create flowchart showing all phases product goes through in its life-cycle

Identify where costs lie in each phase

Collect cost data for each phase

As far as possible, quantify interrelationships between cost factors

Work out a cost equation to help with decision-making process

When to use it
When you or your customers are prepared to buy, based on Life-Cycle Costs for them, rather than just the purchase price.

What you'll achieve
A sophisticated costing approach which trades off expense in the production phase against lower subsequent costs later on. Helps to prevent false economies – savings in one area which cause more expense later on.

When not to use it
Not very useful for complex projects where interrelationships between costs aren't clear, and reliability or failure data isn't available.

And be careful
Often very difficult to get reasonable data for all aspects of costing: concentrate on vital few costs which can be calculated. Needs co-operation along the supply chain.

Training
Training needed for calculating costs and working through interrelationships. Software is available for calculating Life-Cycle Costs for specific products.

Where to find out more
Quality Control Handbook, Juran J, McGraw Hill 1988

Total Quality Control, Feigenbaum A V, McGraw Hill 1983

Example

Life-Cycle Costing is not as widely used as might be supposed by consumers, who tend to assume that processes are designed to optimise Life-Cycle Costs. In fact manufacturers may be only concerned with their small part of the product life-cycle, so that it is up to the customer to work out the total costs.

An example of these calculations is provided by a print shop who want to introduce a Macintosh computer studio. The company lists out all the costs they will face, and considers trade-offs.

Better training would cut down the time staff spend trying to solve technical problems.

Better security would cut down insurance premiums which are extremely high.

And paying now for high-specification machines would prevent call-out charges for installing enhancements when they are needed – which they surely will be.

```
Life-Cycle Costs for Macs in a print shop

Costs

Installation
Hardware
Software
Maintenance agreement
Upgrades
Enhancements
New software
Replacement kit
Opportunity cost of downtime
Time spent by staff by trying to fix problems
Foregone interest on capital invested
Security marking on machines
Better locks and security systems
Higher insurance premiums
Depreciation


Relationships between costs

Training - time spent fixing problems
Security - insurance premiums
High initial specification - enhancements
```

137

Line Graph

Graphic method of showing change over time.

Affinity group: Graphic Tool

Classification • •

Process flowchart

Identify item to track, and collect data

Draw and label axes:
Horizontal: time
Vertical: values

Calculate suitable gradations for both axes

Plot data points on the graph and join by a line

When to use it
When you're looking at data to see trends over time.

What you'll achieve
Clear and easily understood representation of what would otherwise be just a page of figures.

When not to use it
Don't use to emphasise differences between individual data items – use Bar Charts or Histograms instead.

And be careful
Make sure the scale's appropriate and shows up the significance of the data–may need to play around to get right. And interpret by looking at the whole graph, not just individual points.

Training
Line Graphs are easy to create and are now a standard part of word processing.

Where to find out more
Handbook of Quality Tools, Ozeki K and Asaka T, Productivity Press, 1990

Example

Trends over time are very difficult to judge intuitively, since it's always hard to remember exactly what situations were like before.

One company looked up its attendance records to prove or disprove a general feeling at the end of the year among management that absenteeism was growing.

Preparing a Line Graph for the year explained the perception. Attendance patterns did vary, but the variation was seasonal and did not reflect an overall downward trend. Managers were experiencing levels of absence which were higher than earlier in the year, but which were remarkably consistent with the year before.

Line Graph to show patterns of absence over two years

Data table	Year 1	Year 2
January	152	156
February	104	111
March	98	97
April	75	72
May	102	110
June	69	65
July	65	70
August	68	72
September	100	95
October	148	140
November	164	166
December	200	210

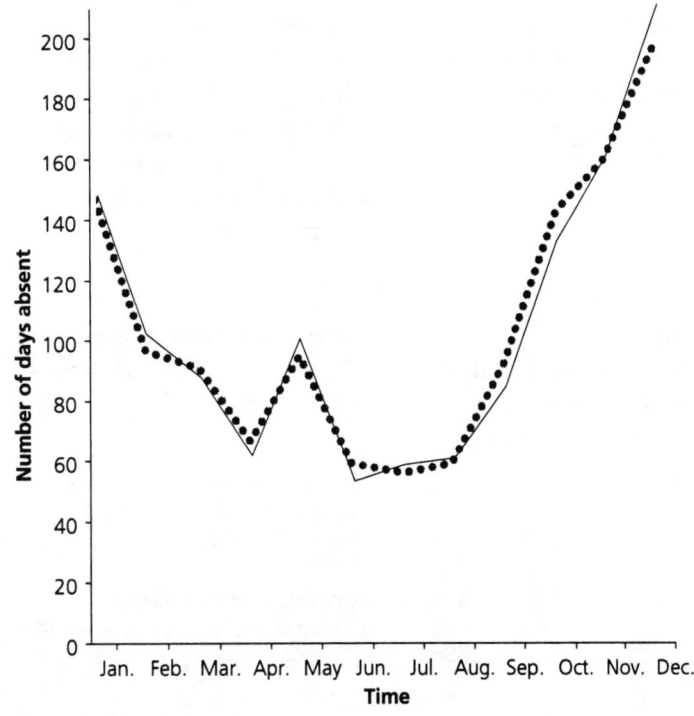

139

Loss Function Analysis

Links deterioration in performance to loss of value to customer.

Affinity group: Product and Process Analysis

Classification • • •

When to use it
Use these calculations for designing specifications and tolerances. A complementary tool to Statistical Process Control.

What you'll achieve
A direct translation of poor performance into money loss – shows that even quite small variations from the design specification matter and that fine-tuning is important.

When not to use it
Don't use for calculating the cost of non-conformances – this is to pick up finer variations.

And be careful
Loss can still seem a notional idea if your customer is internal: make it seem more real by calculating what the knock-on effect to external customers will be.

Training
A measurement and analysis tool which requires some competence in statistics.

Where to find out more
Introduction to Quality Engineering, G Taguchi, Asian productivity Organisation, Tokyo

Quality Control Robust Design and the Taguchi Method, Wadsworth and Brookes, Cole 1989

Total Quality Management, Pera International, Chapman and Hall, 1992

Process flowchart:

Establish measurement points for product or process

Identify target values ie values at which system is designed to operate

Collect measurements of performance and compare with target values

Create Loss Function Diagram, using Taguchi formula

Calculate cost of any deviation from target values

Example

Loss Function Analysis is particularly significant if the process has a number of steps through which the loss function can accumulate.

In engineering processes, even small variations within control limits can cause problems all the way along the line, setting up an incremental deterioration which, viewed as a whole, is worth putting right. This kind of attention to detail has not traditionally been seen as financially worth while. Taguchi argues that it is.

Calculating the cost of Loss Function

The Taguchi formula

L = $k(y-T)^2$
L = loss
k = machine capability
y = measurement of requirement
T = target value

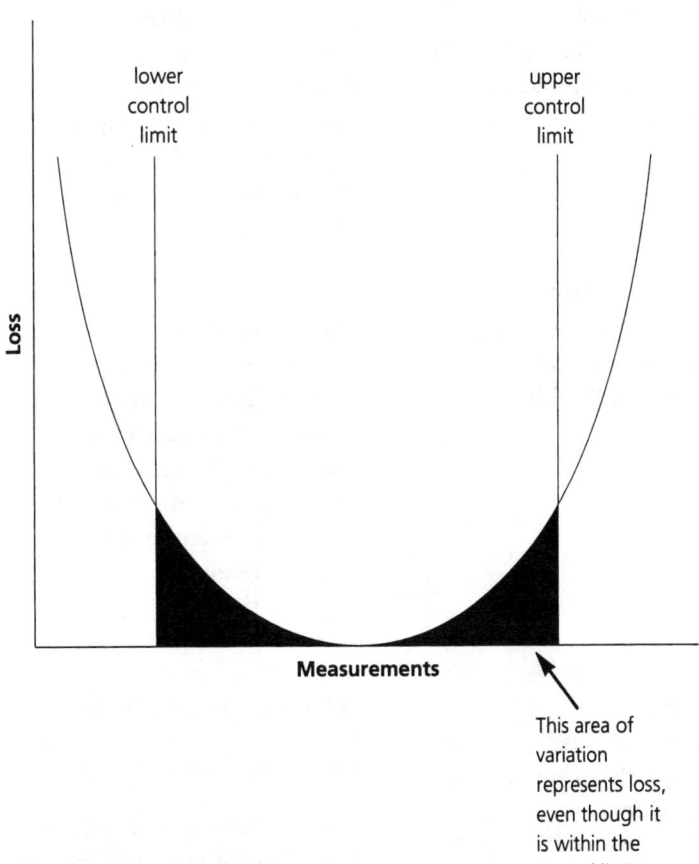

This area of variation represents loss, even though it is within the control limits

Management by Objectives

Way of structuring and assessing management performance by setting objectives.

Affinity group: Strategy

Classification • • • •

When to use it
To focus management effort in directions helpful to the organisation.

When not to use it
Don't use in times of change when managers need to be creative and flexible.

What you'll achieve
MBO should mean that managers are promoted on what they contribute to the organisation rather than who they know or how they behave.

And be careful
Can become bureaucratic and restrictive, taking attention away from real priorities: make sure objectives are simple, important, interesting to the managers concerned, and still relevant to the organisation.

Training
Some training useful on setting good objectives and avoiding bureaucracy.

Where to find out more
The Practice of Management, Drucker P, Butterworth Heinemann, 1994

Management by Objectives, Humble J, British Institution of Management, 1972

Management by Objectives, Applications and Research, Carroll S J, Tosi H L, Macmillan 1973

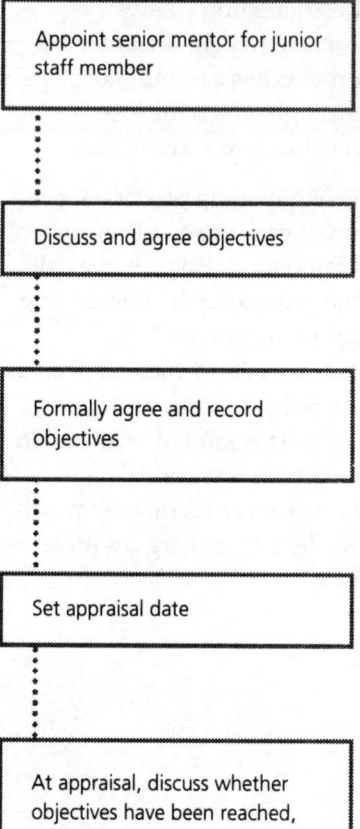

Process flowchart

Appoint senior mentor for junior staff member

Discuss and agree objectives

Formally agree and record objectives

Set appraisal date

At appraisal, discuss whether objectives have been reached, and set new ones

Example

Management by Objectives can work well in situations where managers could develop in a number of directions, all valid. MBO can serve to prioritize these possibilities in the best interests of the organisation as a whole.

An envelope factory which had recently appointed a new production manager used MBO to define his role. The factory badly needed modernisation, both in equipment and attitudes. But where to start?

In his first week, the new production manager agreed with the MD where to focus initial effort. Both agreed that many more issues would arise, but that it would be counterproductive to try to do everything at once.

Although the new production manager concentrated on the objectives he had agreed, he found the first year frustrating as things which needed to be done had to be set aside until later.

```
Management Objectives for the production
manager of an envelope factory


Objective 1
To increase production by around 15% by April 1994.


Objective 2
To reduce waste by up to 5% within three months.


Objective 3
To improve safety both by improving safety awareness
and introducing safety practices, starting immediately.


Objective 4
To show an overall improvement in the efficiency of the
production department by the end of the financial year,
April 1994.
```

Matrix Diagram

Graphic method of showing relationships between a number of inputs and outcomes.

Affinity group: Graphic Tool

Classification • • •

When to use it
Often in production, to show how a range of factors bears on a range of problems. Matrix Diagrams also have a place in quality improvement and process design also has a place.

What you'll achieve
Method of selecting important issues from a number of perspectives: a multi-dimensional approach to analysis.

When not to use it
When you're clear about what causes of problems are, and where they come from.

And be careful
Always check decisions: there is a subjective element in identifying and scoring relationships. Use Matrix Diagram as a working tool, not as an absolute measure.

Training
Training is necessary if people aren't familiar with matrix conventions – there are some quite complicated variations.

Where to find out more
Introduction to Quality Engineering, G Taguchi, Asian Productivity Organisation, Tokyo

Process flowchart

Set up graphic format:
Vertical columns: outcomes
Horizontal columns: inputs

Enter outcomes in vertical columns

List inputs (things related to causes) in horizontal columns

Mark relationships between items with symbols for strong, average and weak

Score relationships

Select most important relationships for analysis

Example

Matrix Diagrams can be used in quite a range of situations where they clarify multidimensional relationships very efficiently.

For example a company may want to consider the impact of ISO9000 on the business. Since both the business and the quality management standard have more than one dimension, there is no simple one to one cause and effect relationship between them.

A Matrix Diagram allows all the dimensions to be considered in relation to each other in turn, and in total.

Of course the way in which the dimensions are scored against each other is not precise.

Matrix to show how ISO9000 relates to company profits

Symbols

Symbol	Description		Value
●	strong relationship	=	3
○	medium relationship	=	2
△	weak relationship	=	1

The business	Mission statement	Quality policy	Procedures	PR
Marketing	○	○	△	●
Sales	△	○	△	●
Internal Processes	△	○	●	△
Procurement	△	●	○	○
HR management	○	○	△	△
Customer Care	△	●	○	○
Total	04	14	08	10

Column header spanning Mission statement, Quality policy, Procedures, PR: **ISO 9000**

Meeting Checklist

Checklist for organising and running meetings effectively.

Affinity group: Planning

Classification •

When to use it
Mostly in large organisations, for organising formal meetings smoothly and effectively.

What you'll achieve
Meetings which don't take longer than they should, and which leave people feeling positive and as if progress has been made.

When not to use it
Don't use for smaller informal meetings where this level of control wouldn't be appropriate. And don't use a meeting at all if there isn't much business to attend to.

And be careful
Judge the way the meeting is going: if it's drifting, keep to the agenda, but if important points are emerging, don't stifle the discussion, and give space to new important points which may arise.

Training
No formal training needed – just discipline.

Where to find out more
The Quality Toolkit, Marsh J, IFS Ltd, 1992

Better Meetings, Open University course P950, Open University 1991.

Making Meetings Work, Barker A, Industrial Society, 1993

Process flowchart

- Organise date and venue 2 weeks before meeting
- Circulate supporting papers and agenda
- Prepare supplement to agenda detailing:
  - decision points for each item
  - time allowed
  - method of delivery for each item
  - leader for each item
  - facilitator
  - etc
- Agree actions and deadlines
- Circulate minutes within three days of meeting

Example

Meetings are very much a part of corporate life, but they can seem time consuming and pointless, particularly when managers are under pressure.

One recently privatised utility seemed to have become completely bogged down in meetings. But although diaries were full of dates, nothing seemed to result from all the meetings. Discussions were generally unstructured, and didn't seem to result in actions. This reflected the uncertainty many managers felt about the implications of the privatisation.

This morale-sapping problem was solved quite simply by introducing guidelines for planning and conducting meetings. The guidelines meant that meetings only dealt with pre-planned, specific issues, and did not become a conduit for general feelings of uncertainty. Any agenda items which could lead to such discussions (such as item 2, opposite) were controlled by appointing a facilitator and by setting a time limit.

Meeting Checklist – supplement to the agenda

```
Date:      Friday 17 May
           10.00-11.30
Venue:     First floor conference room

Present:   V Wright (chair), L Wade, H Seagrove,
           D Jones, P Brooke

Minutes:   B Hart
```

Agenda

1. Agree customer service targets (see attached papers)
   Leader: HS
   Method: presentation of report and discussion
   Time allowed: 25 minutes
   Decision point: Yes

2. Discuss operation of new customer service policies
   (see attached papers)
   Leader: DJ
   Facilitator: VW
   Method: presentation of report and discussion
   Time allowed: 20 minutes
   Decision point: No

3. The annual report - allocating tasks
   Leader: PB
   Method: brainstorm and action plan
   Time allowed: 20 minutes
   Decision point: Yes

4. AOB
   Leader: VW
   Method: suggestions and discussions
   Time allowed: 25 minutes
   Decision point: Yes

Mission Statement

Method of clarifying the purpose of projects and organisations.

Affinity group: Strategy

Classification • • • • •

When to use it
Mission Statements are important particularly at times of organisational change or consolidation, to clarify company direction.

What you'll achieve
A unifying purpose to focus internal policy, and a statement of intent to communicate externally to suppliers and customers.

When not to use it
There won't be much use for Mission Statements when the organisational culture precludes the involvement of stakeholders.

And be careful
Keep the statements short and purposeful: woolly, vague ones are counterproductive. And keep them realistic.

Training
A trained and independent facilitator will be very valuable: these decisions aren't easy.

Where to find out more
Re-engineering the Corporation, Hammer M and Champy J, Nicholas Brealey Publishing, 1993

Process flowchart

Decide who needs to be involved in setting the mission statement, and how you're going to do it

Generate ideas about the vision, mission and values of your project or organisation

Record ideas on a flipchart, and perhaps on file cards

Group ideas into separate categories for vision, mission and values

Decide on the form and wording of the statements

Example

Mission Statements are an important symbol of organisational visions and values.

The reforms in the NHS have been more radical than any made since the creation of the service. A key element has been a focus in each trust on what they are trying to achieve: their key services and the resources which will be needed.

In the development of one key service, co-ordinated nationally from three centres of excellence, setting the direction of the Mission Statement proved crucial in moving from the old to the new. There were many factions for and against change. Sixteen principal staff representing key disciplines were drawn from across the service to draw up a Mission Statement. The principal issue to resolve, and the most controversial, was the question of who the Trust's customers were. One group saw the patient as the customer whom the trust was set up to serve. Another group expected the trust to serve the interests of the clinicians.

Three Mission Statements

Polycell

Polycell aspires to be the best Brand in its trading sector and provide the highest return on sales and investment for its parent William Holdings.

By implication our customers are always foremost in our mind, whether it be for innovation, quality or service. We never assume our markets will remain stable so through the highest standards of communication and training our employees are encouraged to extend the boundaries of excellence in everything they do.

Due to the speed we move, good judgement, honesty and integrity are benchmarks for a culture and Brand that is obsessed with success and continuous improvement.

British Airways

We have a clear ambition. We want British Airways to be the best and most successful airline in the world, because we believe it will be good for our passengers, it will be good for our shareholders, it will be good for the people who work for us and it will be good for the people of Britain. What's wrong with that?

Federal Express

We will deliver the package by 10:30 the next morning.

Multi-Vari Chart

Control chart for products or processes with two or more sources of variability.

Affinity group: Statistical Quality Control

Classification • • •

When to use it
Use the Multi-Vari Chart in monitoring production processes, to show patterns of variability from more than one possible source.

What you'll achieve
An analysis of why individual pieces vary: either each piece is likely to go over the limits, or the variation between pieces is too great, or the quality varies over time. Once you know the cause, you can find the solution.

When not to use it
Don't use for attributes: this chart only works for combinations of variables.

And be careful
Different patterns of variation will have different causes: these need to be understood.

Training
Basic statistical understanding needed.

Where to find out more
Quality Control Handbook, Juran J, McGraw Hill, 1989

Control Charts, Murdoch J, MacMillan, 1979

Statistical Process Control, Oakland J and Followell R, Heinemann Newnes, 1990

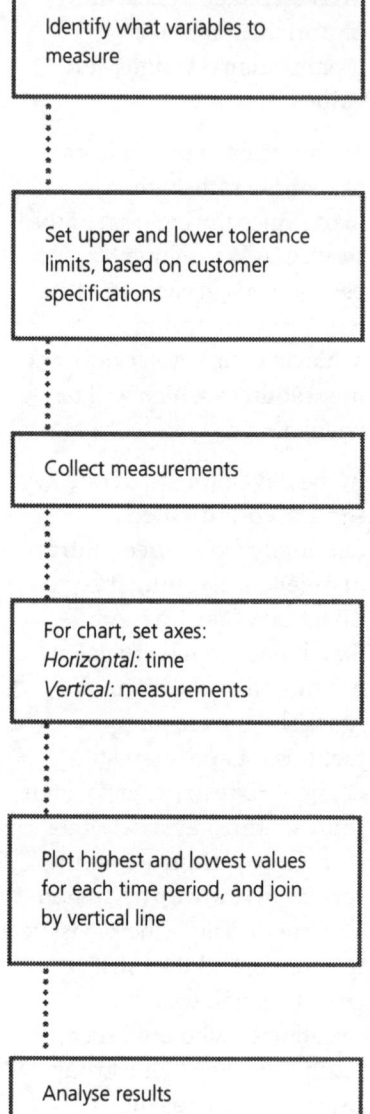

Process flowchart

Identify what variables to measure

Set upper and lower tolerance limits, based on customer specifications

Collect measurements

For chart, set axes:
Horizontal: time
Vertical: measurements

Plot highest and lowest values for each time period, and join by vertical line

Analyse results

Example

A classic use of the Multi-Vari Chart is in the control of cylindrical parts. There are two sources of variability:

- in the comparative diameter of each cylinder (piece-to-piece variation)

- in the consistency of the diameter throughout each cylinder (within piece variation).

Depending on where the variability is, the chart will have a distinctive pattern which makes it easy to identify the particular problem the process is experiencing.

Another example of its use is in controlling heat treatment processes. Once again there are two sources of variability:

- between products

- within each product.

The Multi-Vari Chart can show how the process is performing in relation to both these variables.

Interpreting Multi-Vari Charts

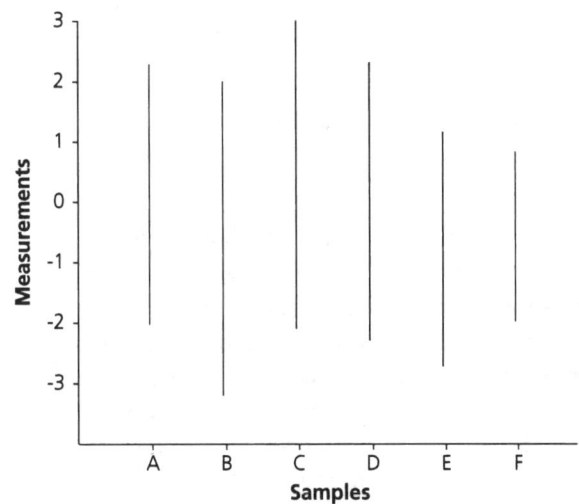

Chart A: variability is too great within each piece.

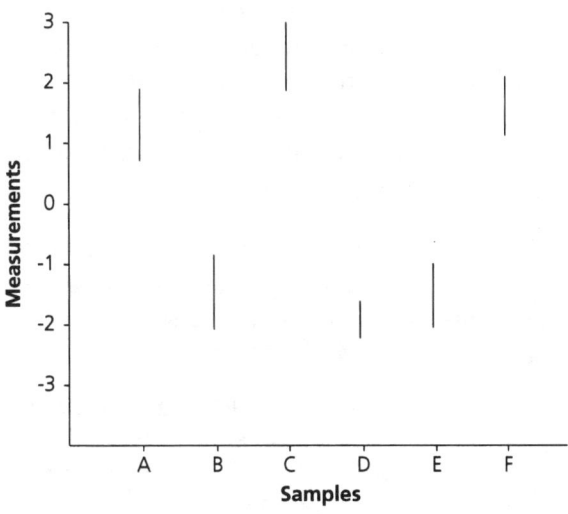

Chart B: variability between pieces is too great.

Nominal Group Technique

Structured decision-making process which helps to reach consensus.

Affinity group: Consensus

Classification • • •

When to use it
For reaching group consensus on decisions where there is a variety of viewpoints and a unanimous decision is unlikely. More consultative than taking a majority decision.

What you'll achieve
Decision-making based on what people think, which minimises the influence of personal or political factors, and makes sure everyone's involved. Should result in a higher level of commitment to decisions.

When not to use it
Don't use with groups which don't have responsibility for the final decision.

And be careful
Facilitator needs to exercise firm control to keep to a structured approach and to stop inappropriate discussions from developing.

Training
Training needed for facilitator, whose role is important for this tool.

Where to find out more
Quality Control Handbook, Juran J, McGraw Hill, 1989

The Memory Jogger, Brassard M and Ritter D, GOAL/QPC, 1994

Generate ideas about a particular problem individually in writing

Record ideas on a flipchart, without discussion

Discuss to clarify meaning of ideas – not for argument

Vote on ideas, rank and prioritise

Discuss results of vote, and take final vote. Check that all group members support decision

Example

The Nominal Group Technique can be used when the ground work – collecting all the facts and figures – has been done. The group doesn't waste time speculating about the facts, but concentrates in an informed way on the issues involved.

In the example, the senior management group of a large multinational company is deciding where to place a new factory. Extensive research has resulted in a short list of 5 sites which fulfil essential criteria and which are not strongly differentiated by cost, or availability of labour.

It is important for everyone to understand how and why the final selection is made, so the Nominal Group Technique is adopted. After the initial votes, each person has a chance to say why they have voted as they have. Although the rankings show considerable variation, it soon becomes obvious that people agree about what the issues are.

By the end of the session the facilitator is happy that everyone understands why Consett has been chosen and that no-one has any serious reservations about it.

```
Choosing a new factory site:
Nominal Group Technique
```

	TF	KM	TS	MA	RF	**Total**
Site						
Milton Keynes	1	1	2	4	1	9
Lyon	3	4	1	1	2	11
Corby	2	2	4	3	5	16
Consett	5	5	5	2	4	21
Leipzig	4	3	3	5	3	18

```
Preferred site:   Consett

Key
1  =   least preferred option
5  =   most preferred option
```

np Chart

Statistical Process Control tool for monitoring the number of defective items in a sample.

Affinity group: Statistical Quality Control

Classification • • •

Calculate sample size

Count number of defects in a selection of samples and calculate average

Calculate upper warning and action lines, using the appropriate formulae

Set up chart and control limits
Horizontal axis:
Samples
Vertical axis:
Number of defects per sample

When to use it
Use in volume production, where quality depends on characteristics known as attributes, to check if the number of defective items is within acceptable limits.

What you'll achieve
A quick and easy way of keeping control: counting defectives is usually quite straightforward to do.

When not to use it
Don't use in safety-critical situations: use 100%, 200% or 300% inspection instead.

And be careful
There can be a subjective element in identifying defects: inspectors should be trained together and cross-check their standards.

Training
Basic statistical understanding needed.

Where to find out more
Quality Control Handbook, Juran J, McGraw Hill, 1989

Statistical Process Control, Oakland J and Followell R, Heinemann Newnes, 1990

A Practical Approach to Quality Control, Caplen R H, Hutchinson Publishing, 1978

Example

np Charts are widely used in the electronics industry where circuit boards and subassemblies are inspected for defects, such as:

• missing parts

• parts inserted the wrong way round

• weak soldering

• breaks in track

Sample sizes will be large – at least 100 – and results will give a general indication of how well the process is working.

The consequences of defects are important, as any one defect means that the unit is rejected. As well as showing trends, the chart will indicate areas for quality improvement.

np Chart in an electronics factory

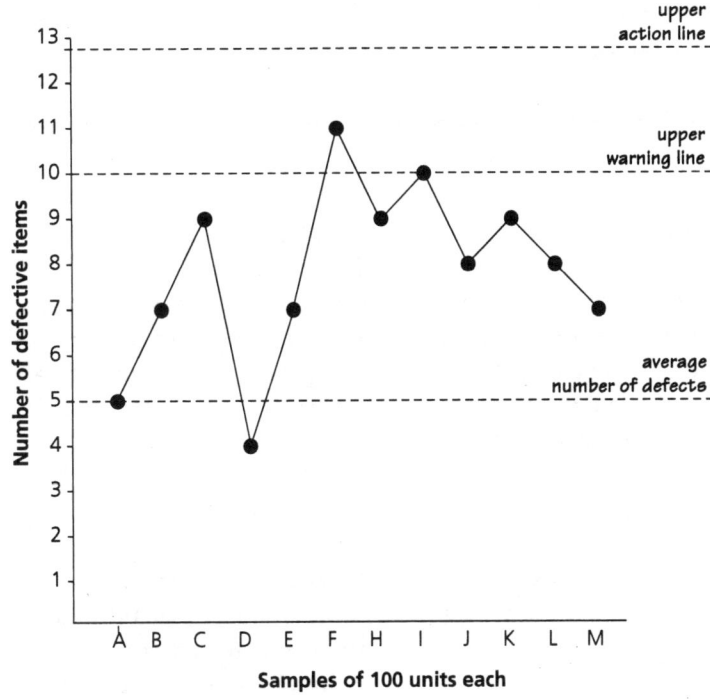

Samples of 100 units each

p Chart

Statistical Process Control tool for monitoring the proportion of defective items in a sample

Affinity group: Statistical Quality Control

Classification • • •

When to use it
For situations in volume production when you want to count and control the number of defective items, but batch sizes differ and it isn't possible to select a standard sample.

What you'll achieve
Information about the proportion of defective items in a group which allows comparisons between different sizes of samples.

When not to use it
Don't use in safety-critical situations: use 100% inspection instead.

And be careful
Make sure inspection standards are constant. And remember to distinguish between single defects and faulty units which may have a number of different defects: use separate charts for each.

Training
Basic statistical understanding needed.

Where to find out more
Quality Control Handbook, Juran J, McGraw Hill, 1989

Statistical Process Control, Oakland J and Followell R, Heinemann Newnes, 1990

A Practical Approach to Quality Control, Caplen R H, Hutchinson Publishing, 1978

Process flowchart

Identify samples for each batch

Count number of defects in each sample and calculate average percentage across samples

Calculate upper warning and action limits, using the appropriate formulae

Create chart
Horizontal axis:
Sample
Vertical axis:
% defects per sample

Example

p Charts provide a way round the problem of selecting samples in an irregular process. By working with percentages, the chart allows different samples to be compared without distorting the results.

This problem occurs in manufacturing or assembly plants which have moved to responsive customer-led, Just-In-Time systems. Since production is demand-led, the balance of work at any one time will be different, with flexible batch sizes and varying specifications on standard lines. So it will not be possible to carry out a standard sampling exercise throughout the plant at any one time.

For example an electronic assembly plant organised in this way, might make a different number of televisions, tape-recorders or videos each week. However the p Chart can show trends in spite of the changing mix.

p Chart in an electronics assembly plant

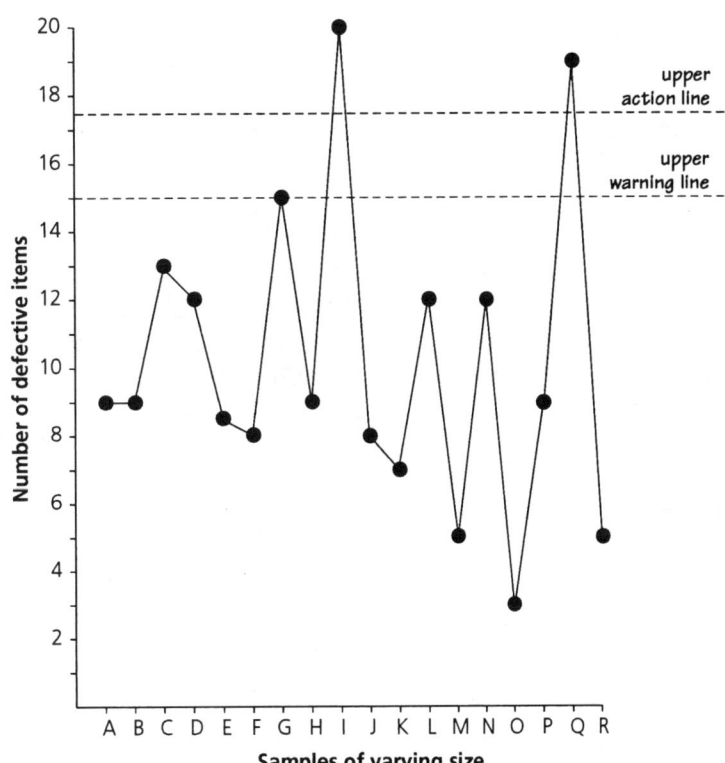

Paired Comparisons

Structured voting method to reach consensus.

Affinity group: Consensus

Classification • •

When to use it

To reach a decision in a logical way, allowing everyone to think through the choices. The scoring process gives everyone an equal say.

When not to use it

Don't bother using such a complicated technique if the decision-makers are happy with open discussion.

What you'll achieve

A format which makes it clear to everyone involved what the issues and choices are. More commitment to the final decision.

And be careful

Judgements about scoring are qualitative and ultimately subjective, so final scores may not bring a consensus without further discussion. Use quantitative measures where possible.

Training

Facilitator needs training to be able to handle feedback, to get the group to the point of agreeing options, and making the final decision.

Where to find out more

The Quality Toolkit, Marsh J, IFS Ltd, 1992

Process flowchart

Draw up numbered list of issues (not more than 10) which relate to the topic under consideration

Issue Paired Comparison forms, which set out all possible ways of pairing issues

Individually circle the preferred option from each pair

Score forms: one point for each time a particular number is circled

Aggregate scores and discuss

Example

Paired Comparisons is a good tool for making choices between similar options, as it provides a way of making a series of small differentiations which then add up to a significant difference.

One small service company decided to improve the way it dealt with customer enquiries. There were a number of different ways the public could get in touch with the company, each with a different manager. Each manager felt that their method of managing customer enquiries was best and should be adopted as the standard.

At a meeting of these managers, it was agreed that the most important thing was for customers to feel as positive as possible about the organisation. This statement headed the Paired Comparison forms, which set out all the different options currently used and asked the managers to rank them against each other.

The results suggested that the public would benefit most from additional resources to the telephone enquiry desk.

Analysing methods of handling customer enquiries

Which method of handling customer enquiries will make customers feel most positive about our organisation? Circle your preference in the vote matrix boxes

Item	Vote Matrix		
1. Telephone enquiry service	① 2	① 3	① 4
2. Postal enquiry service	② 3	2 ④	
3. Enquiry desk	③ 4		
4. Electronic bulletin board			

Results

Item	Total votes
1	3
2	1
3	1
4	1

Pareto Analysis

Method of identifying the vital few causes (typically 20%) which cause 80% of the problems.

Affinity group: Prioritisation

Classification • •

When to use it
Can be used in a wide variety of situations where there are a number of variables contributing to a problem and you need to know which are the most important. Particularly useful at the start of an improvement programme.

What you'll achieve
A strong visual representation of how to prioritise problems, and where to concentrate resources for the best results, which can be understood at all levels of the organisation.

When not to use it
Won't be needed if more sophisticated systems are in place, such as Statistical Process Control.

And be careful
Always important to interpret results carefully. Use common sense as well as data to ascertain causes and priorities.

Training
Basic statistical understanding needed to prepare analysis.

Where to find out more
Quality Control Handbook, Juran J, McGraw Hill, 1989

Managerial Breakthrough, Juran J, McGraw Hill, 1964

Process flowchart

Identify problem and likely causes

Collect information about causes

Prepare Pareto Analysis graph
Horizontal axis:
Causes
Vertical axis:
The problem, expressed as number of occurrences, cost or frequency

Identify the vital few causes

Apply improvement techniques to deal with causes in order of importance

Example

Pareto Analysis works well as an orientation tool at the start of an improvement programme.

One washing machine manufacturer had a quality crisis. A major consumer magazine had ranked their products last in an extensive reliability test and advised consumers not to buy them. The manufacturer's response was to increase the warranty period for its goods and offer customers cash compensation for faults. Clearly however they could not sustain this level of support if faults continued.

The company had kept good records of faults. There were 22 categories reported. However, a Pareto Analysis showed that only 4 were responsible for 83% of the occurrences. Faults in the other categories had only happened occasionally and were reckoned to be rare.

Because the main warranty cost was in call-out and labour, cutting the number of occurrences would also cut the main warranty costs.

Faults in washing machines – a Pareto Analysis

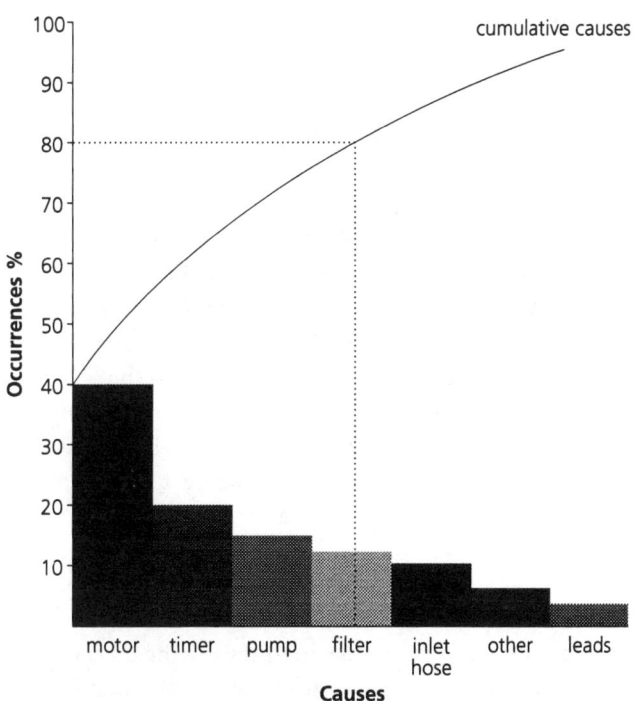

The curve is cumulative, derived by adding the height of each bar as it moves to the right.

Performance Evaluation Review Technique (PERT)

Project planning tool for large projects which include development work.

Affinity group: Planning

Classification • • •

When to use it
For planning complex projects made up of a number of interdependent activities, where the project includes development work for which reliable estimates are not available.

What you'll achieve
An understanding of where delays are likely, and what they will mean for the rest of the project. Means that plans can be adapted to changing circumstances, with delays and the reasons for them made visible.

When not to use it
Not worthwhile for simple sequential dependencies: don't use for its own sake.

And be careful
Keep updating the project plan – there's little point in just using this tool retrospectively to see why delays happened.

Training
Some training will be needed, perhaps from a textbook. Computer programs are now available to make calculations and produce charts.

Where to find out more
Management and Organisation, Sisk H L, South Western Publishing Co, 1973

Process flowchart

List all main project events

Create file cards or boxes for each event

Give three estimated times for each event: optimistic, expected and pessimistic – and calculate expected time, using formula

Work through timings as for Critical Path Analysis

Highlight activities whose finish times affect completion date – mark as Critical Path

Example

A well-known example of PERT is its first application – the building of the Polaris missile. The problem here was the lack of experience or records upon which to build reliable time estimates.

To deal with this problem, PERT uses a series of probability calculations for the activities leading up to each event. The optimistic time assumes that everything goes as planned – a probability of about 1 in 100. The second estimate is for what would be the normal course of events. The third estimate, again a probability of about 1 in 100, is the most pessimistic – if everything goes wrong. From these estimates, a figure for the expected time can be calculated using a statistical formula.

Applying PERT to the design stages of a project

Design stages

1. Design and development planning

    1.1 Design feasibility

    1.1 Design feasibility
    Formula

    $$T = \frac{a + 4m + b}{6}$$

    a = most optimistic time   10 days
    m = most likely time   14 days
    b = most pessimistic time   25 days

    $$\text{Expected time} = \frac{10 + 56 + 25}{6} = 15.17 \text{ days}$$

    1.2 Establish projects

    1.3 Design and development programme

    1.4 Project control documentation

Performance Metrics

Measurements which directly relate to the quality of the product, process or service.

Affinity group: Data Capture

Classification • • •

When to use it
Use Performance Metrics to measure aspects of the business which matter to customers, both internal and external.

What you'll achieve
Objective data on a regular basis, making it possible to set standards, spot deviations, improve performance – in fact, to improve quality.

When not to use it
Don't use Performance Metrics for things which either can't be measured reliably, or which aren't important to customers.

And be careful
Collecting the right measurements isn't always easy, and can be expensive. But don't be tempted to gather just the easy information: be creative to find measurements which are important.

Training
Industry specific training is important so that appropriate measures are adopted.

Where to find out more
Quality Control Handbook, Juran J, McGraw Hill, 1989

Quality Management Library, CCTA, HMSO, 1992

Total Quality Management, Pera International, Chapman and Hall, 1992

Process flowchart

Identify variable characteristics of product or service which relate to its quality

Identify ways of measuring variables

Set up pilot scheme for collecting data

Review ways of analysing and presenting data

Train staff and extend pilot to whole organisation

Example

Performance Metrics vary considerably from industry to industry.

Manufacturing makes use of hard performance measures, such as the number of rejects, cost of rework, inventory levels, or lead times. Important issues are how accurate measurements are, and what level of detail is appropriate.

At the other end of the scale are service industries and professions, whose performance can be judged by customers, but not easily measured. The argument here is about what hard performance measures really mean in, for example, healthcare. Many clinicians would argue that performance metrics are at best irrelevant and at worst damaging to a service which should be judged qualitatively. In simple terms, a long consultation, while uneconomic, is likely to be good for the patient.

Agreeing what to measure, and how to interpret it, is a significant problem for most service industries. All stakeholders have to agree on the assessment process.

Performance Metrics for fast food services

Objective
To see what aspects of our performance in providing fast food services we can measure and reward.

Quantitative Measures
Average waiting time for customers
Average process time from order to delivery
Number of times order is wrong
Number of customers served per member of staff
Average speed of service per customer
Number of customers per seat per day
Amount of car parking spaces
Number of washrooms
Number of times washrooms checked
Number of complaints about washrooms

Qualitative Measures
Friendliness
Helpfulness
Responsiveness
Comfort of environment
Cleanliness of eating area
Cleanliness of washrooms
Quality of food
Choice of menu

Pie Chart

Graphic tool for displaying quantitative information.

Affinity group: Graphic Tool

Classification • •

When to use it
For presenting comparisons in measurement between a number of items.

What you'll achieve
A clear visual representation of the relative size and significance of items, which helps people throughout the organisation to interpret data.

When not to use it
Don't use Pie Charts for showing trends or variability over time: use Histograms or Line Graphs instead.

And be careful
Colouring or patterning the sections of the pie can result in visual illusions – for example dark solids appear larger than light patterns of the same size.

Training
Training might be needed for collecting and interpreting data. Software available for creating the actual pie.

Where to find out more
The Quality Toolkit, Marsh J, IFS Ltd, 1992

Process flowchart

Collect data about all items to be compared and contrasted

Express value of each item as percentage of the whole

Calculate the number of degrees to be assigned to each item

Create Pie Chart, differentiating items from each other

Example

Pie Charts are much used in management circles to present quantitative information easily and attractively.

The board of a large kitchen manufacturer wanted to reduce the cost of after sales service. They asked the customer services manager to make a presentation to them, giving her department's analysis of where the main costs lay.

The key graphic in the presentation was a Pie Chart which showed clearly the seven most frequent types of customer enquiries, and their relative proportions .

The board was immediately struck by the proportion of calls which related to missing components. This gave them their starting point for the cost cutting programme.

Pie Chart showing customer enquiries received by a kitchen manufacturer

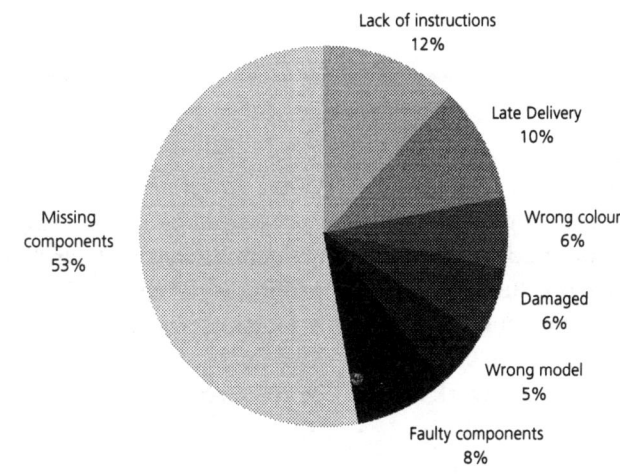

Poka Yoke

Foolproofing devices which prevent problems.

Affinity group: Strategy

Classification • • • •

Set up process flowchart

Identify points at which operator errors occur

When to use it
For manufacturing processes where operator errors can lead to defects in products. Particularly important for JIT relationships, where faulty work will interrupt work flow.

What you'll achieve
Successful Poka Yoke brings an increase in quality and in profits, as re-work and inspection costs fall. Overall lead times and inventories can be reduced.

Brainstorm ways of foolproofing potential error points

When not to use it
Don't use where the cost of foolproofing greatly outweighs the cost of errors. Also will only work when systems are sophisticated. This is not an introductory tool.

And be careful
Control devices which stop the process when they detect an error can cause costly delays. But if the control only raises the alarm, the operator may miss the mistake.

Assess foolproofing ideas for viability

Implement Poka Yoke devices

Training
A simple concept, but one which will need engineering training and experience to put into practice.

Where to find out more
Zero Quality Control: Source Inspection and the Poka Yoke System, Shingo S, Productivity Press, 1986

Example

As part of its quality drive, a toy company which manufactured self-build kits implemented a process control programme. The plant produced a significant number of faulty components, and there had been complaints from customers about incomplete kits.

Using a process flowchart, and available inspection reports, the group identified three main areas where there were consistent problems.

They agreed that the best solution was to foolproof the system so that these problems simply couldn't happen again. This would be expensive, but the company felt it would bring a better return on investment than more conventional strategies of upgrading or replacing machinery for which funds had been set aside.

Suggestions for Poka Yoke devices to prevent quality problems with toy kit production

1. Contact method

   To prevent misshapen components from finding their way into kits.

   As the components are completed, they have to make contact with template shapes. If there are defects in the shapes, the contact pattern will be incomplete and a warning buzzer sounds to alert the operator that something is wrong.

2. Constant number method

   To ensure that the right number of components has been included in each toy kit before it is packaged. Check weigh each kit.

   If the kit is incomplete, the packaging line will stop until the operator takes the faulty kit off. This can slow down the packaging process, but we feel that the incomplete kits damage the reputation of the company so much that this measure is justified.

3. Performance measure method

   To make sure that all the steps in the packaging process are carried out in the right order.

   Using barcode technology, the computer can tell at once if any step has not been carried out and the packaging process will stop.

PRE-control

Operators carry out routine measurements of small samples to pick up potential problems early.

Affinity group: Statistical Quality Control

Classification • • •

When to use it
In production processes where people can observe and measure the characteristics (colour, size, strength) of what they produce.

What you'll achieve
Early warning of problems (hence the name), and operators' involvement in looking after and analysing their own part of the production process.

When not to use it
Remember PRE-control won't tell you how many defects there are in a sample.

And be careful
Follow statistical rules for setting tolerance limits, frequency of sampling and so on. Looks simple, but won't work if you alter the probabilities.

Training
Training in Statistical Process Control needed to set up the charts. Training needed for all operators in PRE-control methods and charts.

Where to find out more
Quality Control Handbook, Juran J, McGraw Hill, 1989

Total Quality Control, Feigenbaum A V, McGraw Hill, 1983

Process flowchart

Identify what to measure

Set upper and lower tolerance limits

Divide tolerance band into target zone and two cautionary zones on either side

Measure two items periodically

If both are outside target zone, adjust machine at once

Example

PRE-control works well when variables are easy to see and measure.

A manufacturer of moulded plastic children's toys introduced PRE-control to give them an early indication of when the moulding process was becoming inaccurate.

The system was set up for them by external consultants who trained all the operators in how to take samples and record them.

The resulting PRE-Control system was very successful in catching variations because measurements were quick and easy to make; operators had no difficulty in carrying them out and interpreting them. The number of wasted parts fell dramatically, particularly for the ball wheels which were very sensitive to the flow of plastic in the mould and could become too thin.

PRE-control record sheet

Measurement Part	Measurement	Checking Rota	Results 1	2	Action
Screw handle	Depth thread	4 hours	2	2.2	✗
Tray mould	Diameter screw hole	1 day	4.8	4.6	✗
Ball wheel	Weight	12 hrs	2.2	1.6	✓

Preventative Maintenance

Strategy for planning maintenance to forestall or remove problems.

Affinity group: Strategy

Classification • • • •

When to use it
For all kinds of production processes, to make sure maintenance is planned and used preventatively, and not just when there's a breakdown.

What you'll achieve
Reduction in the number of unplanned stoppages, leading to increased efficiency and customer service. Also a culture of looking after machinery.

When not to use it
Don't use without reasonable reliability and risk information, from either your own records or suppliers or both.

And be careful
Preventative Maintenance may seem expensive: people may argue for taking the risk and hoping for the best. Use Cost of Quality as a counter-argument.

Training
Training needed for calculating reliability and risk. If maintenance is decentralised, operators will need significant training.

Where to find out more
Quality Control Handbook, Juran J, McGraw Hill, 1989

Process flowchart

Keep records of how equipment behaves: breakdowns and performance levels

Introduce regular maintenance periods, based on predicted levels of reliability

Decentralise maintenance as much as possible to the people who operate the equipment

Consider ways of designing out regular maintenance problems

Provide an effective emergency service to minimise effect of breakdowns

Example

As a result of advances in technology, many businesses who aren't used to owning and maintaining equipment are learning how to do so.

One company took advantage of new printing technologies to bring all its document production in-house.

For the first two years all went well. Then, however, the service seemed beset by technical problems, particularly for colour work. The colour printer had become erratic, on one occasion adopting a default mode of pink and brown.

The service engineer found that the machine had received no maintenance for the last two years – because it hadn't gone wrong. It needed parts and adjustments which should have been done months ago.

The engineer also saw that the volume of work the machine was expected to process had increased considerably, so that it was probably operating at the edges of its capability.

The engineer drew up a Preventative Maintenance schedule, including some training sessions for users in spotting and putting right basic maintenance problems.

How Preventative Maintenance works

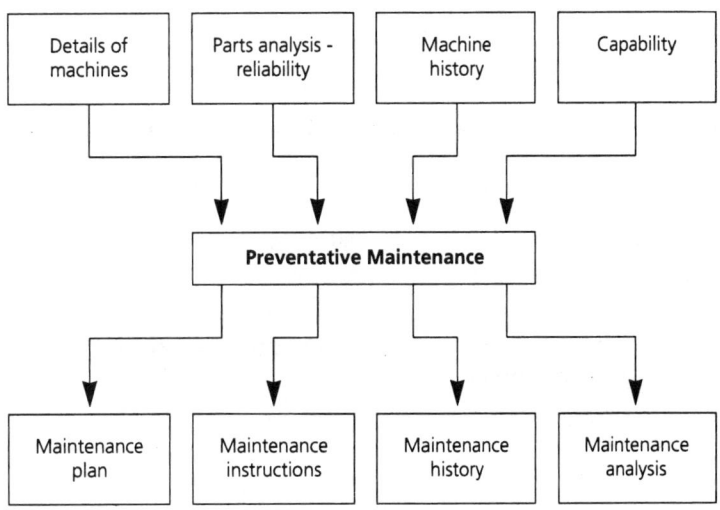

Problem Analysis

Tool for finding the root cause of problems in performance.

Affinity group: Problem Solving

Classification • •

Define problem generally in terms of deviation from specification

Define problem in detail: what, when, where, how much

Identify what could be causing the deviations

List potential causes and work out tests to check which are true

When to use it
When there's a problem in performance – either a production or management process – and it's not clear what's causing it.

What you'll achieve
A formal approach to solving a problem which will otherwise cause ongoing problems.

When not to use it
Don't use the method when the solution is actually quite straightforward.

And be careful
Don't be tempted to cut corners as the analysis gets under way – you may miss something important.

Training
A short training course would be useful.

Where to find out more
Quality Control Handbook, Juran J, McGraw Hill, 1989

Example

Problem Analysis is particularly useful when there are variations in the performance of parallel processes.

A paint manufacturer operated two production lines for its emulsion paints. During one particular week Line A consistently performed less well than Line B. Data was available to quantify the problems. It was now a case of finding out what could be causing them.

Using the Problem Analysis methodology, Line A's performance was compared to Line B's. Then the differences were summarised and related to any known changes which were taking place at the same time.

This analysis suggested two possible causes, which were then verified by further tests. The problem was solved by adjusting the speed of the final mixing drum.

Problem Analysis for a fault in the paint mixing process

Problem definition

Paint from Line A has incorrect consistency.

Problem description

From Friday afternoon, the paint has been on average 10% thinner than specification, and than the paint from Line B.

Distinctive features

Only on Line A.
Probably all the time (all samples show problem).
Precise start time.

Other changes taking place at that time

New colour started on Line A.
Drum maintenance Friday morning before new colour started.

Possible causes

New colour incorrectly mixed.
Timing on drums adjusted but not calibrated.

Assess for most likely cause

New colour now running on Line B without problems, so most likely to be drums.

Verify the cause

Timing on mixing drums out by 10%.
Drums recalibrated.

Process Analysis

Generic tool for analysing processes as a prelude to introducing change or control mechanisms.

Affinity group: Strategy, Product and Process Design

Classification • • •

When to use it
When you need to know more about a process, to improve either efficiency or effectiveness.

What you'll achieve
Insights into what happens at present, and how things could be improved.

When not to use it
Don't use for processes outside the span of your control: the analysis should be a prelude to action.

And be careful
Don't plan to analyse the whole organisation at once – deal with straightforward parts first, and build up gradually in scope and complexity. Stop when the analysis is in danger of getting too large or complex to understand.

Training
Concept not difficult, but a short course will be useful for examining best practice. Software tools are widely available.

Where to find out more
Total Quality Management, Pera International, Chapman and Hall, 1992

Process flowchart

Define process for analysis

Construct outline Block Diagram of process

Construct detailed flowchart of all steps in process

Create task lists for each step

Analyse each task for usefulness and efficiency

Produce Action Plan to carry out improvements

Example

Process Analysis is often the first step to making improvements.

A large engineering company found that it took up to 60 days to prepare competitive tenders while a comparable company took only 16 days.

The company carried out a Process Analysis exercise, taking everyone involved with preparing the tenders on an awayday. The group produced a flowchart of the process and listed all the tasks associated with each step of the process.

This provided the basis for a discussion about how to improve the process.

The flowchart showed the number of times drafts were retyped, and how often they moved between people for comment. It also showed how much material for new drafts was culled from old tenders, suggesting that an indexed bank of tenders would be useful.

It was felt that if engineers had access to CAD to do their own schematics, and to word processing to alter their text, substantial savings would result.

Process Analysis for preparing tenders in the engineering industry

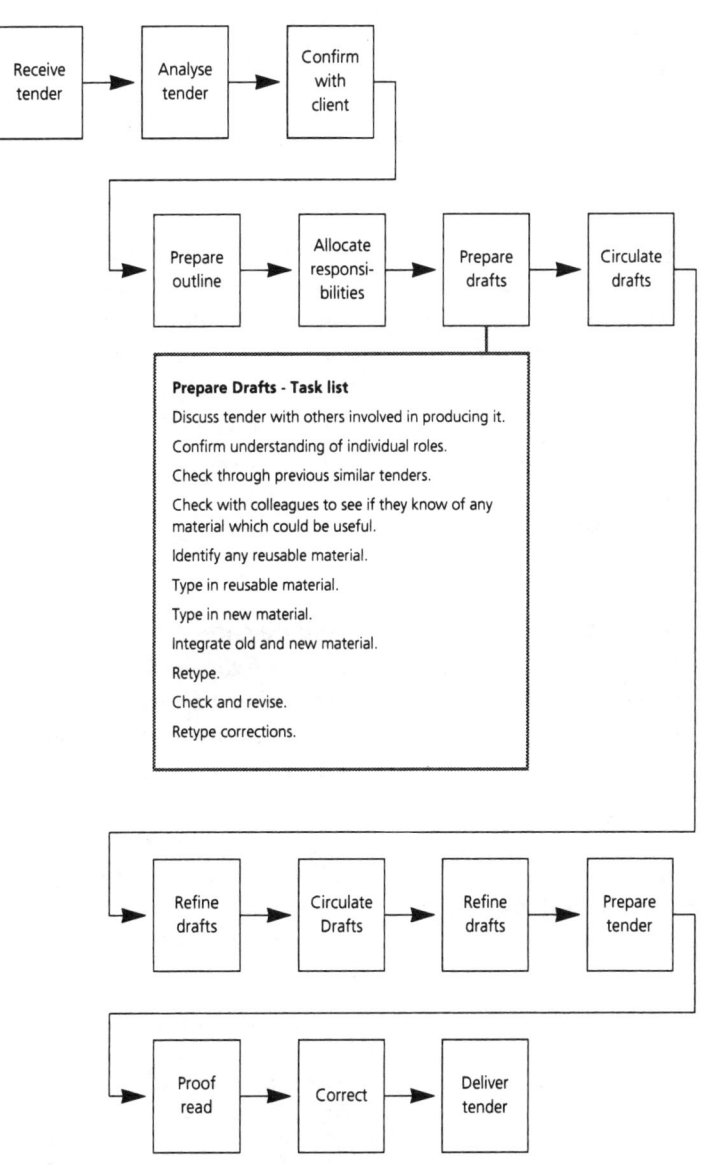

Process Capability Analysis

Method of assessing the performance levels which a particular production process is capable of achieving.

Affinity group: Statistical Quality Control

Classification • • •

Process flowchart

Describe or chart process

Identify variables – people, equipment, materials, environment, etc

Devise ways of specifying and measuring process variables

Take measurements of variables, from sample of representative machines, operators and operating condition

Estimate likely overall variation: 3 standard deviations within specification normally means process considered capable

When to use it
When planning to buy a production plant, changing the use of an existing plant, or setting up or changing production processes. Also use to judge how well subcontractors can fulfil specifications.

What you'll achieve
Reduced risk of production faults and failures typical of processes at their limits. Also helps establish desirable inspection methods and frequencies.

When not to use it
Don't use without access to reliable performance characteristics, including those from suppliers.

And be careful
Measure capability with care: remember comprehensive and accurate measurements will take time to establish.

Training
Competence in statistics essential.

Where to find out more
Quality Control Handbook, Juran J, McGraw Hill, 1989

Total Quality Management, Pera International, Chapman and Hall, 1992

Total Quality Control, Feigenbaum A V, McGraw Hill, 1983

Example

Companies who contract out work should know the process capability of their subcontractors, to keep control along the supply chain.

A building materials manufacturer wanted to contract out for 2 million bricks. They needed to know if the subcontractor's process could meet their specification of no more than 2mm variance in length. A sample size was calculated and the acceptable standard deviation for brick length worked out, using statistical formulae.

When the sampling was carried out, however, it was obvious that the existing variation in the subcontractor's bricks was too great and that the process as it stood was not capable of meeting the contractor's demands.

Process Capability Analysis for brick manufacturing

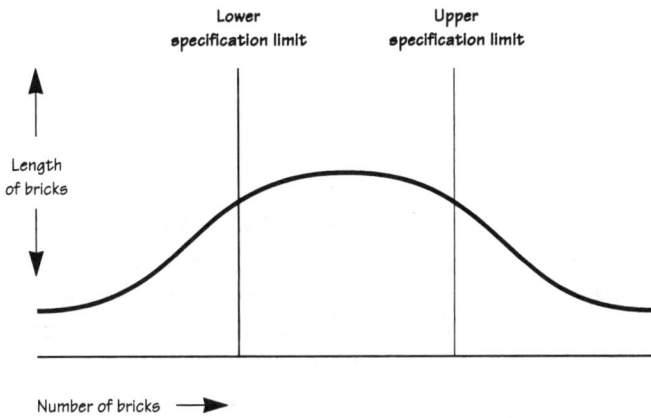

Process Definition

Method of checking that the process, its customers and suppliers are properly aligned.

Affinity group: Planning

Classification • • •

When to use it
Use early on in planning or designing processes, to make sure the process will achieve what it intends.

When not to use it
Don't use without a particular goal in mind – it must be a prelude to action.

Training
Short course could be useful.

What you'll achieve
Overview of what the process is there for, what it does, and what resources it uses. Graphic format makes it easy to see discrepancies and how to adjust them.

And be careful
Keep the analysis clear and broadbrush: it's easy to get bogged down in exceptions and contingencies which don't help at this stage.

Where to find out more
The Quality Toolkit, Marsh J, IFS Ltd, 1992

Process flowchart

Identify process to be defined

List all suppliers and customers

Link outputs to customers, and brainstorm their requirements

Identify all inputs to the process, and all suppliers

Link inputs to suppliers, and brainstorm your requirements

Identify any controls relevant to the process, and resources needed

Example

Process Definition is important in industries where constraints and customer needs change.

A large agricultural enterprise had to revise its processes to take account of falling milk quotas and the pressure from animal rights campaigners to change its relationship with the meat industry.

When all the elements of its present processes had been defined, it could begin to judge what effect the milk quotas would have, and what alternatives there were for dealing with excess calves.

Process Definition for milk production

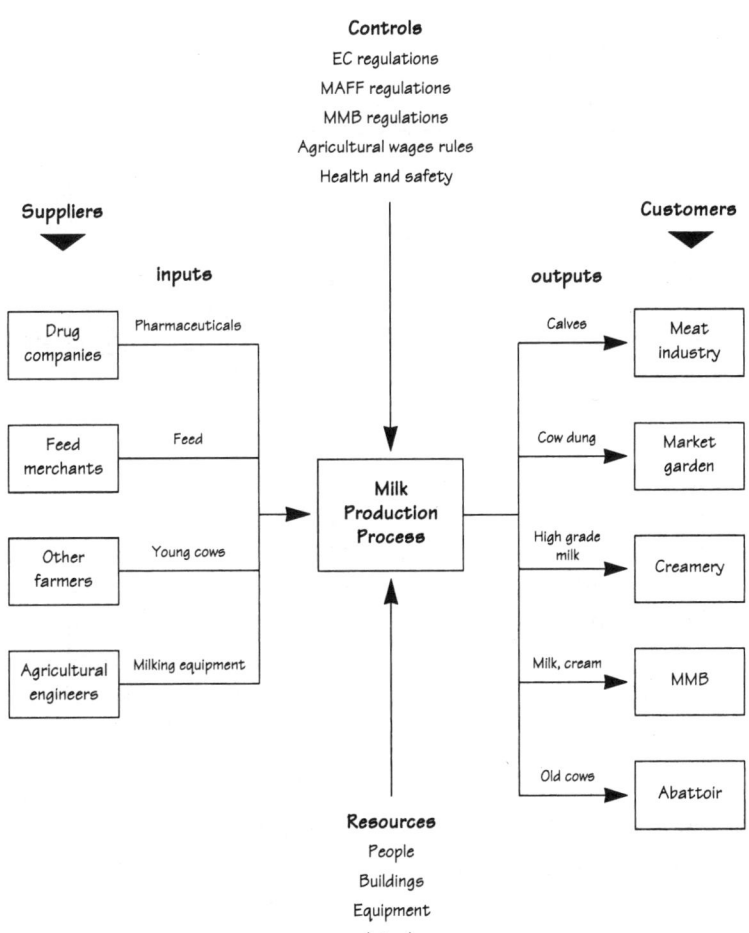

Process Failure Analysis

Method of evaluating control tools and methods.

Affinity group: Problem Solving

Classification • • •

Create flowchart of process, and associated outputs

List possible failure points

List controls you're using at each possible failure point

Classify controls as too little, appropriate or too much and adjust accordingly

When to use it
Use when planning control systems for a new process, or for evaluating the controls already in place.

What you'll achieve
Knowledge of whether the controls you're planning or using are working sufficiently well, and if not why not. Basis for improving key controls.

When not to use it
You won't be able to plan sensible controls in isolation: need to have data collection systems in place.

And be careful
Different kinds of problems need different kinds of controls. Consider for example inspection, training, supplier relationships or mechanical controls.

Training
Some training in analysing processes useful.

Where to find out more
Quality Control Handbook, Juran J, McGraw Hill, 1988

Example

Process Failure Analysis is the first stage in reducing failures in processes.

A telephone company wanted to reduce the number of complaints which followed phone installations. Firstly they charted the installation process. Then they added possible failure points, and listed the controls they used to try to prevent failure at these points. Using data from customer complaints, they could evaluate the controls, and consider improvements.

For example, one possible point of failure was at connection. The control was to use only engineers who had had 4 weeks' training. The evidence suggested that this control was good enough.

Another possible failure point was in people's understanding of how to use their phones. The control was to give them user guides. Here however the evidence suggested that this control was not working well, as customer complaints regularly received calls about basic functions.

The company decided to introduce a walkthrough with the customer and to improve the quality of their user guides.

Process Failure Analysis for phone installations

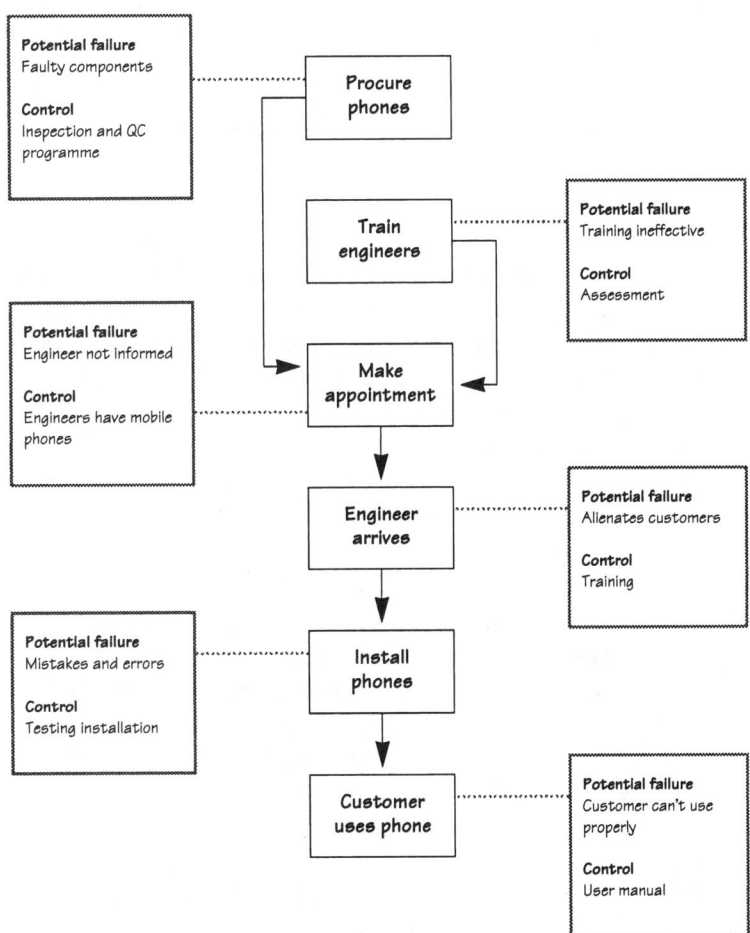

Process Model

Tool for extending Process Definition into sub-processes

Affinity group: Planning

Classification • • •

Process flowchart

Make high level Process Definition

Identify sub-processes and group around process diagram (max 5 per process)

Add output, input, resources and controls to each sub-process

Decompose diagram until all activities are identified, analysed, and related to a higher-level process

When to use it
As a follow on from Process Definition, to get a more detailed picture of the supply chains throughout the organisation. Useful as a basis for quality management system.

What you'll achieve
A complete model of activities, which you can use as a basis for a company-wide analysis. And improved supplier/customer relationships.

When not to use it
As with Process Definition, only use as a prelude to action.

And be careful
Keep control of the diagram – make sure groupings of activities are clear. Discard detail that threatens to obscure the lines of the relationships you're creating.

Training
Short course useful.

Where to find out more
The Quality Toolkit, Marsh J ,IFS Ltd, 1992

Example

Process Modelling takes Process Definition to the next stage. In the example of the farm in Process Definition, Process Modelling starts to look at the sub-processes which surround the central process of producing milk.

As the sub-processes are modelled, the chain of suppliers and customers is also taken to this level, with extra inputs, outputs, resources or constraints added as required.

In the example, the milking process is broken down into four sub-processes which contribute to the overall process of milk production.

Process Model for milk production

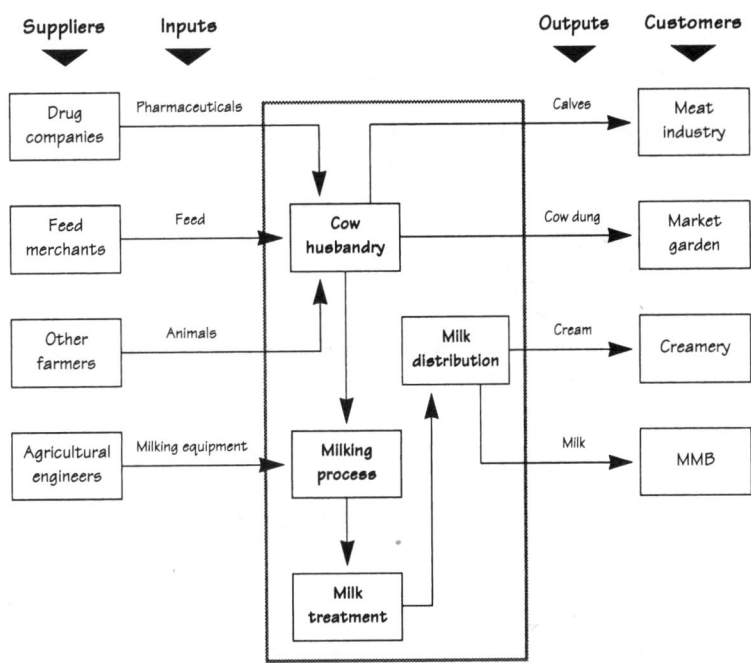

Quality Circle

Group approach to taking responsibility for problem solving

Affinity group: Strategy

Classification • • • •

When to use it
As part of a quality initiative, to help make people responsible for the quality of what they do and what they produce.

What you'll achieve
Not just answers to problems, but a livelier culture and a more responsible and involved workforce.

When not to use it
Don't use when organisational culture is so hierarchical that the group won't have enough autonomy to make changes.

And be careful
Quality Circles need leadership, training and commitment: high failure rate in the UK when they've been talk shops with no real expertise. And successful teams should be rewarded or recognised.

Training
Training is an essential part of successful Quality Circles: all members must be part of long-term training programme in analysis and control techniques and team-working.

Where to find out more
Quality Management Library, CCTA, HMSO, 1992

Quality Control Handbook, Juran J, McGraw Hill, 1989

Handbook of Quality Tools, Ozeki K and Asaka T, Productivity Press, 1990

Process flowchart

Raise general quality awareness throughout organisation with talks from experts, case studies, site visits

Establish Quality Circle in area where people are most interested in quality

Choose one theme or problem and make plans to investigate

Start parallel programme of training in analysis and control techniques

Resolve problem and choose another

Evaluate periodically the work of the circle and consider expanding Quality Circle programme.

Example

Quality Circles succeed when everyone in them is interested and wants to make improvements.

A large photographic studio used Quality Circles successfully, after attempts to impose quality changes from the top down had failed. The company encouraged autonomy and creativity, so the idea of people taking responsibility for improving their own work areas was appropriate. The company culture was also characterised by a high level of interest in the work itself.

Activities undertaken by a Quality Circle for film processing included keeping better records and tracking systems, and an investigation into new chemical products – their costs, availability and effectiveness. The Circle also made links outside the company using the Internet which resulted in a visit to a similar studio in California to compare techniques.

Quality Circle evaluation checklist

Quarterly evaluation of the activities of the film processing Quality Circle

Criterion	Description	Score (0-20)
1. Number of projects	4 (out of 5 planned)	18
2. Relevance of projects	All to do with chemical processing	20
3. Co-operation	All members of the QC participated	20
4. Standardisation	Only one project adopted	8
5. Management rating	Want more info about three of the projects before introducing them: sympathetic to the approach	12

Quality Council

Regular forum for quality professionals to meet and exchange ideas with themselves and with management

Affinity group: Strategy

Classification • • • •

When to use it
As part of infrastructure for quality programme: helps to consolidate initiatives and improve morale of quality staff. Keeps the message going.

What you'll achieve
Makes sure various quality people in the organisation get to talk to each other and share ideas. Also provides a valuable point of contact for senior management.

When not to use it
Don't be afraid to disband Quality Councils when they've run their course.

And be careful
Councils need to feel quality is being taken seriously in the organisation and that decisions will be implemented – mustn't become just a talk shop. But must also have its feet on the ground.

Training
No special training needed.

Where to find out more
Quality is Free, Crosby, P, McGraw Hill, 1979

Process flowchart

- Identify staff with key quality roles in organisation, including key management sponsors where appropriate
- Formally recognise as Quality Council
- Arrange regular meetings
- Allow council complete autonomy: senior management by invitation only
- Make sure decisions have senior management support

Example

Quality Councils can operate effectively in quite an informal way.

One such council was formed in a large printing works after the newly-appointed print quality manager happened by chance to meet someone in administration working independently on quality procedures. The two women started to meet regularly for lunch. The quality manager then discovered that there were a number of other people involved in quality who didn't know each other. She advertised in the company newspaper and received an enthusiastic response from 6 others.

The group approached management for formal recognition as a Quality Council, and set up meetings to give each other support and exchange ideas. The group kept the informal feeling of the first meetings by holding meetings over dinner, and arranging trips and outings. In spite of this informality, the group became very influential and senior management found it an invaluable point of contact. In fact getting an invitation to the Quality Council dinner became quite a prize.

```
Quality Council agenda

Date:    14 June

Time:    7.30 - 10.00pm

Venue:   Ron's Bistro

Agenda

1.  Welcome to Brian Coombes -
    new member from packing department

2.  Address by Andy Watts, Director,
    about the proposed new factory

3.  Update on procedures in the design studio

4.  Visit to Wrenshaw's - any lessons?

5.  Update on the top 10 quality initiatives

6.  Ideas for next year's top 10

7.  Report from editor of quality newsletter

8.  Progress on the idea of a quality award

9.  AOB
```

Quality Function Deployment

Product and process design tool for translating the voice of the customer into characteristics of the product or process.

Affinity group : Graphic Tools, Product and Process Design

Classification • • •

When to use it
For designing or re-designing products or processes to make sure of delivering the product characteristics the customer actually wants. Developed for manufacturing: can work for service processes too.

What you'll achieve
The ability to distinguish between essential and desirable product and process features, so that it's clear where high-cost technological or engineering investment will pay off. Also a framework for assessing impact of changes in product or process.

When not to use it
Don't embark on QFD when priorities are obvious, the process design is efficient, or the design team very experienced.

And be careful
Take time to find out what the voice of the customer really is, maybe through market research. Use Benchmarking.

Training
QFD uses particular conventions for setting out the related matrices and scores for which training will be necessary.

Where to find out more
Quality Management Library, CCTA, HMSO, 1992

Quality Control Handbook, Juran J, McGraw Hill, 1989

Total Quality Management, Pera International. Chapman and Hall, 1992

Process flowchart:

Research customer requirements – the voice of the customer

↓

Identify process design features which match the voice of the customer

↓

Create a matrix plotting customer requirements against design features (a what/how matrix), and score

↓

Select the top 5 or so highest scoring design features

↓

Create matrices for 3 more levels:
- design features and critical part characteristics
- critical part characteristics and manufacturing operations
- manufacturing operations and production requirements.

Example

Using QFD prevents ideas being adopted just because they have a surface validity.

A lawnmower manufacturer recently spent time and money redesigning a control for their most popular mower, only to find that customers were insensitive to the modification. So when they began planning to redesign another of their older models, they wanted to be sure that this time round they would make changes the customer actually wanted.

The company carried out market research to find out their customers' priorities, and a QFD analysis to see what the implications for design and manufacturing were.

The results showed that customers were interested in performance, and that improving the motor, the drive chain and the efficiency of the blades would have far more impact than changing control features had done.

QFD for redesigning a lawnmower

1. Product planning matrix

●	strong relationship	=	3 points
△	medium relationship	=	2 points
○	weak relationship	=	1 point

What	How: Motor	Drive chain	Blades	Handle	Controls	Grass collection
Quiet operation	●	●	△			
Works with wet grass	●	△	●			△
Cuts long grass	●	△	●			
Reliable	●	●			△	○
Light to carry	○	○	○	△		○
Compact for storage				●		●
Safe			●	△	●	○
Total	13	11	12	7	5	8

Further matrices are produced for:

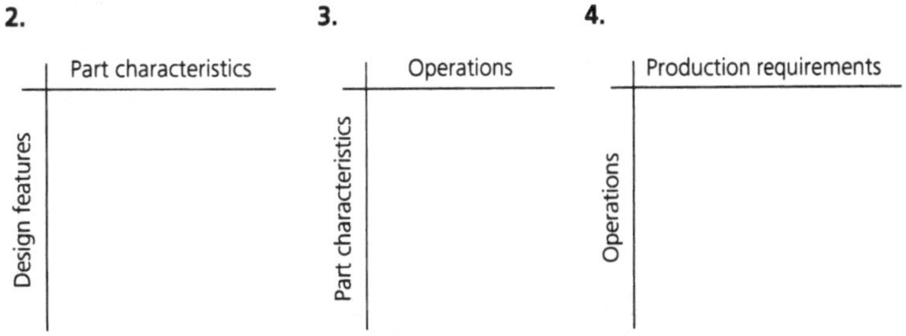
2.
Part characteristics
Design features
3.
Operations
Part characteristics
4.
Production requirements
Operations

Quality Improvement Team

Team put together to carry out particular quality projects.

Affinity group: Quality Management System

Classification • • • •

When to use it
Use QITs for one-off quality projects to find solutions to difficult but clearly defined problems.

When not to use it
Don't use a QIT for everything – only for problems that'll bring greatest savings and benefits. It is not a replacement for good management.

Training
Training for team-working and project management is advisable for first-time teams.

What you'll achieve
Greatly increased chance of finding answers by using a focussed group with the right mix of skills and experience.

And be careful
Teams are sometimes hard to manage, and they're expensive. Make sure group is accountable and has senior management support.

Where to find out more
The Quality Management Library, CCTA, HMSO, 1992

Quality is Free, Crosby P, McGraw Hill, 1979

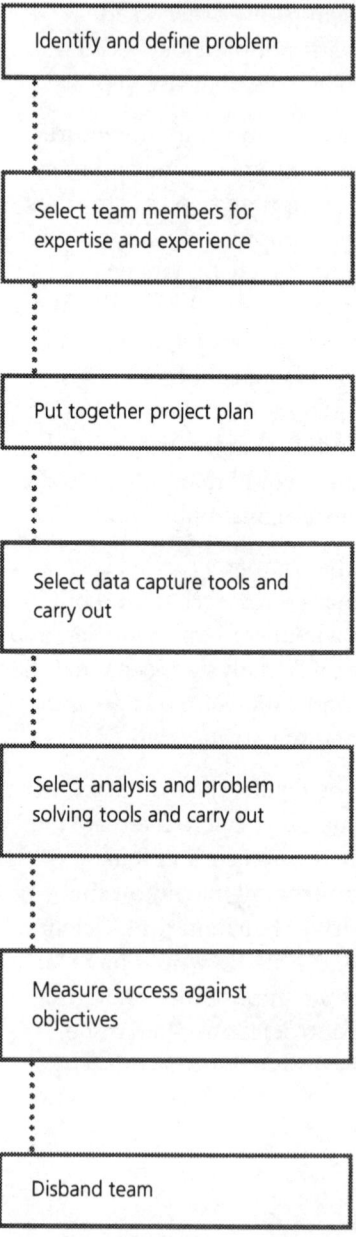

Process flowchart

- Identify and define problem
- Select team members for expertise and experience
- Put together project plan
- Select data capture tools and carry out
- Select analysis and problem solving tools and carry out
- Measure success against objectives
- Disband team

Example

A government IT unit regularly makes use of QITs for problems which fall outside the normal routine of activities. Often these problems are called to their attention through the Help Desk which logs calls from users with problems.

One Help Desk manager became aware of a problem which users of the software package X5 were having. Normal strategies such as rebuilding the desk-top were providing quick fixes, but the problems recurred.

A QIT was formed to look at the evidence, run some tests and solve the problem. The team constituted itself formally with a statement of objectives, time-scale and so on.

Because the team was so focussed it was able to find the solution – an incompatible piece of housekeeping software, which created intermittent faults. The QIT shared a celebratory drink and disbanded.

```
Quality Improvement Team in the IT unit

Name of team
The X5 clean-up team.

Statement of objectives
To find the root cause of recurring problems
with X5, and provide a solution.

Time-scale
Within 2 months.

Resources
Staff RJ, KG, DF, PS and JD.
One staff day per person per week.

Reporting to: BN
```

Quality Objectives

For clarifying the purpose of any quality initiatives.

Affinity group: Quality Management System

Classification • •

Process flowchart
Bring together key players in the quality initiative
Identify desired end results
Agree on performance measurements
State Quality Objectives and success criteria
Check for alignment with business objectives

When to use it
Set objectives every time you plan a quality improvement initiative in the organisation.

What you'll achieve
A definite focus for what can otherwise be a rather wide-ranging activity, particularly in service sector organisations.

When not to use it
Don't use short-term objectives as a substitute for a long-term policy.

And be careful
Make sure Quality Objectives are realistic and not in conflict with other business objectives: for example Quality Objectives can conflict with cost reduction objectives.

Training
Part of training for quality management systems.

Where to find out more
The Quality Toolkit, Marsh J, IFS Ltd, 1992

Example

Estate agents have not traditionally had a reputation for being interested in quality. However with the long-term slump in the housing market, and losses sustained by building societies, attitudes have begun to change as agents have realised that to keep the small amount of business there is, means operating a quality service for both clients and customers.

One large chain started the drive for quality with a set of quality objectives . These focused attention on improvements which would benefit the business and its customers and clients.

The Customer Satisfaction Assessment forms which the agency received three months into the programme gave positive feedback, suggesting that the Quality Objectives were appropriate.

```
Quality Objectives for an estate agency

1. Process all new properties within 24 hours.

2. Increase number of sole-agency agreements by
   at least 10%.

3. Improve the reputation of agency as measured
   by a Customer Satisfaction Assessment exercise.

4. Sell all houses within 10% of asking price.

5. Increase volume of business by 5% per quarter.
```

Questionnaire

For gathering information from a number of people.

Affinity group: Data Capture

Classification •

Process flowchart

```
Define topic and what you want
to know about it
          ⋮
Develop questions using
appropriate types

Open-ended:       How did you?
Multiple choice:  Which do you?
Forced choice:    This or that?
Scaled:           How much?
          ⋮
Send out questionnaires
          ⋮
Analyse and present results
```

When to use it
To find out what an extended group of people is thinking and saying, in an economic way.

What you'll achieve
Information straight from the people who matter: facts about what they're thinking, instead of just impressions.

When not to use it
Not worth using if you can get the information you want from a selection of personal contacts, for example. Use for a wider sample.

And be careful
Phrasing questions takes some thought to get right: check that your questions aren't leading the answers you'll get. And if you're using a database, do a sample verification exercise to check that names are up-to-date and correct.

Training
Training or reading books about how to write questions is important.

Where to find out more
Benchmarking, Camp R, ASQC Quality Press, 1989

Communication for Business, Taylor S, Pitman Publishing, 1993

Questionnaire Design and Attitude Measurement, Oppenheim A N, Gower, 1986

Example

Questionnaires are an important tool for market research.

A university had had a number of complaints from the Student Union about problems with food: its cost, quality and availability. It was considering employing a new company .

However before the company accepted this opportunity, it wanted to know what the students really wanted. Questionnaires were prepared and posted round lecture rooms, common rooms and vending machines. Students are also paid to take the questionnaires round and encourage others to respond.

The results showed that although students would like a better service, they would not guarantee to pay for it, or to use it in the holidays.

The company decided not to operate on the university site, but to increase the advertising for the outlets it already had.

Questionnaire on the availability of university food

1. What do you do for lunch?

	Never	Less than once a month	Once or twice a month	At least once a week	Every day
Sandwiches	☐	☐	☐	☐	☐
Off-campus	☐	☐	☐	☐	☐
On-campus	☐	☐	☐	☐	☐
Vending machines	☐	☐	☐	☐	☐
Snacks from shop	☐	☐	☐	☐	☐

2. What do you typically pay for lunch?

	Never	Less than once a month	Once or twice a month	At least once a week	Every day
Less than £1	☐	☐	☐	☐	☐
£1-2	☐	☐	☐	☐	☐
£2-3	☐	☐	☐	☐	☐
Over £3	☐	☐	☐	☐	☐

3. Where do you eat in the evenings?

	Never	Less than once a month	Once or twice a month	At least once a week	Every day
Digs	☐	☐	☐	☐	☐
On campus	☐	☐	☐	☐	☐
Other	☐	☐	☐	☐	☐

4. Where do you eat your evening meal during the vacations?

	Never	Less than once a month	Once or twice a month	At least once a week	Every day
Home	☐	☐	☐	☐	☐
Digs	☐	☐	☐	☐	☐
Campus	☐	☐	☐	☐	☐
Other	☐	☐	☐	☐	☐

R Chart

Control chart for monitoring the variables in a process.

Affinity group: Statistical Quality Control

Classification • • •

Process flowchart

Decide what variable to measure and when to measure

When to use it
Use in production processes for monitoring the range within which variables operate, and for comparing this with the customer's or manufacturer's specification. Always use with the x̄ chart, plotting them together on the same chart.

What you'll achieve
An understanding of what level of variability is to be expected from your process, and a check on whether, in spite of the variables, the process is still producing items which are within specification. Also the information will indicate areas in need of improvement.

Set up chart

Horizontal axis:
Measurement intervals

Vertical axis:
Range – difference between the maximum and minimum values collected at each time interval

Calculate upper and lower control limits, using formulae. Often upper and lower warning limits are added as well

When not to use it
Don't use for recording defects (ie attributes): use c, u, np or p charts instead.

And be careful
Use with the x̄ chart. Select the right variables, not the ones it's easiest to count, and check findings before taking major action.

Plot measurements and check that range fluctuates randomly within acceptable limits. If not, act

Training
Fundamental understanding of statistics is necessary.

Where to find out more
The Economic Control of Manufacturing Quality, Shewart W, Dover Press, 1936

A Practical Approach to Quality Control, Caplen R H, Hutchinson Publishing Group, 1978

Consider whether average range is within quality target

Example

R Charts are an essential adjunct to $\bar{x}$ Charts. The $\bar{x}$ Chart uses an average figure from each sample to give an overview of the whole process.

By focussing on the range of variation in each sample, the R Chart provides a level of detail which explains more about the process.

In the motorbike components factory described in the $\bar{x}$ example, problems came as much from variability within each sample as from the tendency for the whole process to drift towards the upper control limit. The R Chart showed clearly that the process was much more variable than had been thought.

Causes of variability can require some creativity to discover. The motorbike company now has to look at things like shift patterns, materials and machinery to try to find the reasons for the excessive variation.

R Chart for motorbike components

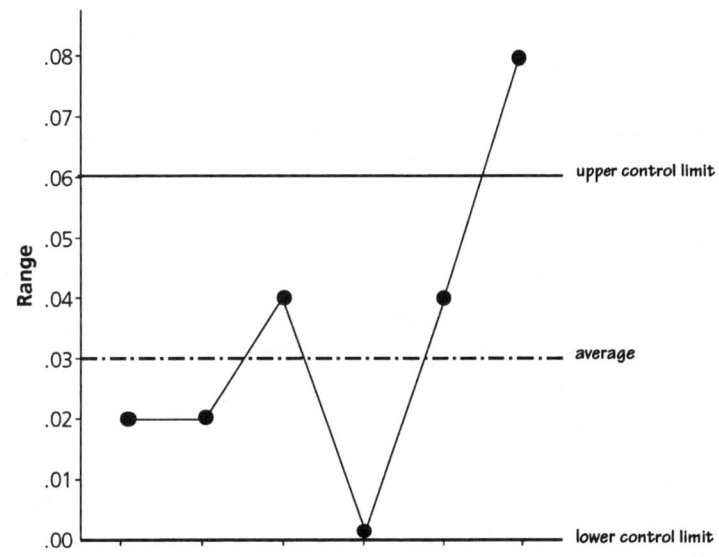

Shift	A	A	A	A	A	A
Time	9.30	11.30	13.30	15.30	17.30	19.30
Date	8 June					
X (max)	.63	.65	.64	.68	.67	.78
X (min)	.61	.63	.60	.68	.63	.70
R	.02	.02	.04	.00	.04	.08

Radar Chart

Graphic tool for rating performance, showing actual and ideal performance

Affinity group: Graphic Tool

Classification • •

When to use it
Use to involve people in evaluating the performance of key areas of the business and in recognising where things could be improved.

What you'll achieve
Company wide picture of perceived strengths and weaknesses against agreed performance targets. An assessment in which everyone involved has to agree.

When not to use it
Don't use without agreement on how to define performance targets.

And be careful
Important to canvas a wide spread of opinion for ratings: ratings by groups of people who work together will tend to be similar.

Training
No specific training needed, but facilitator necessary.

Where to find out more
The Memory Jogger, Brassard M and Ritter D, GOAL/QPC, 1994

Process flowchart

Select between 5-10 areas of performance

Define low and high performance in each area

Construct Radar Chart as wheel:
- equal segments for each performance area
- spokes as measurement scale with high performance on outside edge

Rate performance in each area, individually and as a group

Join together rating scores and fill in performance areas

Select biggest gap in most critical area for improvement programme

Example

The Radar Chart creates a concrete image of the whole organisation: its strengths and weaknesses, and its performance in relation to its goals. It is often used as part of change management programmes.

A kitchen furniture manufacturer had recently been taken over by a competitor. The new management let it be known that improvements in key areas would have to be made if the company were to stay in business. For improvements to take place, it was important for everyone to buy in to new targets and understand the scale of the changes.

All the managers representing the 7 key areas of performance on which the company depended were involved in creating the Radar Chart. Performance targets were discussed and entered on the chart. Managers then rated the present performance of the company. It soon became clear that the company needed better designed products, with greater opportunities for customisation, in order to survive.

Radar Chart for assessing company performance

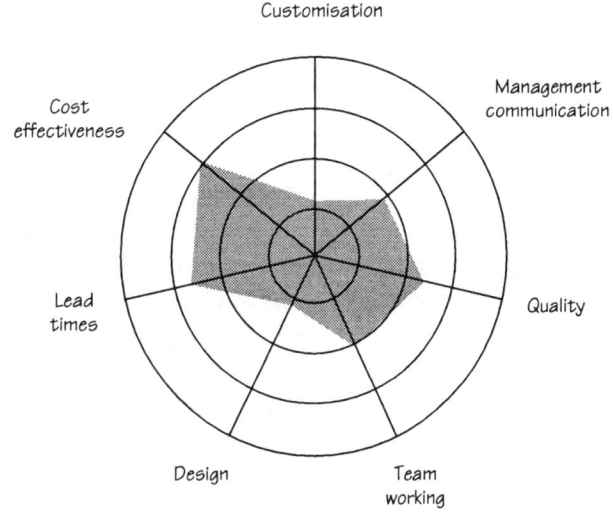

Rating Sheet

Tool for selecting one of a number of options.

Affinity group: Prioritisation

Classification • •

State decision to be made

On Rating Sheet, list criteria that have to be met on left

Create columns to the right for each option being considered

For a basic Rating Sheet, check criteria against options, and choose option that fulfils the most criteria

For weighted Rating Sheet, weight each criterion from 1-10

Multiply scores for each option with weighting factor and choose option with highest score

When to use it
For selecting one from a number of similar options, as part of a formalised selection process.

When not to use it
Don't use when the options are very different and imply different strategies.

Training
Short internal company course could be useful.

What you'll achieve
Objective selection process. Basic Rating Sheet shows up any obvious winners: weighting allows you to fine-tune selection based on particular priorities, such as value for money.

And be careful
Weighting means making some subjective judgements about what's important. Help people to be as explicit as they can about criteria.

Where to find out more
The Quality Toolkit, Marsh J, IFS Ltd, 1992

Total Quality Management, TQM International

Example

Rating does not only apply to selecting products. It can also be applied to broader decisions, provided the criteria are clear.

Often businesses find great difficulty in knowing which projects to support from all those initiated in research and development. Using a rating system provides a method of analysis and selection.

In the example a rating system is applied to five project proposals. The initial basic rating exercise eliminates any obviously unsuitable proposals, such as 'E'.

Those that remain are then rated using a weighting system. There is some discussion about the weightings, but in the end there is unanimous agreement that projects A and D should go ahead. A is very relevant to the business, and D is a low-risk project which could bring good results.

Classification of project proposals A to E

Criteria	A	B	C	D	E
Experience of team	✓	✓	✓	✓	✓
Relevance to core business	✓	✓	✓	✓	✗
Size of investment (under £50k)	✓	✓	✓	✓	✓
Value for money	✓	✓	✓	✓	✗
Feasibility	✓	✓	✓	✓	✓

Weighting of project proposals A to D

Criteria	Weight factor	A	B	C	D	Max score
Experience of team	3	18	9	21	30	30
Relevance to core business	10	80	40	50	40	100
Size of investment	8	64	48	32	72	80
Value for money	6	48	48	24	12	60
Feasibility	7	42	28	49	21	70
Risk	5	20	30	20	30	50
Timescales	4	40	8	8	20	40
Total		312	211	204	225	430

Regression Analysis

Technique for deriving the precise relationship between two sets of data.

Affinity group: Statistical Quality Control

Classification • • •

Select variables you think might be related to each other

Collect data

Create Scatter Diagram

Calculate relationship between variables using regression analysis equations

Substitute values in one variable and predict change in the other

Assess accuracy of prediction by calculating correlation coefficient

When to use it
Use for finding precise relationship between sets of variables, to make predictions about how changes in one variable will affect the other. Particularly useful if one set of changes is reliably known.

What you'll achieve
Potentially accurate predictions of what the effect of change in one variable will be on another. A planning method.

When not to use it
Don't use without strong indication from Scatter Diagram that relationship exists.

And be careful
Interpret correlations carefully – check for reasonableness and for other factors which might be influencing both variables in a similar way.

Training
Basic understanding of statistics needed, and the mathematical ability to calculate the Regression Analysis equation.

Where to find out more
Statistical Methods in Management, Cass T, Cassell, 1969

Example

Regression Analysis is one of the few tools that can be used to provide detailed predictive data.

A shipping warehouse of a large consumer goods company used Regression Analysis to help solve its staffing problems, by establishing mathematically the relationship between seasonal factors and its product mix. This then enabled them to calculate how many staff would be needed.

For example, sales of beach goods were related to hours of sunshine. By using weather forecast information, the company could read off the graph what level of sales to expect, and from this calculate the number of staff hours which would be needed. For example, 60 hours of sunshine would mean sales of £55k of beach goods.

The only drawback was the imprecision of many of the weather forecasts they received, which led to some miscalculations.

Regression Analysis to predict staffing requirements according to sales

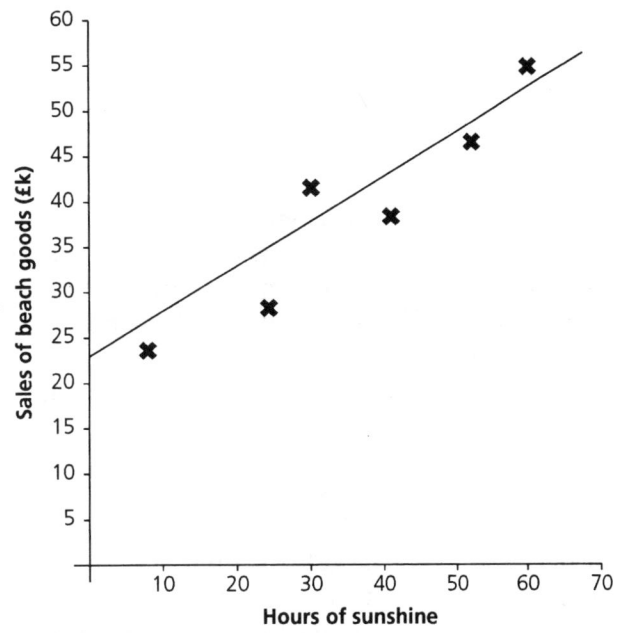

Hours (x)	Sales of beach goods £k (y)
8	23
24	28
30	42
41	38
52	47

Regression equation

$$y = a + bx$$

a is the point at which the line crosses the y axis.

b is the slope of the line.

Relations Diagram

Graphic tool to help analyse problems with complex causes.

Affinity group: Graphic Tools, Problem Solving

Classification • •

Process flowchart

Define problem and write in a box in centre of diagram

List all possible causes

Select primary causes and group them round problem

Place secondary causes behind primary causes

Continue until root causes found

Connect causes and effects with lines and arrows

When to use it
For ordering and relating ideas and information about a subject, to establish whether there is a coherent chain of cause and effect.

What you'll achieve
Comprehensive approach to analysing problems which directs attention to significant root causes rather than wasting time on intermediate measures which won't solve the underlying problem.

When not to use it
Not for fire-fighting situations when a quick solution to an immediate cause is needed.

And be careful
Often difficult to carry out sorting and analysing on the spot: may be best to do this later and present the results to the group for comment.

Training
Can get quite complicated: some training necessary in such cases.

Where to find out more
The Quality Toolkit, Mash J, IFS Ltd, 1992

Handbook of Quality Tools, Ozeki K and Asaka T, Productivity Press, 1990

Example

Relations Diagrams were originally developed for economic engineering, but the clarity with which they show complex interrelationships makes them suitable for a wider range of analyses.

One young company experienced problems with staff not staying late to finish work even when there were deadlines to meet. The management team was not sure how to tackle this problem, or indeed what lay behind it.

The Relations Diagram they produced was helpful in exploring this issue. It showed that the staff, who were mostly young, were taking junior roles, but that the company really needed people who were ambitious and prepared to put their work first.

The company then had the choice of grooming some of the young staff for this position, or employing more experienced staff.

Relations Diagram to explore why staff are unwilling to stay late to meet deadlines

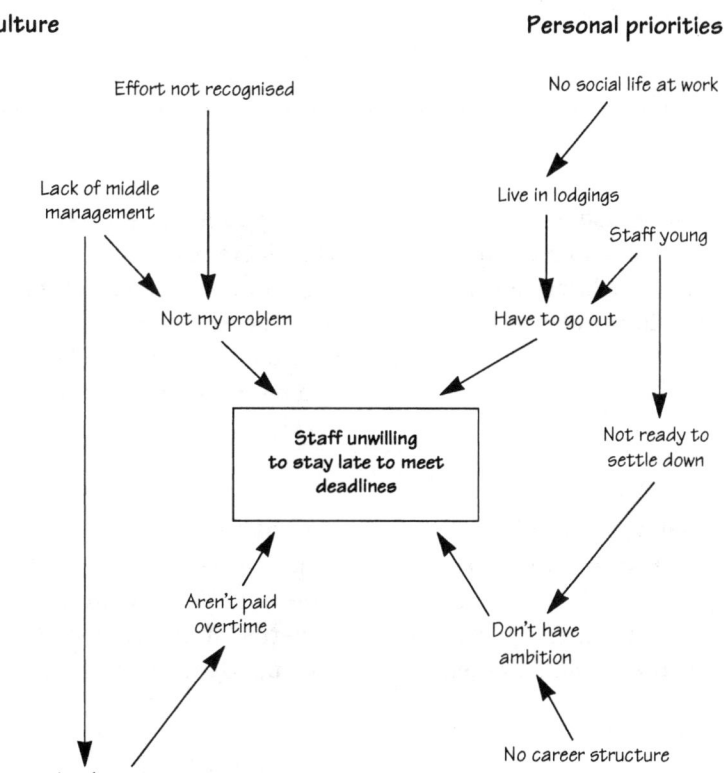

Relevance Tree

Graphic tool for classifying items in a hierarchy.

Affinity group: Graphic Tools, Problem Solving

Classification • • •

Define overall objective and put at top of diagram

Set out major alternative approaches to reaching objectives

Select the preferred approach and break down into actions

Continue to break down the elements of the tree until you reach starting point of action plan

When to use it
Use the diagram to explore a number of different ways of achieving an objective.

What you'll achieve
The diagram sets out in a logical way what approaches could be used to meet objectives, and what actions and resources they will involve.

When not to use it
Don't use for comparing options in a detailed way: the Relevance Tree is for exploring new directions at a general level.

And be careful
Be prepared to go back to the Relevance Tree if your preferred approach doesn't hold up to further analysis.

Training
No formal training needed, but facilitator could be useful.

Where to find out more
Tools for Thought, Waddington C, Johnathan Cape, 1977

Example

The Relevance Tree is a good thinking tool, as it provides a quick way of sketching out ideas in a general way and then adding detail as interesting directions begin to emerge.

A small but expanding company used this tool as a way of thinking about child care for its employees. Many of its employees had started with the company straight from college and now had small children to support. In addition one of the directors had just had a child and was therefore sensitive to the problems involved.

The company held a meeting to examine the options open to them. In this case, providing a creche was the option which everyone wanted. However the Tree showed that there were too many hidden costs and local authority regulations to meet, for the project to be viable.

The company opted for a childcare allowance scheme instead. This would provide choice for parents.

Relevance Tree for providing child care facilities

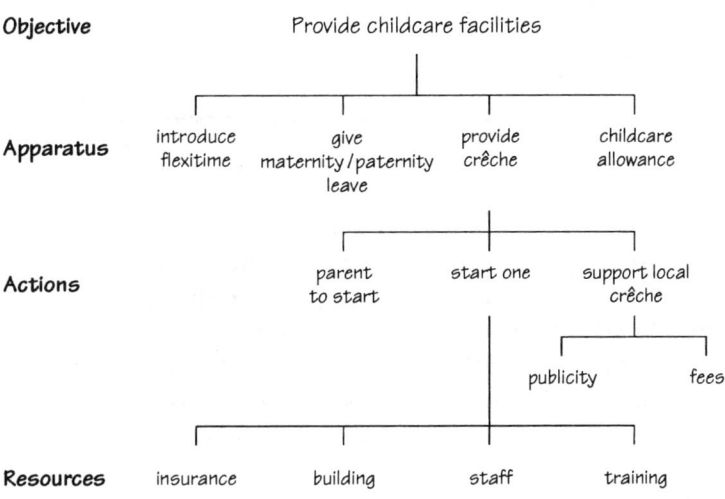

Reliability Prediction & Analysis

Way of predicting how reliable a product will be before making it.

Affinity group: Statistical Quality Control, Product and Process Design

Classification • • •

When to use it
Standard procedure at planning and design stages for manufactured products, to make sure they'll be capable of doing what they're supposed to.

When not to use it
The analysis won't mean much without good sources of reliability data for key components.

Training
Calculating and interpreting reliability data needs statistical ability. Engineers should know the principles involved: a short course could provide context and application.

What you'll achieve
Products that are fit for purpose and that won't be undermined by an unsuspected weak link when people start to use them in appropriate ways.

And be careful
Reliability is a function of both the parts and the whole: make sure all links and connections are included in the analysis.

Where to find out more
Quality Control Handbook, Juran J, McGraw Hill, 1988

Define product in terms of parts and functions, using Block Diagram

Draw reliability Block Diagram, only including functions that affect the way the product works

For each block, list all factors relating to reliability

Estimate using avaliable data, reliability relationships, predicted failure rates etc

Apply predictions and examine for weak areas

Reliability is a quantifiable concept – the length of time a particular component or product will continue to perform at a certain level.

Since it clearly isn't possible to replicate usage to test every component or combination of components, estimations based on sampling are used instead.

But in spite of sophisticated reliability prediction methods, new products or models of old ones still find their way onto the market with unreliable components.

In the car industry, this has led to the conventional wisdom of never buying a new model until all the faults and problems have been found and put right in the second model. There is no real substitute, it seems, for the rigorous reliability testing of actually using the car.

Types of reliability problems in the car industry

Juran cites three periods of use where reliability problems occur, all of which are common in the car industry.

1. **The Infant mortality period**
These are components which fail almost as soon as the car goes into use. They can be as trivial as locking mechanisms or as vital as engine components. Such features are candidates for redesign in the next model. The only way of preventing failures which have slipped through all failure prediction and review nets would be by simulated usage.

2. **The constant failure rate period**
This period shows up features which are poorly designed and therefore only intermittently reliable. A surprising number of car models – even expensive ones – have particular weaknesses such as a tendency for the clutch cable to snap or for wheelbearings to go. Patterns of hard wear or poor maintenance will make these problems worse.

3. **The wear-out period**
These are failures of old age, as the components reach the limits of their lifespan, such as cam belts which are designed to be replaced after a specified mileage. These limits are a subject for quality improvement, but as long as customers know what they are, they can plan to replace the parts affected.

Responsibility Matrix

Graphic tool for clarifying responsibilities in cross-functional activities.

Affinity group: Planning

Classification • •

When to use it
For planning an activity which cuts across normal responsibilities, where there's a danger that people will forget it or not take it seriously.

What you'll achieve
Much better chance of success in making things happen across traditional boundaries: clear allocation of responsibilities, and an overview that lets people see how their contribution fits in.

When not to use it
Don't use cosmetically to pretend to be doing something – responsibilities must be real and realistic.

And be careful
Just allocating responsibilities won't be enough to make things happen. Appoint a senior leader or sponsor to add direction and authority.

Training
No specific training needed.

Where to find out more
Quality Control Handbook, Juran J, McGraw Hill, 1988

Process flowchart

Appoint person in overall charge of activity

Create matrix – actions on left

List roles or departments along top

Assign responsibilities using code
R   primary responsibility
C   contributing responsibility

Example

A common feature of many improvement initiatives is the way they cut across functional boundaries. The Responsibility Matrix is a good way of formalising this.

A benchmarking exercise is a typical example. To gather and analyse information, a number of departments will need to be involved – finance, to analyse company reports and extrapolate cost structures, marketing, to interpret sales literature, or production, to analyse competitor products.

The benchmarking exercise will benefit from the mix of expertise such a cross-functional approach implies, and the organisation will be more committed. Using a Responsibility Matrix shows how these activities are interdependent and how important each one is as part of the larger picture.

Responsibility Matrix for a Benchmarking project

Department	S	M	P	CS	F
Action					
Analyse literature	C	R	-	-	C
Analyse finances	-	-	-	-	R
Analyse products	-	C	R	-	-
Mystery shopper	C	-	-	R	-
Gap analysis	-	R	-	C	C
Recommendations	-	R	C	-	-

Key
R = primary responsibility
C = contributing responsibility

Key to departments
S   = Sales
M   = Marketing
P   = Production
CS = Customer Service
F   = Finance

Root Cause Evaluation Matrix

Graphic tool for prioritising actions to solve problems.

Affinity group: Graphic Tools, Problem Solving

Classification • • •

When to use it
Use as the second stage in solving problems, after you've identified the probable root causes. Can be a technical problem or a more conceptual one.

When not to use it
Don't use without groundwork on finding probable root causes first – you might miss the real cause altogether.

What you'll achieve
A way of setting out and evaluating causes for problems to ensure that the important causes are dealt with first – and not the ones that are easiest to solve.

And be careful
In spite of the matrix, you may not hit on the right cause first time, or the answer may lie in a combination of causes. Be prepared to keep trying, using instinct and experience as well as analysis.

Training
No formal training needed.

Where to find out more
Quality Control Handbook, Juran J, McGraw Hill, 1989

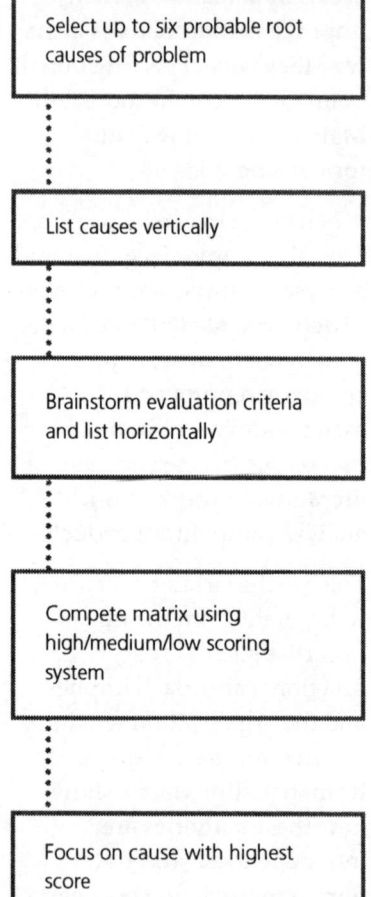

Process flowchart

Select up to six probable root causes of problem

List causes vertically

Brainstorm evaluation criteria and list horizontally

Compete matrix using high/medium/low scoring system

Focus on cause with highest score

Example

Like many tools, the Root Cause Evaluation Matrix provides a way of combining facts with judgement to provide best guess solutions. This tool can apply to general conceptual problems as well as to technical ones.

One group of schools inspectors were concerned about the poor timekeeping of students in a number of schools they had visited. The headteachers in the schools shared this concern, and wanted help to deal with the problem. The inspectors created a Root Cause Evaluation Matrix to help them to talk through the key issues, and to agree a plan of action.

The matrix suggested that the responsibility for dealing with this problem lay with the schools themselves, and that the inspectors needed to work with headteachers in applying sanctions.

Root Cause Evaluation Matrix for lateness in schools

Symbols

●	highly probable relationship	=	3 points
○	possible relationship	=	2 points
△	not a strong relationship	=	1 point

Causes	Certainty	Importance	Solution known	Solution easy	Total
Poor motivation	●	○	△	△	7
Poor transport	○	△	●	△	7
Poor recordkeeping	△	○	●	●	9
Lack of consequences	●	●	●	●	12
Lack of awareness among staff	○	●	●	●	11
Lack of focus on issues	○	○	●	●	10
Lack of system to deal with lateness	△	●	●	●	10

(Evaluation criteria)

Scatter Diagram

Graphic presentation of data to bring out patterns or relationships

Affinity group: Statistical Quality Control

Classification • •

When to use it
Use as part of the investigation of relationships between variables – an important part of quality improvement.

What you'll achieve
Understanding of why particular variations occur, and so how they can be controlled.

When not to use it
Don't use without some reason or probablilty that variables relate.

And be careful
Take time to collect and use your own raw data: approximations worked out statistically will show in distorted results.

Training
An understanding of basic statistics needed.

Where to find out more
Statistical Methods in Management, Cass T, Cassell, 1969

Process flowchart

Select variables you think might be related to each other

Collect data

Create scatter diagram
Horizontal axis:
Cause or independent variable
Vertical axis:
Effect or dependent variable

Plot data points and look for linear relationship

If likely relationship emerges, draw line of best fit to see trend

Example

Scatter Diagrams support insights into the cause and effect relationships which may be responsible for variations in performance.

One such example concerned a sophisticated machine for boring machine parts, which was installed according to instructions and performed well during commissioning. But periodically the accuracy of the machine deteriorated. Extensive testing failed to show any technical problems in the set-up, the hydraulics or the computer controller.

Finally one of the maintenance crew solved the problem. He was a keen fisherman who kept track of tides and who noticed that the times when he was called in to fix the machine coincided with high tide.

The production engineers plotted the machine's failure against high tides – and found a clear correlation.

The factory was built on reclaimed land and tidal pressure had been causing the water table under the factory floor to interfere with the very sensitive machine.

Scatter Diagram to investigate the relationship between the performance of a boring machine and high tide

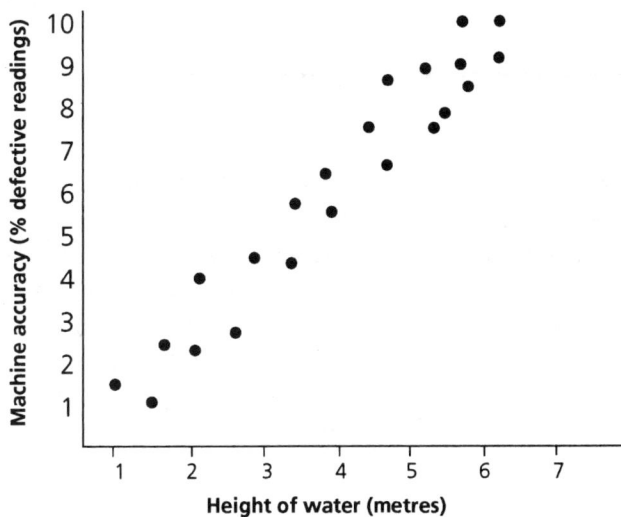

Scenario Writing

Way of predicting the future by imagining how present trends will evolve.

Affinity group: Planning

Classification • •

When to use it
Use at a strategic level in situations vulnerable to change, in the political or technological arena, for example.

What you'll achieve
You'll gain a long-term perspective, and some new insights. Focuses attention on long-term thinking and on the implications of developments which are still in their early stages.

When not to use it
Don't use at the operational level – not a short-term planning tool.

And be careful
Be as specific as you can – otherwise scenarios can be rather fanciful and stray out of the realms of the possible. Can only be 'best guesses' created by peoples' imagination.

Training
No formal training needed.

Where to find out more
Tools for thought, Waddington C, Johnathan Cape, 1977

Process flowchart

Define subject of interest

Describe present-day position

Imagine series of evolutionary steps

Describe future scenario

Develop policies or actions with future scenario in mind

Example

The Internet is the latest technological development to suggest future scenarios vastly different from the ones we know today.

Activities which might reasonably be transformed are:

• shopping – it can already be done at home

• holidays – not just bookings, but images of destinations and conversations with people there

• personal communications – no more letters

• business communications – shortened response times

• education – will teachers be really necessary?

The scenario of how university education could be affected by the Internet should persuade lecturers, at the very least, to master the technology.

But the scenario in the example poses a problem for estates departments. Increasing numbers of students are forcing expansion at the moment, but will the 'virtual' university make these new buildings unnecessary?

Scenario for university education on the Internet

Evolutionary steps

1. All students buy their own computers as a requirement (university can't afford them for all students)

2. All students are automatically linked up to the Internet – issued with codes when they start

3. Tutors communicate with students using e-mail

4. Tutors accept assignments on e-mail

5. Lecturers put lecture notes on e-mail

6. Lecturers publish complete lectures on Internet

7. Students stop coming to lectures – they're on the Internet

8. Lectures cancelled

9. University becomes 'virtual' and worldwide

10. University buildings redundant

Self-Inspection

System whereby the people who make the products or do the job also inspect their own work.

Affinity group: Quality Management System

Classification • • • •

Assess readiness of organisation, perhaps by Attitude Survey

Set specifications, control limits and measurement systems

Carry out comprehensive training programme

Introduce self-inspection in parallel with existing inspection

License competent people and reward or recognise

When to use it
To move responsibility for quality back down the line from inspectors to the people who make the products or deliver the service.

When not to use it
Don't introduce self-inspection early on in the quality programme. Without the right culture, quality will plummet.

What you'll achieve
Self-inspection can mean job enlargement for people who are competent. Erstwhile inspectors can be moved to more positive roles in training.

And be careful
Self-inspection works best when there's clear responsibility for the product or service. Not suitable for highly complex inspection, eg food industry, or microbiological checks.

Training
Training is absolutely essential. Training costs consequently can be high, especially if there is a high turnover of staff. Use short courses and on-the-job training.

Where to find out more
Quality Control Handbook, Juran J, McGraw Hill, 1989

Example

Self-inspection can be useful for easing inspection bottlenecks.

A small cottage industry making knitwear faced increased demand for its garments, putting pressure on the owners of the company who liked to finish and inspect all the garments themselves, to ensure a high standard of quality. To ease this bottleneck, it was decided that homeworkers would take over part of this work.

Each homeworker was shown what to look for and given a checklist to return with the garment.

After a trial period, it became clear that three of the homeworkers could not inspect their own work reliably. However the rest were happy with the extra responsibility (and pay), and felt they were more careful making the garments as a result. The move took a lot of pressure from the finishing staff and decreased order lead times.

Self-inspection checklist for handknitted garments

Check off each item as you complete the inspection.

- ☐ Measurements checked
    - ☐ for sleeve
    - ☐ for back
    - ☐ for fronts

- ☐ Braiding
    - ☐ complete
    - ☐ secure

- ☐ Fairisle correct (colours and design)
    - ☐ on sleeve
    - ☐ on back
    - ☐ on fronts

- ☐ Ends sewn in

- ☐ Checked for faults
    - ☐ knots
    - ☐ dropped stitches
    - ☐ symmetry

Signed   :
Comments :

....
....
....

Solution Effect Analysis

Graphic tool for analysing the likely effects of proposed solutions.

Affinity group: Problem Solving, Planning

Classification • • •

When to use it
Use this analysis when you're proposing changes, so that you can be clear about the consequences of solutions. Use a Cause and Effect Diagram for analysing problems.

What you'll achieve
A way of thinking forward and anticipating what effects proposed changes will have, and a chance to avoid unforeseen consequences.

When not to use it
Don't use when you don't need to – when the changes you're proposing aren't very radical.

And be careful
Don't stop people from making negative predictions about the changes you're committed to: they're not just being difficult – they might be right. Facilitation will be helpful to reduce feelings of threat.

Training
No formal training needed, but facilitation could be useful.

Where to find out more
Total Quality Management, TQM International Ltd

Process flowchart

Write down solution you're thinking of implementing

Place at left of diagram with arrow to the right

Identify all major effects on arrows on either side of main one

Brainstorm all other possible effects and add to diagram

Plan actions to make sure solution is effective

Example

Solution Effect Analysis, as the shape of the diagram suggests, looks at problem solving not in terms of what causes the problem, but in terms of what effect the solution will have.

In this example, a company has decided to introduce flexitime to solve a number of problems – to reduce time lost by staff in commuting, for example, and to make the best use of resources.

As the deadline for the changeover draws near, the personnel department, which is co-ordinating the change, becomes concerned that people have not thought through all the implications. It sets up a series of Solution Effect meetings so that the organisation can engage in thinking through the issues and be better prepared for the new way of working.

Solution Effect Analysis for introducing flexitime

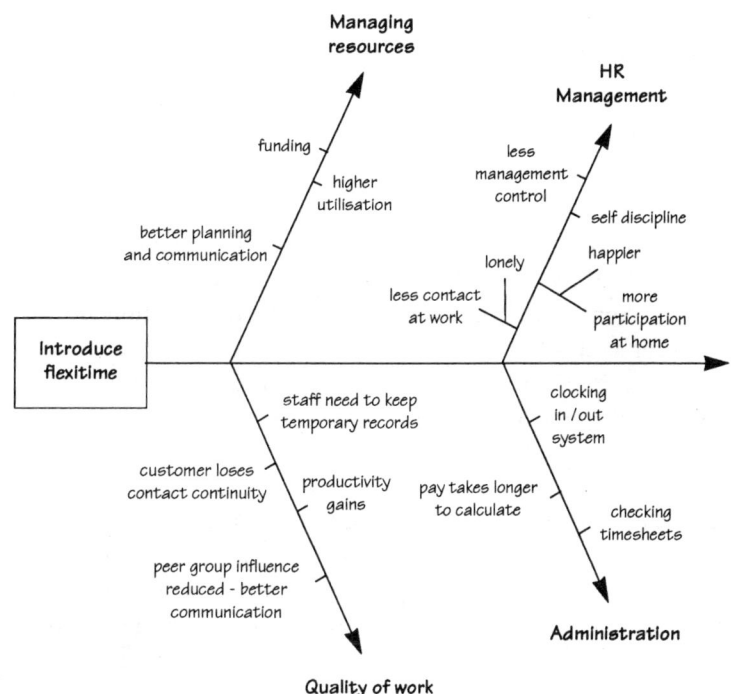

Spider Diagram

Graphic method of structuring thoughts and concepts.

Affinity group: Problem Solving

Classification • •

When to use it
When you need to organise ideas and information, perhaps for a report or presentation. You can also use it as an initial planning tool.

When not to use it
Don't use if you or members of your team have difficulty with creating and understanding diagrams.

Training
No formal training needed, but it needs practice.

What you'll achieve
A flexible method for organising information which allows you to add, adapt and change ideas as you think or talk through the issues.

And be careful
Keep the Spider Diagram under control: when everyone stops understanding it because it's too big, or too abstract, it's no good.

Where to find out more
The Quality Toolkit, Marsh J, IFS Ltd. 1992

Use Your Head, Buzan T, BBC Books 1989

Process flowchart

Define the scope of the topic or project you're planning

Write at the centre of the page

Brainstorm related issues and ideas, perhaps using file cards

Group and connect ideas

Transcribe results as a map with lines joining connecting items

Using Spider Diagrams means that people don't have to think of ideas and how to organise them logically at the same time. It provides more structure than a brainstorm list, but doesn't prevent ideas from a number of directions from being captured. It's also quick to produce.

A group of people who had just moved into new offices were asked for their ideas about how to landscape the courtyard in the centre of the office complex. They had to respond very quickly, so they met over lunch the next day and produced a Spider Diagram which represented their ideas. This took a lot less time than writing a formal structured response, and in this case served the purpose equally well.

Spider Diagram for landscaping an office courtyard

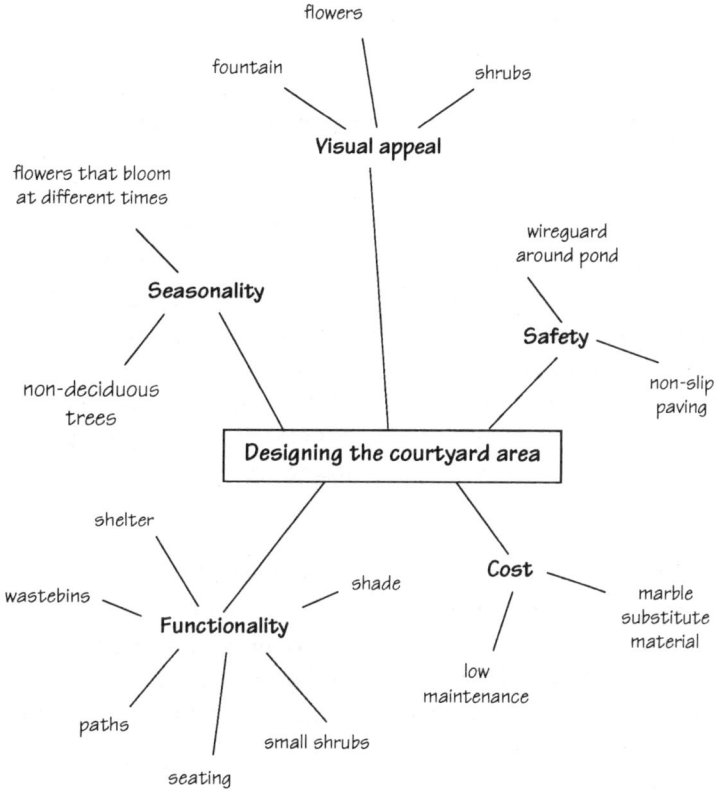

Statistical Process Control

Tool for understanding and improving manufacturing processes.

Affinity group: Statistical Quality Control

Classification • • • •

When to use it

For repetitive processes, from large production runs to small batches, which are producing items to specification and which are subject to some kind of variability.

What you'll achieve

Regular data which reveals how the process is performing – particularly when it's drifting outside acceptable limits. And information to suggest how quality might be improved.

When not to use it

Don't try to use for controlling one-off processes, or project-based work. And do the Cost of Quality calculation: the cost of scrap or re-work must be high enough to make this level of prevention worthwhile.

And be careful

SPC is a sophisticated technique which takes time and expertise to introduce properly. Don't approach this in a casual way.

Training

Setting up SPC is complex and needs a high level of training. Once it's running, Control Charts are relatively easy to maintain and interpret, particularly with the help of the software that's now available.

Where to find out more

Statistical Process Control, Oakland J and Followell R, Heineman Newnes, 1990

Quality Control Handbook, Juran J, McGraw Hill, 1988

Out of the Crisis, Deming WE, Cambridge University Press, 1988

Process flowchart

Define manufacturing process, from inputs to outputs

Identify customer needs, and define upper and lower specification limits

Calculate standard mean and variation from sample of outputs

Set upper and lower control limits

Compare with specification limits to establish process capability

Set up control charts to monitor aspects of process performance

Analyse charts as part of continuous improvement

Statistical Process Control is a highly defined technique which has had a fundamental effect on the way in which many major manufacturing industries operate.

In the car industry, for example, the ability of SPC to keep processes operating within specification has meant that standards can be set and maintained all along the supply chain. Products from a wide range of different manufacturers, including international suppliers, are compatible.

SPC has brought huge advances in the reliability of both machines and processes, helping to control their inherent variability. The ultimate effect for the customer has been better products more cheaply.

A model of Statistical Process Control

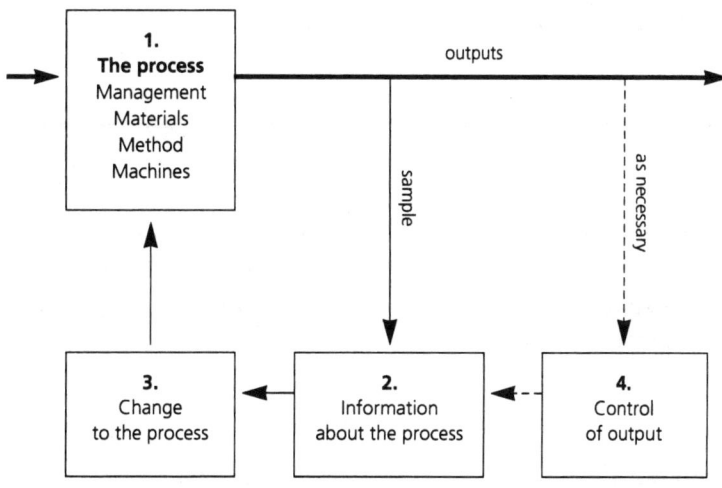

Stratification

Method of analysing data by grouping it in different ways.

Affinity group: Statistical Quality Control

Classification • • •

When to use it
When you're analysing data to find the source of a particular problem with a product or process.

When not to use it
Don't apply to problems which haven't much effect: save for getting to the bottom of the significant few.

Training
Stratification forms part of basic statistics: engineers will be familiar with it.

What you'll achieve
Insight into exactly which factor is causing your problem.

And be careful
Don't pre-judge the outcome: be creative in selecting strata and analyse results with care.

Where to find out more
The Quality Management Library, CCTA, HMSO, 1992

The Quality Toolkit, Marsh J, IFS Ltd, 1992

Total Quality Management, Pera International, Chapman and Hall, 1992

Process flowchart

Collect data about defects etc

Consider potentially significant way of grouping data (stratification)

Put data into graphic format reflecting stratification

Analyse result and try new grouping if necessary

Example

Interpreting data can be a creative process. There are always instances of data which seem to defy a rational explanation: office equipment which works perfectly well one day and won't work at all the next, for example.

Often a suitable stratification will be obvious to the people who work in the industry. The printing process for example is very sensitive to weather conditions – heat and humidity. Drying times can be extended indefinitely in a damp spell.

Humidity will also affect the way a photocopier works. Every photocopier engineer knows to look at changes in weather and paper type when problems recur.

With experience you can build up likely stratifications which will unlock the data.

Types of Stratification

By material
Consider variations in manufacturer, brand, size of consignment, storage time and conditions.

By machine
Look for variations in machine type, make, model, age, position.

By operator
Consider factors such as experience, age, training, gender.

By inspection method
Classify by instruments used, inspection procedure, inspector.

By time
Are the data affected by time of day, season, position in the operation lifecycle?

By weather
Look for changes in humidity and temperature.

Other
Look for significant strata all along the production chain.

Suggestion Schemes

For encouraging staff participation in improving efficiency and effectiveness.

Affinity group: Data Capture

Classification •

When to use it
To involve staff in improving the way things operate – they're the ones who know what's wrong.

When not to use it
No point in introducing Suggestion Schemes in cultures when they'll just be part of the bureaucracy: you'll lose credibility.

What you'll achieve
Good ideas, more involved staff, a culture of improvement, and a more efficient business.

And be careful
There are usually more problems than people know what to do with, and they're tired of telling management when nothing is done. Only start the scheme when you've got the infrastructure to actually carry out the suggestions.

Training
No specific training needed.

Where to find out more
The Quality Management Library, CCTA, HMSO, 1992

Process flowchart

Set up suggestion scheme using:
• pro formas
• suggestion box
• evaluation procedures

Decide whether to have continuous scheme or special promotions

Publicise and promote scheme among staff

Reward staff for best suggestions – not always with money

Example

An ailing chain of toyshops had been taken over by a larger competitor with the closure of a number of stores and the loss of jobs.

The new management had a number of innovative ideas about how to improve the remaining shops. However, rather than telling staff what to do, they wanted to involve them in thinking up ideas.

A Suggestion Scheme promotion was launched with prizes for the best ideas. At first there was very little response, however. Some discreet questioning revealed that the staff were sceptical about the scheme, since in their experience management did not take their ideas seriously.

Eventually a few suggestions were put forward and the new management lost no time in putting them into practice. This encouraged the others, and before long the Suggestion Scheme had produced a flood of suggestions, many of them valuable.

Suggestions for improving our toyshop

Provide toys for the children to play with

Have brighter, more child-oriented uniforms for staff

Give staff training in how the toys work so that they can demonstrate them and answer customer enquiries

Sell all the right batteries

Keep a log of complaints

Keep names of toy repairers

Stage weekly promotions with balloons

Stock a wider range of Lego – there's high demand

Start a mailing list for manufacturers' catalogues addressed to the children

Keep a record of requests for toys not stocked

Increase local advertising

Sponsor local events for children's charities

Supplier Survey

Tool for gathering information about suppliers to predict quality of supplies.

Affinity group: Data Capture

Classification •

When to use it
Before signing up with supplier for contract of significant size – usually manufacturing contracts.

When not to use it
Not worth using such an intensive/expensive procedure for small supplier. Don't insist on a bureaucratic procedure which isn't always needed.

Training
Training in procurement would be useful.

What you'll achieve
Full assessment of supplier's situation: equipment, training, attitude. Better communications with supplier.

And be careful
US studies show that concentrating on supplier's compliance with procedures is no indication of quality: use instead Japanese emphasis on capability to produce the goods.

Where to find out more
Quality Control Handbook, Juran J, McGraw Hill, 1988

Collect information about all previous experiences with supplier

Prepare questionnaire for supplier

Visit supplier: observe and interview

Set up scoring system: criteria on the left, stages of process on the right. Can use weighting system

Set minimum scoring level and accept or reject supplier

232

Example

High street chain stores have put an increasing emphasis on improving the supply chain in recent years.

One chain store with a reputation for demanding very high quality from its suppliers introduced a selection process for new suppliers which involved a Supplier Survey.

During this process, the store would get to know the reputation and capability of its potential supplier very well. Although this was a time consuming process, both sides felt it was worthwhile as any major problems were identified in advance.

For its clothing suppliers, the store used a list of five criteria, from which the suppliers had to score more than 5 out of 10, before they could be accepted.

Supplier Survey for clothing manufacturer

Supplier A

Stages of process	Design	Manufacturing	QC
Criteria			
Procedures	6	8	8
Management	6	8	7
Staff	10	10	10
CAD/CAM	9	10	9
Planning	8	10	9
Plant equipment	9	10	10
Warehousing	–	7	10
Transport	–	8	7
Materials selection	8	7	10
Capacity	5	7	6
Inspection	8	9	10

Recommendation

☑ Pass

☐ Fail

Comments

Good equipment – have invested heavily to get this contract.
Staff have been there for a long time – loyal and experienced.
Some weaknesses in management and procedures though, particularly in the design side. Also some question about capacity even with the new equipment – would be best to try out on relatively small contract first.

Team Briefing

Tool for communicating from the top down through all levels of the organisation.

Affinity group: Strategy

Classification •

Senior management regularly prepares information of general importance on:
• policies
• plans
• progress
• people

Senior management passes information on to next level preferably on the same day

Each level passes on the briefing to the next level, adding in their own brief, preferably on the same or next day

When to use it
As part of internal communication strategy, particularly important at times of change, to tell people what's happening.

What you'll achieve
Efficient and automatic dissemination of information: people feel confident that they're kept informed.

When not to use it
Don't use Team Briefing if you've established less formal but equally effective ways of communicating.

And be careful
Make sure information is concise and well-structured. And carry out spot checks to make sure that information is getting through: one weak link undermines the whole process.

Training
Training in communication techniques highly recommended.

Where to find out more
The Quality Management Library, CCTA, HMSO, 1992

The Manager's Responsibility for Communication, Garnett J, The Industrial Society Press, 1989

Team Briefing is a practical way of setting up a channel of communication right through the organisation. At each level, the original document can be added to or explained, depending on the particular interests in each area.

Team Briefing was successfully adopted in a new hospital trust after serious problems had been caused both in understanding and morale because managers and staff did not feel that they were being kept fully informed about decisions and developments. On more than one occasion, rumours of mergers, staff changes and staff cuts had taken hold before management had had a chance to explain the situation clearly.

By passing information to all staff on the same day, Team Briefing made sure that rumours did not have a chance to grow. The system also made sure that communication didn't get forgotten because of the pressure of work.

Hospital Trust Team Briefing

From: Trust board

To: All section managers

Date: w/e 22.11.94

Item 1
Agreement in principle was reached on merging the two pathology labs - in the main hospital and the maternity hospital - to form one unit on the main site. Discussions will now take place over the next 6 months with all those concerned to work out a detailed plan of action.

Item 2
There will be a visit by the junior Health Minister on the 14th December. Please make arrangements to have a representative available from your speciality during the visit 10:00 - 11:00.

Item 3
It is now hospital policy that hours for junior doctors will be reduced by 15% as from the new year.

Item 4
The nursing computer system has been installed and data is being entered into its databases. Training for all nursing staff will start in the new year.

Item 5
A new appointment: Dr Jane Gladstone to pathology. Dr Gladstone has worked in the London area for the last 6 years and brings a particular expertise in paediatric pathology.

Item 6
Leaving: Bob Vine, our assistant general manager at the main site, who leaves to head his own unit in the Midlands. Our best wishes go with him.

Thinking Hats

Technique for structuring creative thinking.

Affinity group: Problem Solving

Classification • •

When to use it
As part of Brainstorming or Lateral Thinking sessions, to structure creative thinking. Particularly useful for issues which will look very different from different perspectives.

What you'll achieve
Ideas from looking at the problem from all angles – not just the negative ones. People gain insight into other people's roles and perspectives.

When not to use it
Don't use Thinking Hats for problems which require focussed attention, rather than different perspectives.

And be careful
Needs careful facilitating to make sure that people stay in role without becoming self-conscious.

Training
Reading de Bono's book.

Where to find out more
Six Thinking Hats, de Bono E, Penguin, 1990

Process flowchart

Define problem

Provide supply of thinking hats: paper hats in different colours

Initially ask people to put on one colour of hat and think in the appropriate way

Allow change from one hat to another as session progresses

Record and analyse results

Example

The creative arts and media world has a reputation for passion and conflict when different viewpoints meet, particularly when the artisic community meets managers, accountants and shareholders.

A small provincial Opera House experienced this annually when both sides met to discuss the programme for the year. Tensions quickly emerged between artistic ambitions and the reality of what people would pay for, and in fact between idealism and pragmatism in any number of guises.

The Opera House management, who felt they generally came off worst in these exchanges, persuaded the group to adopt the Thinking Hats technique. Perhaps because of its element of theatricality and costume, the group agreed.

The annual battleground was transformed. Although the same debates took place, individuals had a way of talking round the issues without seeming to betray their loyalties – after all, it was the hats talking. It was certainly a more colourful event!

Using Thinking Hats for choosing the next production for the Opera House

Instructions
You will be given a coloured hat to start with.
Anything you say must be in this role.
When the facilitator allows, you can choose other colours and comment from different perspectives.

White Hat   Pure facts and figures.
              Where the opera has been performed before,
              CD sales, popularity elsewhere, cost to
              perform.

Red Hat   Emotions and feelings.
              What feels right for the moment,
              fashions and trends, likes and dislikes,
              gut feeling about what people are ready
              to hear.

Black Hat   Devil's advocate.
              Problems with casting, costing, production
              and promotion.

Yellow Hat Optimism.
              Advantages and opportunities with casting,
              costing, production and promotion.

Green Hat   Creativity, provocation.
              Different angles on traditional themes
              for production and promotion.

Blue Hat   Cool and controlled.
              Objective reflection of what others
              are saying: seeing all sides.

Total Productive Maintenance

Training operators in maintenance so that they can look after their own machines

Affinity group: Strategy

Classification • • • •

- Improve machines until they're working as reliably and efficiently as possible
- Form operators into autonomous maintenance groups
- Set up a system for managing maintenance
- Train operators in monitoring and maintenance
- Provide initial support for managing equipment

When to use it
To develop an aspect of Preventative Maintenance still further, and make sure regular machine maintenance is as efficient and effective as possible.

When not to use it
Don't use without careful thought and planning: it's widely used in Japan but not so much elsewhere. This is because you need the right manufacturing philosophy.

What you'll achieve
Better quality maintenance, lower costs, and a culture of looking after machines which feeds directly into quality improvement programmes. Virtually eliminates unplanned breakdowns. Machines are available and working when needed.

And be careful
Takes 2 to 3 years to implement. Comprehensive training programme needed for staff, and a willingness to put aside traditional demarcations. Must be part of overall move to Japanese approach to manufacturing.

Training
All operators will need extensive training both in the principles of TPM and in how to maintain their machines. Investment in equipment may also be required.

Where to find out more
Quality Management Library, CCTA, HMSO, 1992

Introduction to TPM, Total Productive Maintenance, Nakajima S, Productivity Press, 1988

Total Productive Maintenance for an IT unit

Total Productive Maintenance can relieve overstretched maintenance resources and reduce bottlenecks.

An IT service unit decided to introduce a brand of TPM after a series of futile attempts to keep up with demand from users for routine software maintenance.

The unit spent several months preparing all workstations. Then a selected group from each department was carefully trained for simple maintenance tasks.

The scheme was very successful in moving responsibility for routine tasks away from the specialist IT unit. People expressed relief at being able to solve their own problems rather than feeling helpless whenever anything went wrong.

The IT unit is now considering extending TPM to hardware, although they feel that this will involve much more extensive training, and may create problems with warranty agreements.

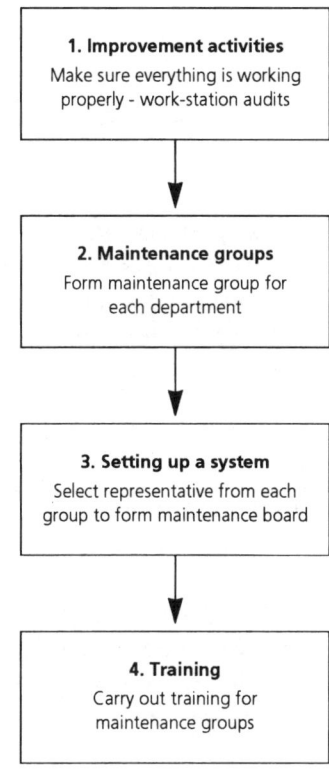

1. **Improvement activities**
Make sure everything is working properly - work-station audits

2. **Maintenance groups**
Form maintenance group for each department

3. **Setting up a system**
Select representative from each group to form maintenance board

4. **Training**
Carry out training for maintenance groups

Training Needs Analysis

Matrix for planning training to match the needs of the organisation.

Affinity group: Strategy

Classification • • •

When to use it
When you're introducing change and new methods of working and you need to plan training to meet potential skills gaps.

When not to use it
Don't use prematurely, before new directions and requirements are fixed.

Training
Personnel departments will be familiar with the technique. Otherwise some training necessary.

What you'll achieve
A way of analysing what skills you need and what you have. Information for aligning training with the needs of the business.

And be careful
Take aptitudes and preferences into account, as well as the needs of the business, when changing people's roles. Training won't solve everything.

Where to find out more
Quality Control Handbook, Juran J, McGraw Hill, 1989

How to Develop and Present Staff Training Courses, Sheal P R, Kogan Page, 1989

Process flowchart

Identify knowledge and skills needed in each department to achieve company objectives

Set up matrix with potential training topics down the side

List staff along the top

Interview departmental managers and tick knowledge and skills staff possess

Arrange training to fill in the gaps

Example

Changes in technology within an organisation should always be supported by a Training Needs Analysis.

A sales and manufacturing organisation introduced personal laptop computers for all its sales force, so that they could prepare their own quotations, write and print their own letters, make stock enquiries on line and join the company's e-mail system. A Training Needs Analysis showed a number of areas for basic training in how to use:
- the operating system
- word processing
- the printer
- e-mail
- the stock enquiry and costing system.

The analysis for each sales person showed exactly how competent they were. Three levels of training were set up – basic for people with no experience, advanced for people with basic experience and training for advanced users in passing on their skills. The laptop computers were a success because the TNA made sure that all staff were trained at the right time and at the right level.

Training Needs Analysis for introducing laptop computers

Sales staff	PD	SS	FE	FT	SM
Training topic					
Operating system	●	✗	✓	✗	✗
Word processing	●	✗	✓	✓	●
Printer	●	✗	✓	✓	●
e-mail	✗	✓	✓	✗	✗
Stock enquiry and costing system	✗	✗	✗	✗	●

Key

✓	advanced experience
●	some experience
✗	no experience

Tree Diagram

A method of classifying ideas in a hierarchy

Affinity group: Graphic Tools, Problem Solving

Classification • • •

When to use it
When there are a number of options in response to a particular problem and you need to see what they all imply and involve.

What you'll achieve
A logical set of proposals at a number of levels which turn a general problem into a set of possible actions.

When not to use it
Don't use for puzzles which have one particular answer, rather than problems which have many.

And be careful
Fill in obvious gaps in logic or sequence missed in the brainstorm. But if ideas won't fit, leave them out.

Training
Training and experience needed in sorting and classifying ideas quickly.

Where to find out more
The Memory Jogger, Brassard M and Ritter D, GOAL/QPC 1994

Process flowchart

State problem

Brainstorm:
• all possible causes
(for a Why Why diagram)
or
• methods of addressing the problem (For a How How diagram)

Start Tree Diagram by putting problem on the left

Select ideas from brainstorm which relate most closely to problem statement, and list to right of it

Select ideas most closely related to each of these and place to right again

Continue until all ideas represented

Example

Tree Diagrams can help to analyse all kinds of problems.

This example was literally sketched on a napkin.

A new restaurant had opened in a small, pretty town in the South Midlands. After the uncertainty of the first weeks, the restaurant began to find its clientele.

It soon became clear however that the restaurant needed to develop a much healthier lunchtime trade if it was to survive. It was not easy to see how this could be done, since the town during the day was populated mainly by young mothers with children – not the target group. Local businesses were served by one or two energetic sandwich shops.

So one day, as the quiet lunchtime period dwindled into the afternoon, the proprietors sat down by their river view to create a Tree Diagram to show how they might begin to build up a lunchtime trade.

Tree Diagram suggesting how to increase lunchtime trade at the restaurant

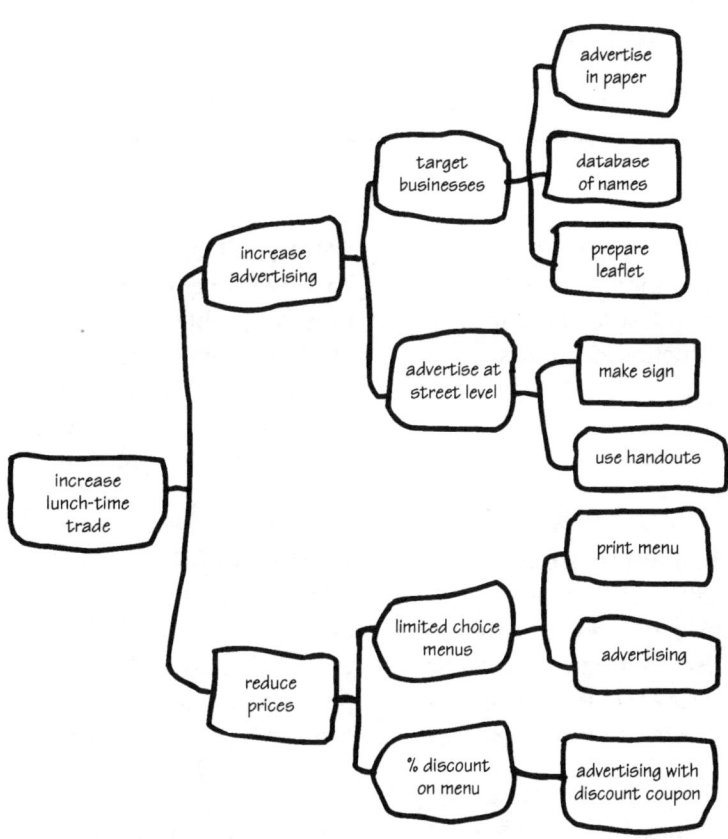

Trend Chart

Chart to monitor processes over time and identify trends.

Affinity group: Statistical Quality Control

Classification • •

When to use it
One of the Control Chart family. Use to monitor production standards.

When not to use it
Don't use for precise information about particular aspects of the process. Trend Charts are only designed for overview information.

Training
Basic understanding of statistics needed.

What you'll achieve
Early warning of trends, for example problems with machinery or materials: you won't have to wait for complaints or breakdowns before seeing the problem.

And be careful
Don't interpret every change as important: focus on long-term shift in overall performance averages and confirm trends before acting.

Where to find out more
Statistical Process Control, Oakland J and Followell R, Heineman Newnes, 1990

Identify key of trends indicators: yield, scrap, machine downtime, number of defects etc

Set up chart
Horizontal axis:
Time
Vertical axis:
Measurement

Collect data, keeping in time order

Plot chart and interpret results

Example

Trend Charts can provide a clear picture for managers and planners.

A large organisation which had just been through a major IS installation used a Trend Chart to monitor the number of Requests for Change immediately following the installation. They had expected a high level initially as the system settled in, and had allowed extra resources to deal with this. They then expected the number to fall to a steady rate. They could then plan the long-term organisation and staffing of the change management operation.

The Trend Chart for RFCs showed a slow start as people started out on the system, followed by a steep rise as problems began to emerge. However after the third week the trend began to reverse and by the end of a ten week period RFCs had stabilised to less than 10 per week.

The long-term change management service could safely be planned around this figure.

Trend Chart to monitor Requests for Change following an IS installation

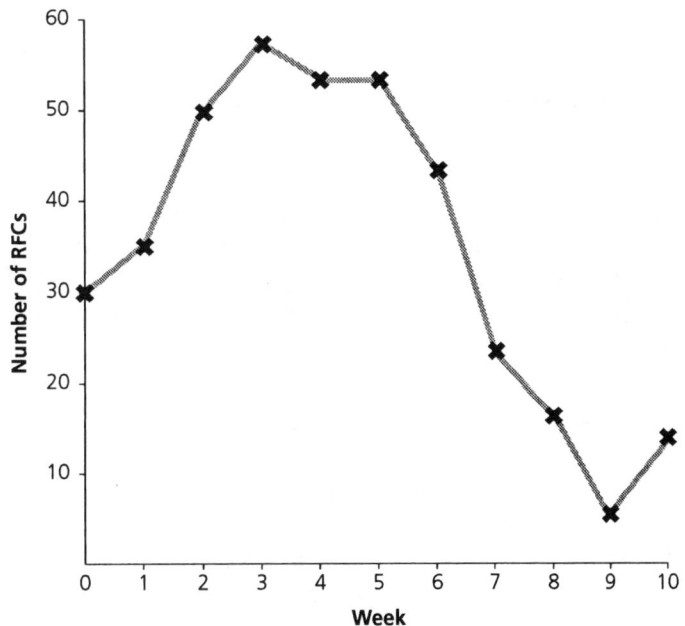

u Chart

Graphic tool for showing the number of defects in a sample of varying size: an attributes measure.

Affinity group: Statistical Quality Control

Classification • • •

When to use it
Use the u Chart for monitoring continuous flow processes where errors or defects won't be in the same place each time. Use where sample size and/or the unit of material inspected varies.

When not to use it
Don't use u Charts for measuring variables.

Training
An understanding of fundamental statistics required.

What you'll achieve
A way of monitoring and comparing quality levels in processes where defects can occur randomly and where sample sizes vary.

And be careful
Be careful of a very wide variation in sample size, because the underlying statistical calculations can change the control limits.

Where to find out more
Quality Control Handbook, Juran J, McGraw Hill, 1989

Statistical Process Control, Oakland J and Followell R, Heineman Newnes 1986

A Practical Approach to Quality Control, Caplen R H, Hutchinson Publishing Group, 1978

Process flowchart

Select and label samples to be checked

Collect data about defects

Create u Chart
Horizontal axis:
Samples checked
Vertical axis:
Number of defects per unit measure of sample

Calculate control limts, where number of defects is too high

Collect data and analyse results

Carpet manufacturing is a process where using u charts as part of Statistical Process Control would be appropriate. Faults in carpet lengths vary in type and position. Carpet lengths themselves vary. So, an absolute measure of an acceptable quality limit cannot be specified. It isn't possible to say that a carpet will be rejected only if it has a certain type and number of faults.

What is important is to make sure that the probability of a high number of faults occurring remains low. This can be done by monitoring the number of defects in selected lengths, and judging the relative performance of the process.

Any trends or variations need to be investigated in the usual way.

Using the u Chart in the carpet industry

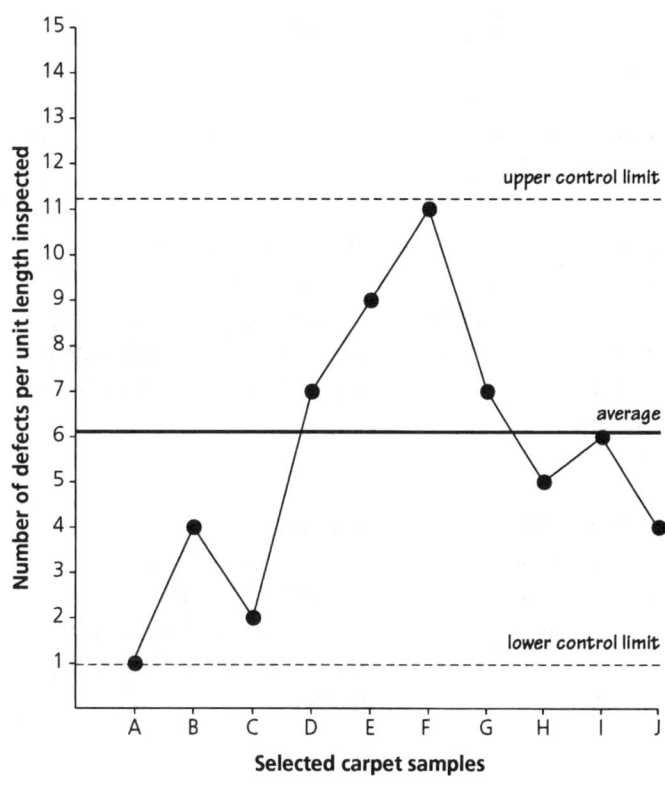

x̄ Chart

Control chart for monitoring the average value of variables in a process.

Affinity group: Statistical Quality Control

Classification • • •

When to use it
Use in production processes for monitoring variables, and making sure variations are within customer's expectation or specification.

What you'll achieve
An understanding of the level of variability of the process, and a check on whether items are within specification limits.

When not to use it
Don't use for monitoring defects (or attributes): use c, u, np or p Charts instead.

And be careful
Use with the R Chart. Select the right variables, not the ones it's easiest to count, and check findings before taking action.

Training
A basic understanding of statistics is necessary.

Where to find out more
The Economic Control of Manufacturing Quality, Shewart W, Dover Press, 1936

Quality Control,Handbook, Juran J, McGraw Hill, 1988

Process flowchart

```
Decide what variable to
measure and when to measure
          ⋮
Set up chart
Horizontal axis:
Measurement intervals over
time
Vertical axis:
Average value at each interval
          ⋮
Calculate upper and lower
control limits, using formulae
          ⋮
Plot measurements and check
that average values are within
upper and lower control limits
```

Example

The x̄ Chart is the simplest form of control chart for monitoring variability in a production process.

An example of the importance of this kind of control is provided by a small engineering company which was set up by a group of enthusiasts to make motorbike components for old-style bikes. Initially the company relied on Acceptance Sampling to make sure the components conformed to specification. However after only a few months in business a consignment of parts was returned by the company's main customer. The parts had passed inspection but were nevertheless causing problems in assembly. The customer made a strong suggestion that the company should introduce Statistical Process Control.

The first x̄ Charts revealed the problem. For the component in question, which consisted mainly of a bar of a specified diameter, average measurements were within specification, but consistently close to the lower control limit. Clearly the manufacturing process needed to be adjusted.

x̄ Chart for motorbike components

Part name	Specification	Sampling Frequency
Retainer	.50 to .90mm	2 every 2 hours

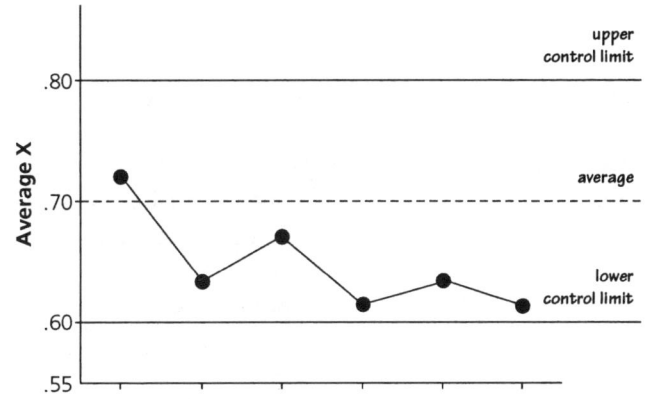

Shift	A	A	A	A	A	A
Time	9.30	11.30	13.30	15.30	17.30	19.30
Date	8 June					
X_1	.78	.63	.68	.60	.65	.61
X_2	.70	.67	.68	.64	.63	.63
Total	1.48	1.30	1.36	1.24	1.28	1.24
x̄	.74	.65	.68	.62	.64	.62

Z Chart

Graphic way of showing progress in achieving objectives.

Affinity group: Graphic Tools

Classification • • •

When to use it
Use to track performance against objectives or benchmarks.

What you'll achieve
You'll have a clear visual representation of what's been achieved and what's still to be done. A good tool for communicating with both senior management and staff.

When not to use it
Don't use when there isn't a summary measurement you can use which everyone accepts as a valid representation of progess.

And be careful
Don't assume that any current increases in performance will automatically continue: examine the basis of your projections carefully.

Training
Easy to use: some basic knowledge needed about how to make graphs.

Where to find out more
Benchmarking, Camp R, ASQC Quality Press, 1989

Handbook of Quality Tools, Ozeki K and Asaka T, Productivity Press, 1990

Process flowchart

Select measurements which reflect goals to be achieved

Collect data on actual situation and ideal position

Plot on same graph
Horizontal axis: time
Vertical axis: measurements

Analyse any gap between actual and projected performance

Develop Action plan to close gap

Example

Using the Z Chart helps managers to keep track of progress towards objectives.

As part of its quality management system, company B set a training target representing 10% of net profit. This level of training was to be achieved from a low base, and would take time to achieve.

The top line of the Z Chart shows what training courses were available to staff in the first seven months of the new targets. The lower line shows how numbers of staff on training courses gradually increased as commitment to the targets grew and staff were able to find time to attend training sessions.

A Z Chart for training objectives

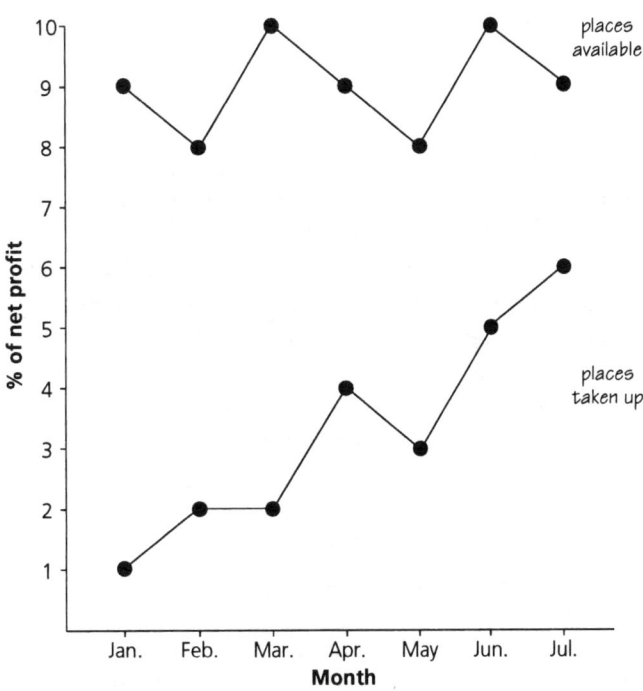

Zero Based Budgeting

Method of calculating resources by working back from your objectives.

Affinity group: Cost Management

Classification • • • •

When to use it
Useful for budgeting new projects, but also important in times of change, such as when an organisation is reduced to its core competancies and needs to establish new budgets.

What you'll achieve
Budgets will reflect the new shape of the organisation, and not perpetrate old ways of working. People won't be held back in critical areas because of outdated patterns of resourcing.

When not to use it
Don't rush into this without thinking through all the practical and political implications: wait till you are sure the organisation's ready.

And be careful
More difficult to apply to existing situations which aren't changing much, but still worth doing: may show up new ways of reaching the same goals.

Training
Training needed for accounting staff.

Where to find out more
Fast Focus on TQM, Barrett D, Productivity Press, 1990

The Budget's New Clothes: A Critique of Planning, Programming, Budgeting and Cost Benefit Analysis, Merewitz L, and Sosnick S H, Rand McNally, 1971

Process flowchart

Set objectives for the budgeting period

Plan best way of reaching objectives

Work out resources of staff and equipment needed, based on actuals and predictions

Prepare budget based on projections, not previous allocations

Example

Training budgets are often calculated by looking at the preceding year's budgets and how they were used. In years of plenty, departments can expect their budgets to be increased across the board: in less affluent years, budgets go down.

Training for introducing a quality management system is company wide, however, and does not relate to previous training patterns. So training costs have to be worked backwards from what will be needed, whatever implications this will have for individual budget-holders.

Training budget for introducing a Quality Management System

Training	Numbers	Cost per capita (£)
Awareness	183	15,189
QMS training	22	4,730
TQM training	40	6,000
Senior management courses	16	24,000
Total budget		**49,919**

Zero Defects

Quality philosophy which states that there is no acceptable level of defects.

Affinity group: Strategy

Classification • • • • •

When to use it
For safety-critical industries such as nuclear power, or industries where professionalism implies perfection.

What you'll achieve
A heightened sensitivity to problems and defects, and a motivating goal to strive for. At its best, can bring about a step change in quality standards and a change in attitude.

When not to use it
Don't embark on a Zero Defects policy without changing attitudes to faults first.

And be careful
Zero Defects controversial philosophy which can lead to an expensive obsession with details which don't really matter to the customer or the business. Don't forget Pareto.

Training
Implementing in a production setting will require extensive training in quality management and quality control.

Where to find out more
Quality is Free, Crosby P, McGraw Hill, 1979

The Quality Management Library, CCTA, HMSO, 1992

Fast Focus on TQM, Barrett D, Productivity Press, 1990

Process flowchart

Identify potential errors for all products and processes

Devise ways of preventing them

Launch campaign to change attitudes to the acceptability of defects

Implement quality improvement programme

Monitor and report progress

254

Example

In safety critical industries the philosophy of Zero Defects is accepted and practised of necessity.

The revolutionary impact of the philosophy is really felt in industries which have traditionally tolerated levels of defects. This was true of the car industry before the Japanese quality revolution. People buying a new car were prepared for faults. If they were lucky these would be rattles and poor adjustments. If they were unlucky, faulty components.

By changing this expectation, the Japanese car industry revolutionised quality standards. People no longer expect their cars to rattle and break down as a matter of course. Much of the technology had always been available: setting new standards needed a new philosophy.

Zero Defects in different industries

The first question to consider is whether the philosophy of Zero Defects is generally applied to an industry.

The second question is if not, why not. It could be irrelevant, or it could be a source of competitive advantage.

We expect zero defects in these industries:
 Nuclear energy
 Aerospace
 Medicine
 Defence
 Chemicals
 Pharmaceuticals.

What would the implications be if we expected Zero Defects in these industries?
 Transport
 Textiles
 Software
 Banking
 Construction
 Hotels and restaurants

References

Barratt, D (1990)
Fast Focus on TQM Productivity Press

Barker, A (1993)
Making Meetings Work The Industrial Society

Brassard, M and Ritter, D (1994)
The Memory Jogger GOAL/QPC

British Standards Institute (1991)
BS6001 Sampling procedures for inspection by attributes BSI

Buzan, T (1989)
Use Your Head BBC Books

Camp, R (1989)
Benchmarking ASQC Quality Press

Caplen, R H (1978)
A Practical Approach to Quality Control Hutchinson Publishing Group

Carroll, S J and Tosi, H L (1973)
Management by Objectives Applications and Research Macmillan

Cass, T (1969)
Statistical Methods in Management Cassell

CCTA (1992)
Quality Management Library HMSO

Cotterman, W M et al (1981)
System Analysis and Design: A Foundation for the 80's Elsevier Science
Publishing Co

Crosby, P (1979)
Quality is Free McGraw Hill

de Bono, E (1982)
Lateral Thinking for Management Penguin

de Bono, E (1990)
Six Thinking Hats Penguin.

Deming, W E (1988)
Out of the Crisis Cambridge University Press

Drucker, P (1994)
The Practice of Management Butterworth Heinemann

Fagan, M E (1976)
Design and Code Inspections to Reduce Errors in Program Development
IBM Systems Journal

Feigenbaum, A V (1983)
Total Quality Control McGraw Hill

References

Fletcher, J (1988)
Effective Interviewing Kogan Page

Garnett, J (1989)
The Manager's Responsibility for Communication The Industrial Society

Griffiths, D N (1990)
Implementing Quality ASQC Quality Press

Hammer, M and Champy, J (1993)
Re-engineering the Corporation Nicholas Brealey Publishing

Huda (1994)
Kaizen: The Understanding and Application of Continuous Improvement
Stanley Thornes

Humble, J (1972)
Management by Objectives British Institute of Management

Imai, M (1989)
Kaizen: The Key to Japans Competitive Success McGraw Hill

Industrial Society (1987)
Managing for Total Quality The Industrial Society

Ishikawa, K (1982)
The Guide to Quality Control Asian Productivity Centre

Juran, J (1964)
Managerial Breakthrough McGraw Hill

Juran, J (1988)
Quality Control Handbook McGraw Hill

Layard R, (1972)
Cost Benefit Analysis Penguin

Lockner, R and Matar, J (1990)
Designing for Quality Chapman and Hall

Lu, D J (1989)
Kanban: Management Begins in the Workplace Productivity Press

Mackenzie Davey, D (1989)
How to be a Good Judge of Character Kogan Page

Marsh, J (1992)
The Quality Toolkit IFS Ltd

Merewitz, L and Sosnick, S H (1971)
The Budget's New Clothes Rand McNally

Morgan, D L (1988)
Focus Groups as Qualitative Research Qualitative Research Methods;
vol 16, Sage

Morris, L N (1967)
Critical Path Construction and Analysis Pergamon Press

Murdoch, J (1979)
Control Charts MacMillan

Nakajima, S (1988)
Introduction to TPM: Total Productive Maintenance Productivity Press

Oakland, J and Followell, R (1990)
Statistical Process Control Heineman Newnes

Open University P950 (1991)
Better Meetings Open University.

Oppenheim, A N (1986)
Questionnaire Design and Attitude Measurement Gower

Ozeki, K and Asaka, T (1990)
Handbook of Quality Tools Productivity Press

Pera International (1992)
Total Quality Management Chapman and Hall

Rawlinson, J G (1986)
Creative Thinking and Brainstorming Wildwood House

Reeve, J T (March 1991)
Applying the Fagan Inspection Technique Quality Forum, vol 17

Sayle, A J (1981)
Management Audits McGraw Hill

Schonberger, R (1982)
Japanese Manufacturing Techniques The Free Press

Sheal, P R (1989)
How to Develop and Present Staff Training Courses Kogan Page

Sherkenbach, W W (1991)
Deming's Road to Continual Improvement SPC Press

Sherkenbach, W W (1989)
The Deming Route to Quality and Productivity Mercury Press

Shewart, W (1936)
The Economic Control of Manufacturing Quality Dover Press

Shingo, S (1986)
Zero Quality Control; Source Inspection and the Poka Yoke System Productivity
Press

Sisk, H L (1973)
Management and Organisation South-Western Publishing Company

References

Taguchi, G (1987)
System of Experimental Design Quality Resources, White Plains

Taguchi, G (1989)
Introduction to Quality Engineering McGraw Hill

Taylor, S (1993)
Communication for Business Pitman Publishing

The Seven New QC Tools Research Group (1984)
The Seven New QC Tools Made Easy JUSE Press Ltd

Thomas Johnson, H and Kaplan, R (1986)
Relevance Lost: The Rise and Fall of Management Accounting Harvard
Business School Press

Towers, S (1994)
Business Process Re-engineering Stanley Thornes

TQM International (1992)
Total Quality Management

Urban, G and Hauser, J (1980)
Design and Marketing of New Products Prentice Hall

Waddington, C H (1977)
Tools For Thought Johnathan Cape

Wadsworth and Brooks (1989)
Quality Control, Robust Design and the Taguchi Method Cole

Watson, G H (1993)
Strategic Benchmarking Wiley

Alphabetical index

Alphabetical Index